I0091200

Eurobondage
The Political Costs of European Monetary Union

Jonathon W. Moses

Published by Rowman & Littlefield International, Ltd.
6 Tinworth Street, London SE11 5AL, United Kingdom
www.rowmaninternational.com

In partnership with the European Consortium for Political Research, Harbour House, 6–8
Hythe Quay, Colchester, CO2 8JF, United Kingdom

Rowman & Littlefield International Ltd.is an affiliate of Rowman & Littlefield
4501 Forbes Boulevard, Suite 200, Lanham, Maryland 20706, USA
With additional offices in Boulder, New York, Toronto (Canada), and Plymouth (UK)
www.rowman.com

British Library Cataloguing in Publication Data
A catalogue record for this book is available from the British Library

Library of Congress Cataloging-in-Publication Data

ISBN: 978-1-78552-256-7 (hardback)
ISBN: 978-1-78552-176-8 (paperback)

'We used up all the wealth we had
To build a ship for fools and mad
And, knowing it proof against all shocks,
Steered it blithely towards the rocks'

Fintan O'Toole's adaptation of Jonathan Swift's obituary poem
(O'Toole 2010:27)

Table of Contents

List of Figures and Tables

Tables

List of Abbreviations

AIB	Allied Irish Banks
Bn	Billion
BoL	Bank of Latvia (Latvia's Central Bank)
CBI	Central Bank of Iceland
CBOI	Central Bank of Ireland
CDS	Credit Default Swap
CHF	Swiss franc (currency)
CIS	Commonwealth of Independent States
CPI	Consumer Price Index
DG	Directorate General (EU)
DIGF	Icelandic Depositors' and Investors' Guarantee Fund [*Tryggingarsjóður*]
EA	Euro area
EBRD	European Bank for Reconstruction and Development
ECB	European Central Bank (EU)
ECOFIN	Economic and Financial Affairs Council (EU)
EEA	European Economic Area
EEC	European Economic Community
EFTA	European Free Trade Area
EIB	European Investment Bank
ELA	Emergency Lending Assistance (EU)
EMS	European Monetary System
EMU	Economic and Monetary Union (EU)
ERM	Exchange Rate Mechanism
EU	European Union
EUR	Euro, € (currency)
FDI	Foreign Direct Investment
FF	*Fianna Fáil* Party in Ireland
FG	*Fine Gael* Party in Ireland
Fidesz	Hungarian Civic Union [*Magyar Polgári Szövetség*]
FME	Iceland's Financial Supervisory Authority [*Fjármálastöðugleikaráð*]
FRED	Federal Reserve Economic Data (US)
FX	Foreign eXchange

GDP	Gross Domestic Product
GIPSIC	Greece, Ireland, Portugal, Spain, Italy, Cyprus
GP	Green Party in Ireland [*Comhaontas Glas*]
HC	Harmony Centre Party in Latvia [*Saskanas Centrs*]
HUF	Hungarian forint (currency)
ICEX	Icelandic Stock Exchange
IFC	International Financial Corporation
IFI	International Financial Institution
IMF	International Monetary Fund
INBS	Irish Nationwide Building Society
IP	Independence Party in Iceland [*Sjálfstæðisflokkurinn*]
ISEQ	Irish Stock Exchange Quotient (Market Index)
ISK	Icelandic króna (currency)
JL	New Era Party in Latvia [*Jaunais laiks*]
Jobbik	'For the Right Hungary' Party [*Jobbik Magyarországért Mozgalom*]
KDNP	Christian Democratic People's Party in Hungary [*Keresztény Demokrata Párt*]
LGM	Left-Green Movement in Iceland [*Vinstrihreyfingin – grænt framboð*]
LMP	'Politics can be Different' Party in Hungary [*Lehet Más a Politika*]
LP	Labour Party of Ireland [*Páirtí an Lucht Oibre*]
LPP/LC	Latvia's First Party/Latvian Way [*Latvijas Pirmā partija/Latvijas Ceļš*]
LVL	Latvian lat (currency)
MDF	Hungarian Democratic Forum [*Magyar Demokrata Fórum*]
MNB	Hungarian Central Bank [*Magyar Nemzeti Bank*]
MNC	Multinational Corporation
MP	Member of Parliament
MSZP	Hungarian Socialist Party [*Magyar Szocialista Párt*]
NA	National Alliance 'All For Latvia!' Party in Latvia [*Nacionālā apvienība 'Visu Latvijai!'*]
NAMA	National Asset Management Agency (Ireland)
OCA	Optimum Currency Area
OSP	Office of the Special Prosecutor in Iceland
PD	Progressive Democrats Party in Ireland [*An Páirtí Daonlathach*]
PM	Prime Minister
PP	Progressive Party in Iceland [*Framsóknarflokkurinn*]
PS	Civic Union Party in Latvia [*Pilsoniskā savienība*]
PPS	Post-Programme Surveillance (IMF)

R&D	Research and Development
RP	Reform Party in Latvia [*Reformu partija*]
SDA	Social Democratic Alliance in Iceland [*Samfylkingin*]
SDP	Social Democratic Party in Iceland [*Alþýðuflokkurinn*]
SDR	Special Drawing Rights
SGP	Stability and Growth Pact (EU)
SIC	Special Investigative Commission in Iceland
SZDSZ	Alliance of Free Democrats in Hungary [*Szabad Demokraták Szövetsége*]
TARP	Toxic Asset Relief Programme (US)
TB/LNNK	For Fatherland and Freedom/LNNK Party in Latvia [*Tēvzemei un Brīvībai/ LNNK*]
TD	*Teachta Dála*, Member of Irish Parliament
TP	People's Party in Latvia [*Tautas Partija*]
TSCG	Treaty on Stability, Coordination and Governance (EU)
UK	United Kingdom
ULC	Unit Labour Costs
Unity	Unity Party in Latvia [*Vienotība*]
US	United States
USSR	Union of Soviet Socialist Republics (aka Soviet Union)
WSJ	*Wall Street Journal*
WTO	World Trade Organisation
ZRP	Zatlers' Reform Party in Latvia
ZZS	Union of Greens and Farmers Party in Latvia [*Zaļo un Zemnieku savienība*]

Preface and Acknowledgements

The impetus for this project was a commissioned chapter for an anthology edited by Jim Caporaso and Martin Rhodes (2016). Contributors to this collection met on at least three different occasions (Boulder, Seattle, Washington DC) to present our work and exchange ideas and comments. I am indebted to the collection editors and workshop organisers (Jim and Martin) for inviting me to join this group, and to all the workshop participants for their useful comments along the way.

This project ended up very different from the one originally planned when I first attended the 2013 workshop in Boulder. This difference can be explained, in large party by the help and encouragement from others in the project. In particular, I would like to thank Christine Ingebritsen, Erik Jones, Kate McNamara and Richard Wesley for their useful comments and exchanges on earlier drafts. It was at one of these meetings that Rachel Epstein suggested that I should look into the Hungarian case, and this little nudge got me thinking about a larger comparative project. Thank you Rachel!

I have been lucky to have friends and colleagues who were brave enough to read all or portions of the finished manuscript, in hopes that they could help me uncover factual errors or unfair characterisations/depictions. These include Michael Alvarez, Erik Jones and Bjørn Letnes. I am extremely grateful for their help and guidance, and the work is clearly stronger as a result. But these friends and colleagues cannot, and should not, be blamed for the end result. That responsibility is all mine.

A comparative project of this sort is challenging on a number of fronts, as the countries (and languages) are too diverse for any one researcher to pursue primary sources in all of the cases. For that reason, I have had to rely heavily on the secondary literature in English, the quality and quantity of which varied substantially from case to case. Worse, these countries are sufficiently diverse that they do not join the same sorts of clubs. Hence collecting comparative data, over longer runs of time, was much more difficult than I originally anticipated. Since Iceland decided against joining the EU, Eurostat seems to have lost interest in most things Icelandic, and as Latvia is not a part of the OECD, it is seldom included in their datasets. Consequently, I have had to search for common sources of data, and/or patch together compatible dataruns to facilitate comparisons.

Another unexpected challenge came in the form of obfuscation. Political elites tend toward euphemisms when describing national responses to the crisis. This has not made my job any easier. Not only did I have to try to find English sources, but I then had to translate many of the concepts from Eurospeak to something more comprehensible (and honest). I considered the inclusion of an interpretive glossary (e.g. wage flexibility = pay cuts; fiscal adjustment = budget cuts; front loading = shock therapy…), but decided against it at the last minute. I will leave it to the reader to decide if my translation effort was successful, and the concepts are now more accessible.

Finally, a note on data sources. I have included full references for most of the data in the bibliography. On occasion, however, I have simply pulled comparative data from the Eurostat dataportal to support a claim. As Eurostat's dataverse is in constant flux, I have found it more useful to cite the specific variable name, rather than a URL address. In these cases, I include the variable name in brackets (e.g., [migr_emi2]), to make it easier to track down the statistic(s) from Eurostat's homepage.

Chapter One

Bound to the Mast

Listen with care
To this, now, and a god will arm your mind.
Square in your ship's path are Seirênês, crying
beauty to bewitch men coasting by;
woe to the innocent who hears that sound!
He will not see his lady nor his children in joy,
crowding about him, home from sea;
the Seirênês will sing his mind away
on their sweet meadow lolling. There are bones
of dead men rotting in a pile beside them
and flayed skins shrivel around the spot.

Steer wide;
keep well to seaward; plug your oarsmen's ears
with beeswax kneaded soft; none of the rest
should hear that song.

But if you wish to listen,
let the men tie you in the lugger, hand
and foot, back to the mast, lashed to the mast,
so you may hear those harpies' thrilling voices;
shout as you will, begging to be untied,
your crew must only twist more line around you
and keep their stroke up, till the singers fade...
(Homer 1963: 210–11)

This warning, from Homer's *Odyssey*, was given by Lady Kirkê to Ulysses, so that she might prevent his 'suffering from misadventure either by land or sea.' In our own time, this myth came to play an important role in convincing Europeans about the benefit of jettisoning their national monetary policies and joining a common monetary union.[1]

---

1. During the run up to European Economic and Monetary Union (EMU), references to 'tying one's hands' were commonplace in the media, among policy makers, and even among academic economists. Giavazzi and Pagano (1988) is, perhaps, the most famous example from the time, but the myth is still used for rhetorical leverage. See also Schelkle (2006).

Like the threat from the Seirênês, whose crying beauty bewitches sailors far from home, Europeans were warned that inflation and/or devaluation might tempt the vote-lonely politician. Following Ulysses' bold example, Europeans came to believe that we would be better off tying our public officials to a rigid mark. Economists, policy makers and the broader public became convinced that political authority could not be trusted with monetary policy, as it might be lured into grounding the economic ship of state on the shoals of public opinion. Taking the form of a shared euro (€), Europe's monetary policy was designed to be rule-bound and isolated from political forces: hence, Eurobondage.

Obviously, it takes more than Homer's *Odyssey* to create a common currency. Indeed, there were a number of political and economic arguments forwarded in support of the Eurozone. On the political front, it was hoped that a shared currency might bind together the sundry states of Europe into a cohesive political whole. At the end of the twentieth century, European statesmen, such as Jean-Claude Juncker and Helmut Kohl spoke of how a common currency would create a common European identity or sense of patriotism (Streeck 2015:11).[2] Instead of centuries of internecine warfare, an economic and monetary union promised an *Even Closer Union* and *A Perpetual Peace* (Dinan 1999; Kant 1917 [1795]).

Economic arguments for a common currency were even more audible: by creating a Eurozone, member states could kick-start economic growth. In creating a continental marketplace and by minimising transaction costs within that marketplace, companies and travellers would be spared the inconvenience and risk of foreign exchange transactions, and consumers would find it easier to compare prices across national markets, now sold in the same currency. In the doing, a larger market would generate greater efficiencies of scale.

There were also other, more amorphous, economic arguments circulating in Europe at the time. At the turn of the millennium, many economists and policy makers came to believe that advances in central banking had tamed the business cycle. Modern central banks, now freed from political and financial influences, could pursue policies (such as those derived from the Taylor Principle) that would flatten the business cycle (or so it was held). To followers of this 'Great Moderation', an activist monetary policy was not only unnecessary, but it was outright counterproductive.

The Great Moderation took root in a broader ideological context where economists were seen to suffer from a 'failure of collective imagination'.[3] By relying on fanciful models, inhabited by rational actors endowed with perfect foresight, economists came to believe that markets work best when left to their own devices; government policy would only knock markets off balance. In this

---

2. At the time, Juncker was Prime Minister of Luxembourg, while Kohl was an ex-Chancellor of Germany. Today, Kohl is retired, while Juncker is President of the European Commission at the time of this writing.

3. This is the memorable response from a group of eminent economists to the Queen of England's (2008) visit to the London School of Economics, where she asked why the economics profession had been unable to see the financial crisis coming. See Besley and Hennessy (2009: 3).

ideological light, national monetary policies were seen as a relic of the past: it was better to let the market work its magic unhindered. Politicians, fearing the electoral costs of poor governance, willingly abdicated their power.

Of course, not everyone agreed about the economic benefits to monetary union.[4] American economists, in particular, were sceptical that Europe constituted anything close to an Optimum Currency Area (OCA), as its component regions lacked the price flexibility, factor mobility and federal fiscal transfers that held the American monetary union together (Jonung and Drea 2009). In the absence of adequate adjustment mechanisms, regions that shared a common currency would have little recourse to correct local economic imbalances. In response to this critical view, a new, more optimistic (and politically opportune) approach to currency union began to gain momentum.[5] In this approach, increased economic integration, borne of a common currency area, would further reduce the need for national (monetary) policy autonomy.[6] All in all, then, a consensus developed, in which the economic benefits of currency union exceeded its costs.

Even if they did not succeed in changing the course of events, a number of important concerns were raised about the economic costs of monetary union. The same cannot be said about the *political* costs of joining a monetary union. Indeed, there has been remarkably little discussion of the political costs to jettisoning national currencies.[7] This lacuna is odd, if only because monetary policy was the principle means by which governments stabilised their economies in the post-war period.

After all, most students of macroeconomics begin their study with closed-economy models where political authorities are able to respond to local economic conditions by affecting the amount of money in circulation (and with it its price, or interest rate). During periods of economic recession, interest rates are lowered to encourage investment in real economic activity and to fend off rising levels of

---

4.   In the wake of the Eurocrisis, there has been more discussion about the economic costs of monetary union, and the design shortcomings of the Eurozone. Academic commentators have pointed to the problems that arose due the absence of a banking union (Caporaso and Rhodes 2016), a corresponding fiscal union (Jabko 2015), the challenges of increased financial union (Jones 2015), and the fact that Europe's monetary union was not properly embedded in a political union (McNamara 2015)...but these costs were not clearly evident in the run-up to the Eurozone; nor did they influence political debate at the time.

5.   In particular, European policy makers came to embrace 'endogenous business cycle theory': where increased economic integration would wash away the regional differences that necessitate local economic responses. As the market became larger, and more integrated, Europeans could expect greater synchronisation of their regional/national business cycles (Frankel and Rose 1997; 1998; EC 1990). See, e.g., Wagner (2014). For a review of the literature that questions whether monetary union drives convergence, see Eichengreen (2012: 298f).

6.   I should point out that this interpretation was countered by many contemporaries, and has not stood the test of time. In particular, economic integration can *increase* regional specialisation (and the need for regional policy autonomy), as regional economies exploit their comparative advantage and/or build economic clusters. See, e.g., Krugman (1993); Bayoumi and Eichengreen (1993); Clark and van Wincoop (2001); and Kalemi-Ozcan et al. (2001).

7.   One recent and important exception is Stiglitz (2016).

unemployment. During periods of runaway growth, authorities increase the interest rate, discouraging investment (and subsequent economic activity). These closed-economy conditions describe the core characteristics of the international economy for most of the post-war period. The institutional contours of this international economy were secured by a *political* bargain at Bretton Woods in 1944.

At the end of World War II, there was broad agreement over the need to secure democratic legitimacy for, and control over, markets. A fear of violent revolution, from either the left or the right, motivated the victorious allies to create a system that would provide policy makers with the stability derived from full employment. In particular, the Bretton Woods regime secured an international order characterised by free trade, fixed exchange rates, and limited capital mobility, so that domestic political authorities could secure *stable* national economies, characterised by full employment. To secure this order, one factor of production needed to take a back seat to another: the needs of labour were allowed to trump those of capital. Recognising the necessity of placing markets at the service of states, the Bretton Woods agreement secured a context of embedded liberalism (Ruggie 1982; following Polanyi 2001 [1944]).

The need to stabilise the local (national) economy and secure full employment was a common point of departure for economists and policy makers alike.[8] This post-war consensus was the product of a new political understanding, produced by the failures of the interwar economy, which rested on three precepts: 1) faith in the notion of a self-correcting market had been undermined by the Great Depression; 2) an economic context that produced massive unemployment and human suffering would not be tolerated (as it would spark political protest, even revolution); and 3) the long-term stability of modern states (and the status quo) rested on the capacity of national officials to deliver full employment and economic growth.

With the close of the twentieth century, this consensus had evaporated and been largely forgotten. A self-regulating market was back in vogue; political elites began to fear the fury of capital markets more than the threat of the unemployed; and elected officials were no longer held responsible for the failures of the real economy, over which they allegedly governed.

A snake in the system

By 1999, after the Bretton Woods order had imploded around them, Europeans jettisoned their national monetary policy autonomy, and bound their monies together in a common currency area. The reason for this significant change in course was a growing realisation of the diminished utility of national monetary policies. This realisation was particularly strong in Europe's smaller states, who often found their currencies exposed to attacks by roving herds of speculators. Europe jettisoned its national monetary policies in part because it came to embrace an economic ideology of free markets (described above), and in part because of

---

8. As we shall see in the chapter that follows, this holds for the original authors of OCA theory as well.

the lessons it had learned from recent history. To return to our opening analogy, Europeans had lost faith in their skippers' capacity to manoeuvre in treacherous economic waters.

Both of these instigators of change reflect a shift in the underlying balance of class power between labour and capital in Europe. By the end of the twentieth century, the power and influence of financial capital had eclipsed that of organised labour, and the objectives of government policy reflected this new balance of power. Policy was increasingly aimed at securing the blessing of global financial actors, at the expense of democratic constituents. This was the rise of Saskia Sassen's (1996) economic citizenry, where bigger, less regulated markets could trump democratic control over local (smaller) markets.

This tension between the demands of international finance and the needs of domestic voters was increasingly evident in Europe, as the twentieth century came to a close. The relative mobility of capital, especially finance capital, across sovereign regulatory boundaries, provided it with an effective veto over undesirable policies. States that pursued unpopular (read left-leaning) policies were punished by capital flight and speculative runs on the national currency.

If proof was needed, it came in 1981 – when France elected its first Socialist President to the Fifth Republic. Upon election, François Mitterrand championed an expansionary Keynesian policy (along with an ambitious nationalisation plan), in an all-out effort to reduce French unemployment levels at a time when much of Europe was saddled by recession.[9] Here was an explicit attempt by a major European power to prioritise the needs of its domestic constituents over the apparent demands of global markets. By all accounts, the Mitterrand experiment was a spectacular failure: from the start his policies were resisted by international markets (which focused massive speculative activity against the franc) and by a steady outflow of French capital.[10] Among many on the Left, the failed Mitterrand experiment came to symbolise the end of national policy autonomy, embedded liberalism, and the rising power of global finance (Helleiner 1995: 327).

The nature of this trade-off between international and domestic interests was also evident in the difficulty that Europe had in trying to secure a fixed exchange rate system, before the introduction of the Eurozone. A stable European exchange rate agreement was difficult to secure because elected officials still had some ambition to steer their domestic markets and deliver full employment for voting constituents. The progressive deregulation of financial markets was making this increasingly difficult, allowing international investors/speculators to take advantage of perceived disequilibria.

As a consequence, the road to the euro was a bumpy one. Although the Bretton Woods system was beginning to show signs of strain in the 1960s, it was Nixon's closing of the gold window in 1971 (Gowa 1983), and the resulting exchange rate instability (facilitated by increased capital mobility and financial

---

9. See, e.g., Lombard (1995); Bauchard (1986); and Schmidt (1996).

10. Whether the disaster was the fault of Mitterrand's policy, or the exchange rate system that was the harbinger to the euro, remains unclear, however. See Lombard (1995).

market deregulation) that prompted a string of unsuccessful attempts at European currency coordination. As the international economy lumbered under the weight of stagflation and oil price shocks, it proved impossible to hold these sundry European economies on the same economic trajectory. One subsequent arrangement after the other (e.g., the Snake-in-the-Tunnel; the Snake; the European Monetary System (EMS), with its Exchange Rate Mechanism (ERM)) was battered by speculators, increasing the short-term volatility of exchange rates across European currencies. The main problem was one of conflicting signals: on the one hand, national policy makers were trying to stabilise their domestic economies to secure full employment; on the other hand, European exchange rate agreements obliged monetary policy officials to maintain relatively fixed exchange rates between diverging economies.

Consider the nature of the economic relationship between Germany and the UK at the turn of the century. The German economy had just undergone a remarkable transformation, having united what were once two independent countries: East and West Germany. To help pay for the costs of reunification, the German government had (understandably) increased its domestic spending; this, in turn, forced the German central bank (the Bundesbank) to print more money – causing prices in Germany to grow (i.e. increased inflation). In the United Kingdom, by contrast, the economy appeared to be exhausted after a long bout of Thatcherism. In the early 1990s, Britain was experiencing the longest official recession since the 1930s' Great Depression; it was in desperate need of stimulus. By April 1993, when growth finally returned to the British economy, nearly three million people found themselves unemployed.

In effect, in the early 1990s, the German and British economies were heading in two very different directions. Yet both countries, like many others in Europe, had agreed to tie the external value of their currencies together in the ERM. The original participants in the ERM (France, Germany, Italy, the Netherlands, Belgium, Denmark, Ireland and Luxembourg) agreed to defend fixed rates of exchange within a 2.25 per cent fluctuation band (above or below each bilateral central rate). The UK joined this arrangement in 1990, with a broader fluctuation band (+/- 6 per cent).

The problem is that pegged exchange rates require the participant central banks to pursue parallel interest-rate policies (this is sometimes referred to as Irving Fisher's interest rate parity theory). So, when the Bundesbank began to raise interest rates to address the problem of rising domestic inflation (the result of reunification), it put upward pressure on the German mark. This forced other central banks, who were participating in the ERM, to also increase their interest rates – regardless of domestic economic conditions. In short, the ERM required Britain to increase interest rates (to defend its fixed exchange rate with the German mark, +/-6 per cent), even though economic conditions in Britain necessitated just the opposite economic prescription: lower interest rates!

The same tension lies at the core of today's Eurozone crisis. The desire for a fixed exchange rate regime (in the context of free capital mobility) conflicts with the inherent needs of the very different domestic economies that joined the agreement. At this earlier juncture, in 1992, the nature of the fixed exchange rate was still not set in stone – it was still being tested. It was the fictitious nature of this 'fixed' exchange rate that emboldened Georg Soros to bet all of his money (and that of his Quantum Fund) on a short sell that the Bank of England would not be willing to follow Germany in increasing its interest rates. In September 1992, Soros bet that the English central bank would prioritise the needs of the British economy over that of a European exchange rate agreement – and his bet paid off. When the Bank of England announced that it would float the pound and leave the ERM on what came to be known as 'Black Wednesday', Soros and the band of investors that followed his lead, demonstrated how vulnerable central banks were to speculative attacks.[11]

Small currencies were especially vulnerable to such speculative attacks, as they lacked the financial wherewithal (even with international assistance agreements) to defend their exchange rates. The Swedish response to Black Wednesday is especially noteworthy: in order to defend the Swedish krona against a speculative attack (like the one led by Soros against the British pound), the Swedish central bank (Riksbanken) was forced to raise its marginal lending rate briefly to a shockingly high 500 per cent!

In this period, before the creation of a common currency in Europe, markets were willing to bet against political agreements that would demand real economic adjustments. Markets realised that it made little economic sense to fix rates of exchange between national economies that varied so significantly, and that politicians (even central bankers) would not be willing (or able) to defend the agreement, at the expense of local economic conditions. After all, how long could the Swedish authorities maintain a 500 per cent interest rate in order to maintain a fixed exchange rate to the German mark?!

It is in this context that the European Union came to be seen as the last line of defence, behind which democratic policies might take refuge. If individual nation states were too small to oppose international financial markets, they might ban together in a common union, in order to create a political counterbalance to the rising power of global markets. It was at the supranational level that the forces of democracy would circle their wagons and fight off global capitalism.

In short, by the closing decade of the twentieth century, people came to believe that there was little scope left for autonomous national monetary policies. Some of this belief was fuelled by a new panglossian approach to markets, others recognised that financial markets had become more powerful than national monetary authorities – leaving the latter with precious little room for policy autonomy. Even if the touted economic and political benefits of monetary union were perhaps exaggerated, it still made sense for policy makers to bind themselves

---

11. As the pound continued to depreciate (to nearly 15 per cent against the German mark), Soros made a killing – estimated to be worth a billion dollars (Ferguson 2009). This part of the story is well known. What has been largely forgotten is that the depreciation of the pound increased the international competitiveness of British firms, bringing about the end of the long recession, described above.

to the euro. If there was no utility to be had in maintaining a national monetary policy, what harm could be done by following the example of Ulysses?

A view from the deck

I've been around boats all of my life, and I've sailed in my fair share of treacherous waters. This is probably the reason that I am drawn to Lady Kirkê, and the ways her advice has been used to convince political authorities to jettison a once significant tool of democratic governance. The providence and timelessness of Homer's myth gives it weight and currency; but its nautical content is pure rubbish. From the perspective of a deckhand, Ulysses' decision – and the advice that it inspires – is completely bogus.

When navigating any difficult passage, whatever the nature of the challenge, the last thing that any qualified skipper should do is limit his or her options and fix the rudder. There are simply too many independent forces, beyond the control of the helmsperson, which will require an immediate and unique response. In other words, the skilful skipper needs to prepare for the threat of currents, winds, hidden shallows and pirates, in addition to the lure of the Seirênês.[12] Skippers that allow themselves to be bound to the mast while sailing through treacherous waters will soon face a mutiny by their crews (and should be charged with incompetence, and relieved from their positions, by the ship's owners or relevant authorities).

As a political economist, and a democrat,[13] I've marvelled at the currency of a myth that would have policy makers blatantly ignore the will of the people (and have the ears of their constituents filled with beeswax, no less!). In what other arena do we encourage policy makers to ignore their constituents and bind themselves to a particular (unswerving) path? Even Plato, no friend of democracy, recognised the utility of a skilled navigator at the helm of our ship of state (*The Republic*, Book VI, 488e–489d). Limiting political authority in this way leads us down a slippery slope: in trying to protect democracy from its shortcomings, we can easily undermine the very foundations of democratic rule (Elster 1979: 93–6). Indeed, an erosion of democratic accountability is already evident in several of the EU's responses to the current crisis: whether it is the imposition of constraints on member states' fiscal policy (by way of the two-pack, the six-pack, the Treaty on Stability, Coordination and Governance (TSCG), etc.), or by the replacement of elected government officials with appointed technocrats, who will prioritise international demands when they conflict with domestic interests.

As a sailor and a democrat, I have good reasons to doubt the sagacity of using Homer's analogy to inform European monetary policy. Indeed, it seems to me that great harm has been inflicted by prioritising myth over deliberation. Evidence of

---

12. As John Elster (1979: 90) puts it: '[W]ould Ulysses let himself be bound to the mast if he knew that the shallow waters around the Sirens' island were too difficult for anyone else but him to master?'

13. In Chapter Two I elaborate on the meaning of democracy as it applies to questions of economic, especially monetary, policy.

this harm is clearly seen in the broad swath of unemployment that now stretches across Europe. While policy makers fret over the threat of inflation or the size of the government's deficits and debt burden, a whole generation of European workers searches unsuccessfully for work.[14] In response to the inability of member states to manage their domestic economies, hundreds of thousands of Europeans have been forced to leave home in search of work in other member states.[15] This is the economic and moral backdrop to the analysis that follows.

As a political economist, I am curious about the baseline assumption of European monetary union: is it really true that states – especially small states – no longer have recourse to autonomous monetary policies? If not, what are the political costs of following Lady Kirkê's advice? What happens when skippers remain at the helm, and respond to the call of the demos? To answer these questions, we need to consider the degree to which states benefited (or not) from the use of an autonomous monetary policy, during periods of crisis. After all, if monetary policy autonomy is to mean anything, its meaning should be most evident in response to one of the largest crises in modern economic history.

This book investigates the ways in which four states responded to the financial crisis: the options that were available, the choices that were taken, and the consequences of those choices. By illustrating the degree to which monetary policy autonomy still plays an effective role in responding to economic shocks, I intend to document the substantial sacrifices that states have made in joining a suboptimal currency area. These are the political costs of monetary union in Europe.

Case selection strategy

I hope that the reader now shares my interest in the need to investigate whether states are still able to pursue independent monetary policies in Europe. In order to do this, we want to compare the economic achievements of states that have joined the Eurozone against those that have stayed outside the Eurozone (and maintained an independent currency). In particular, we want to see how states were able to respond to the biggest economic crisis in the post-war period: the 2008 financial crisis. As small states are especially exposed to the whims of international markets (and lack the foreign reserves and influence to defend against a determined attack), it makes sense to focus our attention on how small states responded to that crisis.

To test the degree to which Europe's monetary union limits the political autonomy of participant states, we can compare the responses of three small states

14. In the summer of 2015, nearly a quarter of all European youth (on average) were unemployed, whereas the level of youth unemployment (twenty-five years old or younger) exceeded 40 per cent in Spain, Greece, Croatia and Italy (Eurostat, [une_rt_m]).

15. Using the OECD's (2013) standardised migration statistics, which cover only permanent migration movements across borders within OECD Europe, there were more than 900,000 internal migrants in 2011. Obviously, not all of these were desperate economic migrants, but the share of those being pushed out from under-performing labour markets has increased significantly after the crisis (see Jauer et al. 2014).

to the current crisis: Ireland, Latvia and Iceland. These cases were chosen with reference to three basic characteristics: country size, economic predicament and their relationship to the euro. This sampling strategy draws on J. S. Mill's (2002 [1891]) method of difference: these three countries are shown to be similar in the most relevant respects (size, nature of the economic predicament), but differ in their relationship to the euro. Hence any variance in outcome (degree of policy autonomy) can be explained by the variance in their relationship to the euro, *ceteris paribus*.

Let us begin with the similarities: size and economic predicament. Even though all three states are small, Iceland is *very* small (with roughly 320,000 people in 2013) compared to Latvia (*circa* two million) and Ireland (*circa* 4.6 million). When studying monetary policy autonomy, small states represent critical cases. The benefits of monetary union should be greatest for states such as these. As I suggested in the preceding section, small-country currencies are especially vulnerable to speculative attacks. If the analysis demonstrates that small states are able to secure policy autonomy outside the Eurozone, we can expect larger states to be able to do so as well. I make this argument cautiously, and recognise that large states also have to consider the systemic effects of their policies (whereas smaller states do not).

In addition to being small, these countries share a number of relevant economic conditions: each experienced a significant financial bubble in real estate and stock markets (inflated by mobile capital in Europe); domestic banks in each country relied on the international lending market to keep solvent (and when that market dried up the state stepped in); each state was forced to turn to the international community for help out of the crisis; and each country incurred significant government debts in order to bail out their financial sectors (whereas they had relatively little government debt before the crisis).

For most states in Europe, the economic crisis grew out of a bank and financial crisis. This financial crisis became a sovereign debt crisis when states rushed-in to bail-out their failed financial (and banking) markets. Ireland, Latvia and Iceland all threw significant amounts of money at failed banks – as their ballooning government debt levels attest (*see* Figure 3.4, below).[16] In Laeven and Valencia's (2011) influential study of international bank crises, Iceland, Latvia and Ireland are shown to have experienced deep and systemic banking crises.[17]

---

16. As we shall see in subsequent chapters, comparing these three states is complicated by the fact their banking sectors were structured in very different ways (e.g., some used a branch-expansion strategy; others relied on subsidiaries), and they relied to varying degrees on foreign banks. In addition, both Latvia and Hungary participated in the Vienna Initiative, where the home countries of the international banks servicing several East European countries provided support for their banks (and their subsidiaries in these countries).

17. The authors define a systemic banking crisis as cases where at least three of a list of various interventions (extensive liquidity support; significant guarantees on liabilities; significant restructuring costs; significant asset purchases; and significant nationalisations) occur. A borderline case is one that almost, but not entirely, meets their criteria. See Laeven and Valencia (2012: 6).

To illustrate these differences, we can compare the level of public intervention in the banking sector, as a percentage of GDP. Table 1.1 presents the headline figures for each of the three cases, the Eurozone average and Hungary (for reasons that will become obvious shortly).[18] From Table 1.1, we can see that in Iceland and Ireland – and to a lesser degree Latvia – the state was forced to turn to international lenders (e.g. the International Monetary Fund, or IMF; the European Central Bank, or ECB; and the European Commission) to secure the funds necessary (in the form of both capital and guarantees) to keep their banking systems afloat. In the doing, these states became heavily indebted.

Table 1.1: Public interventions in the banking sector

	Recapitalisation	
	Amount pledged	**Amount used**
Hungary	1.1	0.1
Iceland	24	13
Ireland	7.6	4.6
Latvia	2.5	2.5

Note: Figures in per cent of GDP
Source: Laeven and Valencia (2011: 25).

A similar pattern is evident when we compare the direct fiscal costs of the financial crisis over the 2007–09 period, as a percentage of (nominal) 2009 GDP. This is done in Figure 1.1, which includes states from both within Europe and beyond. Here we see that Ireland and Iceland have suffered the most expensive financial meltdowns. In Ireland, especially, the costs were staggering: almost 50 per cent of GDP. The cost of the crisis in Latvia, by comparison, seem relatively modest – but these were still substantial – at 4.9 per cent of GDP – and even greater than that experienced in the United States. The costs of the crisis in Hungary were significantly lower.

While Ireland, Iceland and Latvia are relatively small, and suffered relatively similar fates during the recent economic crisis, they are very different in one particular way: they differ in regards to their relationship to the Eurozone: Ireland, as a member of the Eurozone, was bound to a monetary policy emanating from Frankfurt (home of the ECB). Iceland, by contrast, maintained an independent currency that allowed it much greater scope for policy autonomy. Latvia, as an EU member state considering membership in the Eurozone, was in a middling

---

18. The European Commission (EC 2009: 63) has a more exhaustive comparison of the size of the public interventions, and one that includes the Eurozone average. But this comparison was done relatively early in the crisis, and did not include Iceland. I might note that the European Commission calculated that the total public intervention (effective, not approved) in the banking sectors was about 0.1 per cent of GDP in Hungary, 227.3 per cent in Ireland, 8.9 per cent in Latvia, and 11.1 per cent for the Eurozone average. In other words, the ranking is the same as we see in the Laeven and Valencia data, even if the overall numbers differ.

Figure 1.1: Direct fiscal costs of the financial crisis over 2007–09

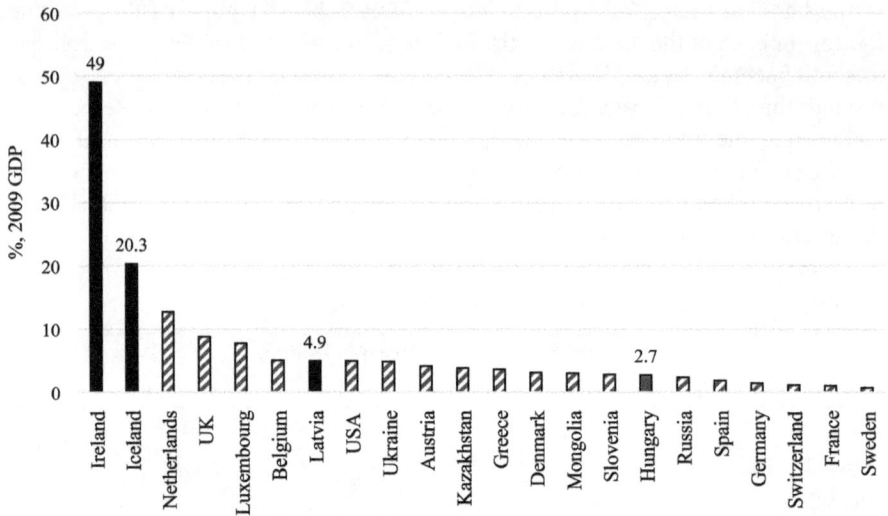

Note: See original sources for more information on how the indicators were generated.
Source: Laeven and Valencia (2010) and OECD (2011a: 20)

position: it had the option of pursuing a more independent monetary policy, or binding itself firmly to the euro.[19]

By including three small countries (Iceland, Ireland and Latvia) that suffered under very similar conditions – but maintained very different relationships to the Eurozone – we can trace how their relationship to the euro affected the opportunities and choices available to each. Given their common points of departure, any variance we find in their policy outcomes can be explained by each country's relationship to the euro. While it is unlikely that the patterns I uncover are solely the result of a country's relationship to the euro, the patterns will reveal some of the political (and economic) costs of jettisoning an important instrument for managing the domestic economy.

Their relationship to the euro is not the only thing that distinguishes these countries from one another. Each country enjoys a distinct historical trajectory, political culture, and unique political institutions that have developed alongside those distinctive contexts. As these factors can play an important role in facilitating (or deterring) economic adjustment in each context, it is unfortunate that we have no means to control for this additional variation. Such is the nature of the political world.

In short, this sample was selected with an eye on controlling for the effects of euro membership on policy autonomy, but it cannot adequately control for all unwanted variation. In particular, some of the variance we uncover might be the

---

19. At the time of the crisis. Latvia joined the Eurozone in 2014.

result of indigenous institutions and political cultures. Despite these shortcomings, the research design allows us to generate strong (if tempered) expectations that are subsequently tested in the empirical chapters that follow.

This comparative study of three cases would probably suffice, but it ignored the elephant in the room: Hungary. In two relevant regards, Hungary is very different from the other cases: it is larger (population, *circa* ten million), and it did not suffer from the same sort of financial collapse as did Iceland, Latvia and Ireland. More to the point, Hungary has maintained an independent currency, and used it to successfully navigate the financial crisis and to map out its own, radically independent, political course. By including Hungary in the study, I hope to shine some additional light on the role that an independent currency can play under a very different set of circumstances.

To do this, we need to understand how Hungary's point of departure was so different from the other three cases. Most importantly, Hungary did not suffer from the same sort of financial collapse (and requisite bail-out) as we saw in the other cases. In Table 1.1, Hungary's recapitalisation effort was minimal (0.1 per cent of GDP), compared to the other cases.[20] Indeed, Laeven and Valencia (2011) describe Hungary's predicament as being less precarious than in the other cases: while Iceland, Latvia and Ireland were all categorised as having experienced systemic banking crises; Hungary's crisis was listed as only borderline systemic. Just as importantly, Hungary was already suffering from a heavy level of government debt (unlike the other cases), prior to the crisis – and this level of debt became increasingly difficult (expensive) to finance once the international financial crisis hit.

In a way, Hungary's challenges are more conventional: its debt was the result of years of economic mismanagement, rather than a hasty response to a global financial crisis, per se. The challenges facing Hungary would probably have happened, sooner or later, even in the absence of a major financial crisis. The Hungarian authorities were not dealing with an existential crisis, but the international crisis was making it more difficult for them to continue financing their government debt burden. In short, the financial crisis simply made it more difficult to continue funding the country's string of budget deficits. Consequently, Hungary found itself in a situation that paralleled Latvia's: it had to choose between following the path being blazed by the ECB for the Eurozone, or branching off on its own political path. While Latvia followed Ireland and strengthened its commitment to the euro, Hungary followed Iceland and chose its own path forward through the crisis.

The comparative case study reveals a very clear pattern, but its lesson is limited to small states that experienced severe financial crises. By adding Hungary to the mix, we can juxtapose the lessons generated by the comparative study of very small states against the experiences of a larger state. In many ways, however, the Hungarian authorities found themselves in a situation that was similar to Latvia's: they were EU members, on-track to joining the Eurozone. Like Latvia, Hungary

---

20. And in the European Commission report, Hungary's total bail-out was equally small, relative to the Eurozone average and the other cases (EC 2009: 63). *See* footnote 18 above.

needed to decide whether to commit to a fixed exchange rate (and pursue a so-called 'internal devaluation' as a result), or allow the forint to float – and enjoy the political autonomy that resulted. The Hungarians chose the latter strategy, and started down one of the most autonomous (and controversial) policy paths in Europe. By looking closer at the Hungarian case, we can see how even larger states are able to employ an independent currency to secure autonomous (if not always successful) policy outcomes.

This sort of comparative design allows us to generate a better understanding of what is possible for states to achieve, and to critically evaluate the uniqueness (or not) of their particular situation. Most existing studies of the crisis tend to focus on individual states, often by people who have a close relationship to the events taking place. As a result, they tend to suffer from a certain degree of myopia: they assume that the choices made were the only ones possible, or that their particular situation was especially difficult or challenging.[21] By comparing country responses, we can overcome this shortcoming and get a fuller understanding of the *real* options that were available to states in response to the crisis.

The empirical study reveals that non-Eurozone states enjoy better economic outcomes and more policy freedom than Eurozone states. Iceland exhibits a monetary policy that reflects popular opinion, and which has the broadest spectrum of policy options from which to choose; Ireland exhibits the least popular outcomes, with the narrowest choice of policy options; and the Latvian outcome and choices lie somewhere in between. Although Hungary faced a different set of challenges, the choices it made reflect a degree of policy autonomy that parallels what we find in Iceland. Those countries that chose to stay outside the Eurozone enjoy more degrees of policy latitude, even if this latitude is not always maximised to best effect. The alternative (losing control over monetary policy), however, leaves states pursuing policies that hurt the most vulnerable in society, delay the economic recovery, and are unpopular with voters. Worse, elections in Eurozone countries proved ineffective in changing the policy paths, as the most important tools of economic management lay beyond the reach of democratically-elected officials.

Chapter outline

This project aims to measure the political costs of monetary union. These costs are introduced and described in the following chapter. The political costs of monetary union are associated with the loss of democratic control over economic outcomes – especially the state's capacity to stabilise the national economy. In

---

21. For example, Donovan and Murphy (2014: 262) writing about the high cost of default in the Irish case, argue that: 'In Ireland's case, they would be particularly damaging, given its extremely open economy, its very high dependence on private capital inflows and the potential risk of capital flight. While default may appear superficially attractive to some, it is a wholly unrealistic option for a country in Ireland's position.' As we shall see in subsequent chapters, the Icelandic economy shares these very same characteristics, yet seems to have benefited from default.

an era characterised by increased income inequality and growing radicalisation, we need to be more aware of the political cost of economic solutions steeped in austerity. Chapter Two describes these political costs and how they are incurred in a monetary union; it then generates explicit expectations for the sort of crisis responses we can expect to find in states that have maintained a degree of monetary policy autonomy (and those that have not).

Expectations generated from this approach are tested in the empirical chapters that follow. We first examine whether policy choices result in outcomes that benefit the weakest members of the community (a surrogate indicator for democratic accountability). This is done in Chapter Three, which paints the general economic context in the Eurozone and how the four cases relate to the Eurozone average. Here we get a sense of how deep the crisis was in each of the four cases (and that conditions in Hungary were very different from in Iceland, Ireland and Latvia). More to the point, Chapter Three examines the social costs of national responses to the financial crisis, by looking at how the crisis has affected the unemployment, income inequality, social expenditures and emigration levels in each case. This is done to gauge the degree to which policy makers prioritised the needs of domestic constituents over those of international financial interests and institutions.

Chapters Four–Six examine the political contexts in each of the three cases for comparison (Iceland, Ireland and Latvia) – to gauge the degree to which a broader set of policy options were constrained by participation in a common currency area. In each case I describe the nature of the country's relationship to the Eurozone, and the way in which political pressure was brought to bear (or not) on national policy makers. In the doing, we are able to ask: to what extent were policy makers able to respond to democratic pressures (or chose to prioritise international interests above those of domestic constituents)? In contrasting these three cases, the implicit comparative design rests on J.S. Mill's method of difference: they all share central features (small states suffering from deep financial crises that result in mountains of sovereign debt), but they differ in one essential regard – their relationship to the euro (and, hence, their degree of monetary policy autonomy). This one central difference explains the remarkable variance in their ability to navigate and respond to the crisis.

Chapter Seven then steps outside of this comparative design to consider an altogether different case: Hungary. Hungary is larger than the other states, and its economy did not suffer from the same magnitude of financial meltdown. But the financial crisis brought its own challenges to Hungary, which found it increasingly difficult (read expensive) to fund its tendency to live beyond its means. As the political conditions attached to international support began to accumulate, Hungarians responded with a radical political alternative: their own third way, or *sonderweg*. As Chapter Seven reveals, this alternative was secured by means of an independent monetary policy.

The concluding chapter, Chapter Eight, begins by analysing the patterns that were revealed in the preceding empirical chapters to show how the variance in national outcomes associated with an independent currency (and central bank) provided European states with substantial policy latitude. This latitude allowed

Iceland more options than those states that were bound to the euro. In the Icelandic response, politics clearly trumped economics.

We find the exact opposite in the Irish case: elected officials defended European institutions and international lenders, despite a clear mandate from their constituents to oppose these policies. In the cases of Latvia and Hungary, we find more room for manoeuvre. In the Latvian case, that latitude was used to secure a stronger relationship to Brussels and Frankfurt; in Hungary, the resulting political latitude was used to secure a more nationalistic policy. Although Hungary started from a different place than the other cases under study, its ability to leverage the greater autonomy it enjoyed (from maintaining an independent forint), offers a nice contrast with the Icelandic case. In doing so, we are reminded that policy autonomy does not ensure any particular type of policy (good, moral, leftist, etc.) – merely policies that reflect constituent interests.

The study concludes that some small states in Europe were able to secure a degree of monetary policy autonomy, and this autonomy was used to prioritise the needs of domestic constituents over those of international markets. Eurozone member states, by contrast, pursued policies that prioritised the (long-term) needs of international lenders and European institutions, at the (short-term) expense of their own constituents. Contrary to popular and academic perception, there is still much scope for monetary policy autonomy, and policy makers that jettison this important tool risk delaying economic recovery and even sinking their economies.

This conclusion needs to be placed in a larger context. For some readers, the attractiveness of a shared European market (whether it is due to the promised economic gains, a sense of greater European identity, or an ideological commitment to free markets, etc.) may still outweigh the benefits of national monetary policy autonomy. For these readers, the path to future action is clear: it is necessary to recognise the significant political costs to membership in a common European currency area and develop endogenous (EU) institutions that can help to minimise those costs.

Other readers may wish to prioritise the need for democratic accountability and political stability. For these readers, transferring more political authority away from locally-elected politicians is hardly a desirable solution, especially if the authority is transferred to institutions that lack democratic legitimacy and are seen to be captured by international interests. Such readers can employ the conclusions of this analysis to question the utility of any further concentration of economic and political power in Europe.

Chapter Two

The Political Costs of Monetary Union

Most arguments for creating a monetary union in Europe rested upon three important beliefs: 1) a monetary union would generate economic growth by reducing risk and transaction costs; 2) a monetary union would create a greater sense of union or community in Europe; and 3) the political costs of joining a monetary union were small, as individual member states had already lost their capacity to pursue an autonomous monetary policy (as witnessed most dramatically by the failed Mitterrand experiment).

Although each of these beliefs was widely held at the birth of the Eurozone, they have become much more difficult to embrace in light of recent developments. The first two beliefs are challenged in the daily headlines of the world's press, where the inadequacies of the Eurozone are blamed for the continent's economic malaise and the growth of a xenophobic nationalism that threatens the European project. The third belief will be tested in the pages that follow: whether small European states managed to maintain a degree of monetary policy autonomy outside the Eurozone, and whether this autonomy was used to secure political (popular and just) objectives. This chapter lays the groundwork for that test by describing the political costs of monetary union, and how these can be operationalised.

This chapter is divided into three parts. I begin by justifying a more political approach to monetary policy. This is necessary, if only because so much of the policy discussion (and its supporting academic analysis) has focused on questions of efficiency. By ignoring or downplaying the distributional consequences of their decisions, policy makers can threaten the legitimacy and stability of democratic regimes. While austerity and internal devaluations may generate economic growth over the long run, they can also create the sort of political instability that will jeopardise those long-term economic gains. As di Muzio and Robbins (2016: 99) point out, 'what leading economists and banks call "austerity" is, in reality, a "taking" from others.' To secure long-term, sustainable and stable outcomes, policy makers must balance the needs of both efficiency *and* justice.

The second part of the chapter focuses-in on the political effects of monetary policy. It does this by defining monetary policy in very broad terms and then elaborating on the distributional consequences of various monetary policy choices. While economists tend to argue that monetary policy needs to focus on aggregate demand (and fiscal policy should be used to affect distributional outcomes), this section points to the important distributional consequences associated with monetary policy decisions. At a time of rising inequality and radicalisation, it is important to be aware of these distributional consequences.

The chapter's third part leverages this discussion to reveal the potential political costs of membership in a monetary union. In joining a monetary union, political authorities effectively jettison their political responsibility for economic management (at the regional/national level). Consequently, their citizens become more exposed to markets and the burden of economic adjustment lands most heavily on the shoulders of society's weakest members. Regional adjustments are secured by (downward) wage flexibility, market-driven labour mobility, and shrinking (local) budgets for public services. On the other hand, the main beneficiary of this change is a small, elite and international group of mobile asset holders. This opens up an important distributional gap with significant political consequences.

In light of this discussion, we can generate expectations about the political costs of joining a monetary union: members of a monetary union must adopt a one-size-fits-all form of monetary policy that prioritises the interests of traders and money changers. States that avoid monetary union enjoy the opportunity to pursue more popular and just policies, to the benefit of their constituents. They can, of course, use their autonomy to deliver poor and inappropriate policies as well. We can measure this political effect in two ways: by comparing the capacity of states to deliver economic outcomes for society's most vulnerable members; and by seeing which states are able to deliver popular policies (those embraced/demanded by their constituents).

In the end analysis, Europeans may wish to prioritise the potential for economic gain that is promised by monetary union. In doing so, however, we need to be aware of the significant political costs involved.

Balancing efficiency with justice

By the political costs of monetary policy, I mean the loss of democratic influence on economic decisions (and outcomes). Beneath this definition lies a belief that elected officials should be held responsible for economic outcomes, that they are responsible for protecting the most vulnerable segments of their population, and that they need the appropriate tools to secure those outcomes. When democratic officials are unable to direct economic policy in accordance with national/domestic demands or needs – or worse, when they willingly discard those tools in the name of market freedoms – then we face a significant challenge to democratic governance.

Our willingness to ignore the political effects of monetary policy is remarkable, given the important role that monetary policy played as a central measure for taming the business cycle in the post-war economy. There are probably three reasons why we have let our elected officials jettison this responsibility. First, and as hinted in the introduction, there was a growing consensus that changes in the international economy had undermined the scope for autonomous monetary policy. This important belief will be tested in the chapters that follow. Second, many economists are ideologically predisposed to believe that the political effects of a policy decision are irrelevant to the cost/benefit analysis. Although this is slowly changing, and it is possible to find a renewed interest in inequality and distributional issues among economists and policy makers, the analytical approach of many economists still makes a false distinction between economic and political spheres (with their analysis being limited to the former). In order to maximise economic gains, politics is often side-lined in exchange for more rule-based and technocratic solutions.[1] A majority of economists honestly believe that re-distributional issues are best secured by fiscal policy, and that monetary policy should be dedicated to influencing aggregate demand.[2] In the doing it is implied that the distributional consequences of monetary policy are insignificant. Also, when countries join a monetary union, they lose the capacity to wield many of these additional policy tools. Finally, many analysts simply (albeit implicitly) assume that the political benefits of monetary policy follow directly from the economic benefits.

For the democratic citizenry, however, there are at least two good reasons to maintain political influence over monetary policy. The first reason is normative and the most important: governance is not just about efficiency; it is also about justice and vision. Because decisions about monetary policy have important distributional consequences, constituents should expect the polices of *their* elected officials to reflect democratic priorities (and that there will be political repercussions for unpopular policies). After all, some of the most pressing political issues of the day (e.g. unemployment, debt-relief, income inequality, economic stagnation) are affected by monetary policies. When policy decisions result in significant political repercussions, they should not be isolated from political influence, and policy makers should not pretend that they can be resolved by the application of technical expertise. Alternatively, if central banks are to be independent, they should be independent of the financial interests whose fate they help to secure. It is precisely because monetary policy has the potential to generate outcomes with significant consequences for the relative material well-being of different groups of citizens that it cannot, and should not, be isolated from democratic influence (yet should be isolated from narrow economic interests).

In arguing that monetary policy should generate fair outcomes, I mean that it needs to reflect the interests of the broader population and the most vulnerable among us. In democratic states, we do this (in part) by creating institutions that depend on votes and other expressions of preference.[3] To ensure just and

---

1. The choice between rules and discretion has been central to the academic literature on the conduct of monetary policy since Simons (1936). See also Kydland and Prescott (1977) and Fischer (1990).

2. Many also harbour rather patronizing views of elected officials, who 'pander' to voters. Sinn (2014: 59) is exemplary: 'This is apparently the problem with democracy. A government commits to agreements and sticks to its promise of fulfilling them, but its successor dumps the commitments in favour of pandering to the current needs of voters, instead of doing something for future generations, perhaps even secretly speculating on its neighbours' eventually accepting joint liability for its debts.'

3. For example, Robert Dahl (1971: 1) holds that the fundamental democratic principle is 'the continuing responsiveness of the government to the preferences of its citizens, considered as

democratic outcomes, the authority to conduct monetary policy should lie in institutions that matter and are responsive to their democratic constituents. There are two components to this argument, as elaborated below: 1) removing popular control over monetary policy is inherently problematic from a democratic perspective; and 2) removing democratic control over monetary policy has distributional consequences – it benefits some groups, at the expense of others. Should democratic institutions prove to be less efficient than other arrangements, the political community needs to balance the desire for democratic legitimacy against the desire for increased efficiency.

We should expect democratic policy makers to pursue policies that deliver just outcomes. As a rough surrogate for just outcomes, we can measure the results of that policy on the most vulnerable members of society.[4] In short, economic analysts and the finance sector prioritise the need to secure economic growth, minimise inflation, public deficit and public debt levels. Consequently, this is where most of public attention has been focused. But it is also legitimate to consider the effects of the crisis on another set of indicators, such as the levels of inequality, unemployment, social expenditures and emigration. These indicators are particularly interesting as they reflect the ability and willingness of a state to take care of its most vulnerable citizens. Of course, the two types of indicators (efficient/just) are related to one another, and connected by a significant lag. Hence, it may take some time before the economic gains trickle down to society's most vulnerable members; in the meantime, we need to know how they fare.

There are no simple answers to the questions being asked. If a policy decision (such as central bank independence) can be shown to generate superior economic outcomes (for the benefit of the people), is it legitimate to insulate central bank governors from democratic pressure? What if the resulting economic gains benefit one group of people more than others (e.g., lenders over borrowers)? If there is a trade-off between economic efficiency and democratic responsiveness, should we always prioritise economic gain? Cannot the same argument be made about fiscal policy? Or governance in general? Think of the money, time and effort we could save if we got rid of regular elections and instead chose our governors by way of an algorithm (or some other measure of technical or expert competence)!

---

political equals.' Dahl's eight institutional arrangements for securing democracy include: freedom to form and join organisations; freedom of expression; right to vote; right of political leaders to compete for support; alternative sources of information; eligibility for public office; free and fair elections; and *institutions for making government policies depend on votes and other expressions of preference.*

4. Operationalising justice in this way will be familiar to readers of Rawls (1970), in that it employs a (max-i-min) approach to justice. But Rawls arrives at his position in a radically different way: by way of a thought experiment that involves the veil of ignorance. In short, for Rawls, individuals would rationally choose a society that maximises the position of those who are most vulnerable (as they don't know which rung in society they will occupy, when deciding on the social contract behind a veil of ignorance). What I am proposing is much different: a simple attempt to measure the degree to which policy outcomes benefit (or not) the most vulnerable groups, and use this as a surrogate measure for just outcomes.

In opening up this Pandora's Box, I aim to demonstrate that difficult trade-offs are involved, and that we need to make people more aware of the political costs associated with those trade-offs. Making such difficult decisions is precisely the strength of democratic forms of governance: they allow communities a peaceful, legitimate and just means of resolving tricky decisions.

This brings me to the second argument for a more political approach to monetary policy. While the first argument rests on a normative embrace of democratic values, the second argument is more instrumental, as it concerns political stability. This argument draws on Karl Polanyi's (2001 [1944]) caveat about the necessity of embedding economic exchange in their requisite social and political contexts. When the values of economic exchange are allowed to trump political and social conventions, especially as they regard the markets for 'fictitious' commodities (such as labour and capital), we can expect strong political and social reactions.

Every attempt to create 'free' and unfettered markets has clear and detrimental political consequences, as spelled out by Fred Block in his introduction to Polanyi's *Great Transformation*:

'The fictitious commodities explain the impossibility of disembedding the economy. Real market societies *need* the state to play an active role in managing markets, and that role requires political decision making; it cannot be reduced to some kind of technical or administrative function. When state policies move in the direction of disembedding through placing greater reliance on market self-regulation, ordinary people are forced to bear higher costs. Workers and their families are made more vulnerable to unemployment, farmers are exposed to greater competition from imports, and both groups are required to get by with reduced entitlement assistance. It often takes *greater* state efforts to assure that these groups will bear these increased costs without engaging in disruptive political actions. This is part of what Polanyi means by his claim that "laissez-faire was planned"; it requires statecraft and repression to impose the logic of the market and its attendant risk on ordinary people' (Block 2001: xxvi-xxvii, emphasis in original).

I'm sure readers will recognise that Block is describing precisely the sort of populist backlash that now tears Europe asunder. Long-term economic solutions that exacerbate income inequality, and demand greater austerity from those who can least afford it, are not sustainable over time. They will be met by political opposition and increased radicalisation, even the threat of revolution. The rise of fascism and communism, in response to the failures of the liberal interwar regime, are examples of this type of radical reaction. Between 1929 and 1933, German wages plummeted by 27 per cent, while unemployment rose to 30 per cent (Sinn 2014: 139). While other countries used devaluations to de-link from the Gold Standard (and, with them, the austerity plans and internal devaluations required of that commitment), Germany chose the more austere route and its internal devaluation pushed the country to the brink of civil war and its eventual embrace of Fascism. Europe today faces a similar challenge. To navigate these tricky economic waters, policy makers need to steer a middle course that balances economic and political objectives.

To generate fair, stable and legitimate outcomes, it is necessary to secure democratic influence over important policy decisions (and the institutions in which they are made). When a country abdicates political control of its monetary policy to distant (and politically isolated) institutions, it pays a significant political cost – in that it loses influence over outcomes that can be seen as unfair, resulting in increased political instability.

In the end, the political costs of monetary policy decisions, whether large or small, still need to be weighed against the potential gains (both political and economic) from that decision. It is possible to imagine four possible outcomes, as outlined in the matrix below (Figure 2.1).

Figure 2.1: The policy makers' decision matrix

		Political	
		Costs	**Benefits**
Economic	**Costs**	1 (Inferior)	2 (Embedded)
	Benefits	3 (Faustian)	4 (Superior)

Of the four options, the first (option 1) is not very attractive, and will be avoided at all costs. On the other hand, option 4 is superior in the sense that the country's economic and political objectives are seen to go hand-in-hand. This implies that a state can chose a monetary regime that secures both economic and political gain. As suggested above, this seems to be the implied position of many policy makers today. In option 2, a state chooses to prioritise the domestic needs of its constituencies over the price of greater economic reward. With a nod to Polanyi, I refer to this as an Embedded Strategy, where economic exchange is a means to achieve (more just) political ends.[5] Option 3 embraces an inverse set of priorities. This option is akin to a Faustian Bargain, where states are willing to sell their democratic autonomy in exchange for the promise of greater economic reward.

This larger cost/benefit analysis lies beyond the scope of the current study, but I see it to be the rightful task of elected policy makers, responding to their democratic constituents. It is entirely possible to recognise the political costs of monetary union, and still believe in the desirability of a currency union in Europe – because (for example) the economic, political and ideological gains are sufficiently large to cover any potential political costs. But I worry that the pursuit of these economic gains will result in significant political costs that will, eventually, dwarf any promised returns.

---

5. This option could also be called a Conservative Strategy, as it is reminiscent of the logic of American Federalists who consciously designed an inefficient constitutional structure, in order to protect against the possibility of capture by a particular faction (or tyrant). In other words, policy makers may find that there are more important concerns than the promise of economic gain, and choose a less efficient regime in order to optimise the political benefits.

The distributional consequences of monetary policy

In order to measure the political costs of monetary union we need to first delineate the scope of monetary policy autonomy. This requires that we are clear about what actually constitutes monetary policy (and autonomy).

At the most general level, monetary policy aims to influence the size and the rate of growth of the domestic money supply (both internally and externally), and with it, its price (the interest rate and exchange rate, respectively). Given this definition, the relevant authority for conducting monetary policy will necessarily vary from country to country (but will usually include the central bank and the ministry of finance). Likewise, we can expect that the specific tools and targets for a country's monetary policy will vary with the preferences of its constituents, and the underlying nature of the economy. Whatever the mix of objectives and instruments, monetary authorities aim to ensure that there is sufficient liquidity to fuel economic growth and a current account balance,[6] but not so much (little) liquidity as to overfeed (starve) the domestic economy. This definition of monetary policy is broader than most, in that it incorporates concerns about foreign money (and its price). But in a globalised economy, monetary authorities must keep a vigilant eye on both the internal and external markets for money, simultaneously, as they are intricately linked.

In any open market, the price of a good/service is determined by its relative supply (given a fixed level of demand): the more readily available a thing, the lower its price. The same general rule applies to money. Monetary authorities can affect the price of money (its interest rate) by determining how much of that money is available in the market. Thus, monetary authorities can affect the domestic interest rate by influencing the amount of money in circulation via so-called open-market operations;[7] likewise, they can affect the external price (the exchange rate) of that currency by buying and selling foreign exchange in the market (with its foreign reserves).[8] As if to complicate matters even more, the interest rate and the exchange rate are linked, in a context characterised by free capital mobility, so that raising the interest rate for domestic money will strengthen the domestic currency, relative to global currencies.[9]

---

6. The current account balance captures a country's aggregate net trade in goods and services, the net earnings from other factor services (such as rents, interest, profits and dividends) and net transfer payments (e.g. returns from investment funds and net workers' remittances abroad). It is connected to the domestic monetary supply by way of the two prices mentioned above (the interest rate and exchange rate). A rise in the domestic interest rate, *ceteris paribus*, will appreciate the currency's exchange rate.

7. Open-market operations refer to a nation's central bank buying or selling government securities in the open market, in an attempt to expand or contract the national money supply.

8. Buy selling foreign exchange, and buying domestic money, the authorities are taking domestic money out of the market, hence increasing its price on international markets.

9. *Ceteris paribus*, assuming an exchange rate regime that allows for such flexibility. As we shall see, when the exchange rate is not allowed to change, the adjustment is forced back onto individual prices (and wages) in the domestic economy.

Monetary authorities have access to a whole spectrum of policy components (and within them, sundry instruments) with which to influence the amount of money in circulation (and, consequently, its price). Rather than try and list the various instruments of monetary policy, we can focus our attention on four distinct components of a country's monetary policy, distributed across two dimensions: external and internal. These four components of monetary policy can be used in a variety of ways, as some are better adapted to address short-term needs, like managing the business cycle, while others are better at providing a long-term defensive bulwark, or to deter crises by encouraging less risky activities (e.g. requiring that banks have sufficient reserves to cover their lending activity). The most important thing to recognise is that policy decisions with respect to each of these components entail both efficiency and distributional concerns. Let us consider the latter (the distributional concerns) in more detail.

Foreign money

To mediate external imbalances, and to control the amount of money entering and leaving their country, monetary authorities can employ capital controls and different types of exchange rate regimes. In choosing whether (and how) to employ these components, the monetary authorities balance the needs and desirability for stable international exchange, against the need for and desirability of protecting the domestic economy. Whatever the decision, there will always be winners and losers, but the main lines of cleavage tend to break out across sectors (exposed/sheltered) and levels of economic security (privileged/vulnerable).

Capital controls

By imposing capital controls, the authorities are able to secure full control over the amount of money in domestic circulation (and hence can direct monetary policy to meet domestic needs, without concern for its effect on the exchange rate). States position themselves along a continuum, which stretches from little or no controls (on the one end) to an extensive network of capital controls (on the other), or anywhere in between. Quite simply, the greater the scope of capital controls, the greater the degree of monetary policy autonomy for the state.

There are two main distributional cleavages affected by the choice of capital controls: one is factor based (labour/capital), the other is sector based (public/private). In lifting controls on capital mobility, the authorities are granting greater opportunity for capital owners, relative to labour. After all: ordinary citizens, especially workers who have only negligible financial assets, do not benefit directly from freer capital mobility. To demonstrate how workers are hurt (relative to capital) by freer capital mobility regimes, consider two parallel scenarios. In a country with capital controls, we can expect that the workers' productive input creates extra value for their firm. With proper incentives in place, this excess capital is re-invested at home to create a better future/jobs for those workers and their children. In the same country without capital controls, workers have no guarantee that their contribution to excess capital will end up as a beneficial investment: the excess capital can be freely invested abroad, by the private decisions of capital owners in search of greater returns. If that excess capital had not been exported, it might have fuelled domestic demand and created more jobs at home. To put it simply, the greatest gains from free capital mobility go to those with capital.

Worse, the threat of exit provides capital owners with a de-facto veto power over important government policies.[10] In the absence of capital controls, states find it more difficult to impose regulations that can protect domestic workers (and the environment), or to secure tax-based revenues that the state needs to help society's less fortunate members. In a context of free capital mobility, states are forced to compete with one another to offer more attractive investment environments. A shrinking source of government revenue leaves less money for public programs such as health, education, social security and pensions, and poverty relief. Finally, during times of crisis, capital controls can be used to stop larger (herd like) capital flows, which can have significant destabilising effects on the national economy. For all these reasons, the decision to lift capital controls can be seen as detrimental to workers and the broader population that benefits from public spending and domestic investment.

At its root, these distributional cleavages result from the ease with which financial capital can traverse national boundaries (relative to labour). Workers prefer to find well-paid jobs near friends and family: the personal and social costs of moving to a new job in a new country will always be a significant deterrent. Financial asset holders, by contrast, benefit from larger markets, shrinking transaction costs, and fewer regulatory hindrances: they will gladly chase down a larger reward on the other side of the market, as the 'costs of distance' are negligible for them.

By focusing on the distributional cleavages that are generated by lifting capital controls, we should not be distracted from the potential economic effects. Over the long run, it may be true that freer capital mobility can increase productive activity to the benefit of workers in the countries involved. This argument may be especially strong in less-developed economies that hope to attract foreign capital for investment. But recent experience in Europe should make us leery of such promises, as much of the (pre-crisis) capital flows went to Europe's poorer regions, but with little apparent (long-term) benefit. For example, much of the foreign (e.g., French and German) capital that flowed into Spain was wasted in the ruins that now surround Spanish cities – as the demand for its housing boom never materialised (Sinn 2014: 99). It is for this reason that economists usually discount future returns (and grandparents everywhere proclaim that 'it is better to have a bird in the hand than two in the bush'), as there is a good chance that promised rewards won't appear as promised.

---

10. A threat that labour cannot wield as successfully, as it is much more difficult for workers to pack up and leave.

Exchange rate regime choice

The choice of an exchange rate regime also signals a commitment to prioritise the exposed (or sheltered) sector of the home economy. Here too, choices can be lined up along an imaginary continuum that stretches from fixed to floating regimes (and different levels of commitment within each regime type). A decision to join a monetary union is the most extreme form of a fixed exchange rate regime, as a country discards all opportunities for using the exchange rate to adjust external imbalances. At the fixed exchange rate end of this continuum, exporters and importers enjoy stable prices, but domestic wages and prices are forced to accommodate for any imbalance in the current account. Even John Maynard Keynes (1953 [1936]: 266–7) and Milton Friedman (1953: 173), who agreed on little else, agreed on the difficulty of orchestrating wide-ranging wage cuts to improve a nation's competitiveness (internal devaluations). At the flexible exchange rate end of the continuum, by contrast, states are able to make external adjustments in a way that spreads the cost across the entire economy: a country can depreciate its currency rather than raise its unemployment rate (or appreciate rather than inflate) when facing a current account imbalance.

Milton Friedman provided a useful way of contrasting these two regime types by comparing the choice of exchange rate regime with strategies for dealing with daylight savings time:

> 'The argument for a flexible exchange rate is, strange to say, very nearly identical with the argument for daylight savings time. Isn't it absurd to change the clock in summer when exactly the same result could be achieved by having each individual change his habits? All that is required is that everyone decide to come to his office an hour earlier, have lunch an hour earlier, etc. But obviously it is much simpler to change the clock that guides all than to have each individual separately change his pattern of reaction to the clock, even though all want to do so. The situation is exactly the same in the exchange market. It is far simpler to allow one price to change, namely, the price of foreign exchange, than to rely upon changes in the multitude of prices that together constitute the internal price structure' (Friedman 1953: 173).

When used in addition to capital controls, a fixed exchange rate regime can lay the foundation for a strong international economic system (e.g., the Bretton Woods order): it can encourage trade, but allows for significant monetary policy autonomy (as changes in the domestic interest rate will have less influence on the exchange rate). But when combined with a free capital mobility regime (no capital controls), a fixed exchange rate regime severely limits the state's capacity for policy autonomy, as interest rates must be used to secure the fixed exchange rate (rather than address domestic economic conditions). A more flexible exchange rate regime allows states to make corrections when suffering under a current account imbalance. Rather than force workers across the economy to submit to lower wages, a devaluation can cut prices (relative to international competitors) across the board, so that all groups are affected equally.[11]

There is another advantage to using exchange rate adjustments when correcting current account imbalances: the effects from a re/devaluation are almost immediate. By contrast, the alternative adjustment strategy (a so-called internal devaluation, where wages and prices are forced down to increase international competitiveness) takes a long time to work its way through the economy. In the meantime, workers and voters are forced to suffer. As with capital controls, there are noteworthy distributional consequences to this temporal trade-off. As some groups are better positioned than others to withstand long-term economic adjustments, policy makers need to consider the distributional consequences of an adjustment path that is shorter (and hence less painful for those at the bottom of the economic hierarchy), compared to one that takes longer, *ceteris paribus*.

The choice of exchange rate regime matters, as it determines how a country will respond to current account imbalances (and who will pay for them). Countries that maintain a rigid fix (e.g. states sharing a currency union) are forced to adopt internal adjustment strategies that hit workers and the most vulnerable especially hard. These strategies aim to deflate domestic prices and wages by depressing wages and government expenditures and by imposing significant structural reforms (e.g., undermining unions) to make domestic products more competitive (internationally) and to reduce demand for imports. Indeed, much work in political economy has argued that these sorts of internal adjustments are particularly hard to achieve in democratic countries, because the median voter will be negatively affected by this strategy (e.g, Simmons 1994; Eichengreen 1996; Bearce and Hallerberg 2011).

On the other hand, states that maintain their own currencies (and can adjust their exchange rate) are able to respond to current account deficits with a downward exchange rate adjustment (devaluation or depreciation). This strategy has very different distributional consequences.[12] While the purchasing power of all workers will fall in response to the depreciation (the degree to which this happens

---

11. Bergström (1991: 299–301) writes of a how a devaluation sinks real wages anonymously, via inflation; making the adjustment easier than a nominal decrease in wages (or increase in taxes). It has long been a rule-of-thumb among policy makers that choosing a flexible exchange rate, in a context with free capital mobility, allows states to maintain some autonomy in their domestic interest rate policies (the so-called Mundell-Fleming conditions, or Unholy Trinity). See Cohen (1996). Recent research by Rey (2013) has questioned whether this advantage still exists if not buffeted by reduced capital mobility.

12. For example, Streeck (2014: 182) notes: '…in making its imports more expensive, the devaluing country makes it more difficult for its better-off citizens to buy foreign goods while at the same time it helps its wage-earning population to secure higher pay, without necessarily making what they produce more expensive abroad and thereby putting their jobs in danger. To put it another way: the option of devaluation prevents "competitive" countries from forcing "less competitive" ones to cut the income of their less well-to-do citizens so that their more well-to-do can buy their BMWs at a fixed price from producers in "competitive countries".'

depends on the capacity of the state to minimise the inflationary consequences of that deprecation), the change in prices has an immediate effect on the current account, by making exports cheaper (and imports more expensive). This stimulates domestic economic activity, for the benefit of all, as consumers replace imports with domestically-produced goods, and exports increase. In general, then, the overall effects of the external adjustment tend to be less painful for citizens (than those of an internal adjustment).

As with the use of capital controls, we have focused on the distributional issues, while largely ignoring the economic costs/benefits associated with fixed and floating regimes. While firms and travellers surely benefit from reduced fees for money changing, and while there may be efficiency gains reaped by the creation of a larger market (minus exchange rate risks), policy makers and citizens need to ask whether those gains are worth the cost of losing the capacity to stabilise the local economy. In choosing a fixed exchange rate regime (and joining a monetary union), states are clearly prioritising the needs of those that benefit from international exchange (traders and money changers) at the expense of those who can benefit from a more active stabilisation policy.

Domestic money

While the most important distributional cleavages over foreign money concern the exposed sector and whether there should be collective or individual responses to (necessary) international adjustments, the most important distributional cleavages over domestic money pit investors and savers against workers and borrowers.

To stabilise the domestic economy, monetary policy authorities influence the amount of money in circulation. For an economy to grow, it requires sufficient liquidity: too much liquidity, and the economy can tip over into inflation; too little liquidity and the economy can suffocate. Either option incurs political costs and benefits. As most people have only a tangential relationship to financial markets,[13] our focus should be on the real economy, where citizens will feel the effects strongest. With an expansive monetary policy, authorities encourage more liquidity (and with it lower interest rates) that will encourage productive investment (and with it, job growth), and provide assistance to those with significant debts (read homeowners and students). If an expansive policy creates a higher level of inflation, this tends to benefit those with significant debt (e.g., workers labouring under large student debt and mortgages loads), as the inflation erodes away the debt-burden. Of course, no one benefits from a very high (or worse, unstable/fluctuating) rate of inflation, but the level of inflation (e.g., whether it is 0.5 per cent of six per cent) has *very* significant distributional consequences.

By contrast, a restrictive monetary policy benefits investors who fear that inflation will undermine the value of their investments, and who can enjoy the benefits of higher returns generated by increased interest rates. Low inflation

---

13. To see how skewed the share of euro-area financial asset holdings are (by wealth percentages), see ECB HFCS (2013) and Claeys *et al.* (2015: 4).

benefits holders of interest-bearing wealth: keeping inflation low ensures that banks and other lenders are repaid in money whose value is close to that lent. As the restrictive policy is aimed to decrease economic activity, those who rely on gainful employment suffer (relative to the rentier). There are two main monetary policy components that the authorities can use to affect this internal balance: financial/banking regulation and central bank independence.

Financial/banking regulation

By creating a stronger or laxer system of financial regulations, the authorities can influence the ease of access to capital (and with it, its price). The regulatory tool box can include many diverse tools (e.g., determining the size of the fractional reserve requirement, establishing deposit insurance programs – and who needs to provide them, etc.), but their end effect is roughly the same: to make it more or less expensive to access money. We can expect that the vast majority of citizens (who rely on paid employment for their livelihood, and who do have excess money with which to invest/gamble) desire a financial system that encourages social and economic stability. It should not be controversial to suggest that these worker-citizens would prefer a regulatory framework that secures safe, local and productive investments (even if it generates lower returns), while penalising more speculative financial ventures (in which they are unlikely to partake) with the potential to threaten the real economy.

In a global economy (with free capital flows), these regulations can impose additional costs on the domestic financial sector, making it less competitive. Although many economists believe that reduced regulation is good for the economy, it can also create great economic turmoil (as witnessed by the Great Recession), so the overall economic gains of reduced financial regulation are unclear.[14] On the other hand, rigorous regulation is associated with greater stability and can provide states with tools that help in effectively managing the economy. Consequently, the distributional consequences of financial regulation are similar to those that we saw with respect to capital controls, as (foreign) capital controls are merely another form of financial regulation.

Degree of central bank independence

The final component of a country's monetary policy is the one that is probably most familiar to readers: the political responsiveness of the central bank. Here there are many variants, including whether the central bank is responsive to elected officials, the scope of its mandate (does it aim to secure full employment,

---

14. Consider US Senator Elizabeth Warren's questioning of Leonard Chanin, at the Banking Hearing on Consumer Finance Regulations on 5 April 2016: 'Now, according to the Dallas Fed, that [financial] crisis cost the American economy an estimated $14 trillion. It cost millions of families their homes, their jobs, their savings—it devastated communities across America. So when you talk about how certain regulations are too costly or too difficult to comply with…' See Warren (2016: 1.25 minutes).

a low inflationary context, economic growth?), and the number and type of tools that it has at its disposal to influence the domestic monetary supply (e.g., moral persuasion; the discount rate; open-market operations).

For most of the immediate post-war period, central banks were placed under direct political control, because voters were no longer willing to accept the enormous political (and economic) costs associated with their independence during the interwar period. In the late 1970s, the ideological tide began to shift, as most developed states adopted independent central banks with more narrowly defined (low inflation) targets. Whatever the economic costs/benefits of central bank independence and the utility of rule-bound (as opposed to discretionary, or politically-responsive) monetary policy, there can be little doubt that granting central banks independence from political pressure diminished the public's opportunity to influence and manage the domestic economy.

Decisions about central bank independence affect factor holders differently. At root is a question of perceptions about the domestic economy: is the economy on the verge of recovery, or does it require additional stimulus (or, in other words, what do we fear worse, unemployment or inflation)? As Keynes (1924: 40, emphasis in the original) pointed out almost a century ago, this pits the interests of the rentier against those of the worker:

> 'Thus Inflation is unjust, and Deflation is inexpedient. Of the two, perhaps, Deflation is, if we rule out exaggerated inflations such as that of Germany, the worse; because it is worse, in an impoverished world, to provoke unemployment than to disappoint the *rentier*.'

Those who live off the returns from invested income worry that inflation will undermine the value of their wealth; they are less concerned about the level of unemployment (so long as inflation is kept in check). For this reason, investors would prefer that the central bank proceeds cautiously, and pursues a more restrictive policy. Workers land on the other side of this distributional divide: they need jobs to pay their bills and debts (mortgages, credit-cards, cars and student loans). Indeed, as my parents' generation was lucky enough to experience: a little inflation can help them pay down these debts. This group – by far the largest group in any society – would prefer the central bank to be more expansionary: prioritising the need for jobs over its fear of inflation.

The political costs of monetary union

In developing their national monetary policy, authorities can pick and choose among these different components to secure the right balance of political control and economic benefit. Only in this way can policy makers meet the unique needs and preferences of their constituents. In some states, the interests of capital (or the exposed sector) will be especially strong, and we should expect policy makers to design a monetary policy that best satisfies those interests. In other states, however the power of labour (or the sheltered sector) may be stronger, and we should expect policy makers to design a monetary policy that reflects that (different) balance of power. Given the number of different economic types (e.g., some states rely heavily on agriculture, others on industry or services…), and the even wider variance in preferences (e.g. some states prefer more free-market approaches, others more managed approaches), it is not possible to find a single monetary policy that best suits each and every country. The world would not make for an optimum currency area.

In recognising the existence of these significant differences, it should be clear that joining a monetary union entails substantial political costs, as it imposes a single monetary policy on states that will differ in their economic strengths, structures and preferences.[15] These costs can be seen in the two different ways in which states lose control over their capacity to manage their (national) economy, and the distributional consequences that result.

The first is the most obvious. Joining a monetary union means jettisoning the national currency in exchange for a single currency shared with other political entities. This means that the diverse components of a nation's monetary policy (the capacity to use capital controls, exchange rate changes, financial/banking regulation and central bank independence) are all taken from the nation state (and its democratically-elected officials) and delegated to federal-like (or supranational) institutions that are (by their very design) more removed from the people they are supposed to serve.[16] Consequently, when elected officials need to stabilise the national economy in response to a crisis or a business cycle fluctuation, they cannot employ monetary policy.

This concentration of monetary policy-making authority also means that local interests (at the national level) may not be strong enough to influence policy choices and outcomes at a higher level of aggregation (at the EU level).[17] Consequently,

---

15. This is not a secret, and the argument has been made explicitly by the leadership of the European Central Bank. For example, José Manuel González-Páramo (2005), then member of the Executive Board at the ECB, said 'First, there is a broad consensus among academics, observers and policy-makers that monetary policy should focus on maintaining price stability in the single currency area as a whole. Thus, monetary policy should anchor inflation expectations and increase market transparency, thereby facilitating the necessary adjustment of relative prices across different countries or sectors in the presence of economic shocks. By contrast, it is widely recognised that assigning to monetary policy the additional role of directly addressing the relative balance between the sectors or regions of the single currency area in the process of adjustment to shocks would overburden monetary policy to the detriment of its primary role.' Similarly, Lucas Papademos (2007), then Vice President of the ECB, noted 'Needless to say, but I will say it anyway to make it abundantly clear, the single monetary policy cannot address the ULC [unit labour costs] growth and inflation divergence in individual countries. And since it cannot do it, it should not attempt to do it and it will not do it.'

16. This is true of mature monetary unions. As we shall see, states still enjoyed some domestic regulatory capacity in the European monetary union, prior to and during the crisis. This autonomy is now being erased with the introduction of a banking union and the ambition of introducing a stronger political union in Europe.

17. This is not a question of Friedman versus Keynes, but of Montesquieu versus Madison. In his influential *Spirit of the Laws*, Montesquieu argues that small states are best equipped to overcome capture by special interests. In the *Federalist Papers* (especially number 10), Madison argued just the opposite: that larger states are less likely to capture by factions.

the (common) monetary policy is likely to be affected by only the most powerful interests (capable of being heard at the aggregate level of decision making), at the expense of local (smaller) interests. As Paul de Grauwe (2011: 5) noted, 'In a monetary union, financial markets acquire tremendous power and can force any member on its knees.' Worse, other tools for managing the national economy (such as the size of state budget deficits) are also jettisoned in order to make the union function properly.[18]

From this first perspective, monetary policy autonomy can be understood as a reflection of the national interest (as operationalised by democratic elections). An autonomous monetary policy would reflect the interest of the majority and be freed from special influence, whether it comes from specialised interests within the country (e.g., the finance or banking sector) or external interests (e.g., neighbouring states, international organisations). As long as different political communities have different preferences with respect to balancing their sundry economic interests/needs, then an autonomous monetary policy should reflect that variance. In a monetary union, this sort of policy autonomy is not possible.

The second issue is trickier and concerns economic structures and the appropriate scope (or geographic range) of a currency union. The economic character of every state[19] is a product of a complex historical process, whereby the natural advantages of that particular economy (e.g. it enjoys a navigable coastline with deep harbours; an abundance of fertile soils; a very large population…) have been tempered by the political decisions of previous generations (e.g. developing an educational system, infrastructure, regulatory and legal environment, etc.). Because of this, the economic character of every nation state is unique, and it will continue to be so for some time into the foreseeable future. These real economic differences requires substantively different types of monetary policies, and no degree of wishful thinking will erase them entirely.[20]

---

18. In Europe, for example, we have the two-pack and the six-pack, which have become enshrined in the Treaty on Stability, Coordination and Governance (TSCG) of 2012 and Regulation No. 473/2013 on monitoring draft budgetary plans, adopted by the European Council and ratified by the European Parliament.

19. In political matters it is common to use the nation as a sort of surrogate for community, as nation-states have been the primary means by which communities have organised (and defended) themselves. Over time, this political organisation has created economic patterns that correspond with national borders. The economic trajectory of one nation state depends partly on geography, geology and climate, and partly on those patterns or regulation that developed with the nation state.

20. Since the very beginning of discussions about a Western European currency union, there has been a difference of opinion among those who believe that economic convergence and factor mobility are prerequisites for an optimum currency union (e.g., Meade 1957) and those who believe that the creation of a currency union would create the required convergence and factor mobility to make it work (e.g. Scitovsky 1958). See Mundell (1961: 661). As we saw in the introduction, this difference continued while the euro was coming to be, as EU officials and aligned academics embraced an endogenous business cycle approach, while independent economists emphasised the degree to which economic specialisation (rather than convergence) was a normal characteristic of international integration. See Wagner (2014).

Consider Norway's relationship to the Eurozone. Norway is an oil- and gas-producing state, which exports most of its petroleum to world markets, including the EU. The rest of Europe mostly imports oil and gas (from Norway and elsewhere). This means that when the price of oil or gas goes up, it is a good thing for the Norwegian economy, and a bad thing for most economies in Europe. Alternatively, when the price of oil or gas goes down, it is a bad thing for Norway, but a good thing for the rest of Europe.

Now imagine an economic environment where the global price of oil has fallen dramatically (this is not difficult to imagine at the time of this writing). In Norway, the authorities need to worry about the recession that falling oil prices will induce, and consider ways to stimulate the economy. With respect to monetary policy, this means generating more liquidity and lowering interest rates in an effort to encourage greater economic activity (creating new jobs for the oil-sector workers who will soon find themselves out of work). But this sort of expansionary monetary policy is exactly the opposite of what the rest of Europe would need, as the price of an important energy input has fallen dramatically, stimulating greater economic activity. In short, it makes no sense for Norway and Europe to share a currency, as their economies sing to very different tunes. Norwegian monetary policy needs to be sufficiently autonomous to respond to these unique (Norwegian) economic conditions.[21]

The same sort of conflict will occur when residents of different states in a common monetary union want to pursue different types of policy, or harbour different preferences. This sort of regional economic asymmetry occurs even when states have been tied together in a political and monetary union for decades. Despite sharing a currency for over 150 years, the United States continue to experience these types of regional economic variances, and elected officials at the state level have very little authority to do anything about it.

This second challenge is especially problematic, in that states need to find other ways to adjust their external balances (when they lack their own monetary policy). Indeed, much of the subsequent literature on OCAs has been aimed at studying how existing currency areas have compensated for the absence of regional stabilisation policies. Much of this work has looked at the United States, to emphasise the role that internal price (wage) flexibility, factor (capital and labour) mobility, and federal fiscal transfers play in accommodating for regional economic variation within a common currency area.[22] In effect, members of a currency union are locked into rigidly fixed exchange rates, with all the adjustment burdens described in the preceding section. In order for a currency union to succeed,

---

21. The same sort of variation in needs can be seen in the short history of the Eurozone. Before the recent financial crisis, the so-called GIPSIC countries (Greece, Ireland, Portugal, Spain, Italy, Cyprus) enjoyed explosive growth, at a time when Germany was suffering from very high levels of unemployment. After the crisis, we see an inverse pattern: Germany seems to benefiting from European monetary policy, while the GIPSICs are suffering. One common monetary policy for both these groups of countries was neither possible nor feasible. See Sinn (2014: Chapter 3).

22. See, e.g. Eichengreen (1997) and de Grauwe (2014).

regional economies need to find other ways to adjust to asymmetric shocks. As a result, the responsibility for economic adjustment is shifted from elected policy makers over to workers (in the form of shrinking wages, higher unemployment and economically-induced migration) and those who depend upon public services (which are no longer affordable). When the supranational state is underdeveloped (as it is in the EU), and lacks significant fiscal transfers across regions that share a common currency, then even more of the burden is transferred to those who can afford it least.[23]

Given the variance in national economic structures and preferences, there can be significant costs (both economic and political) in creating a common currency area. When the author of the seminal piece on Optimum Currency Areas, Robert Mundell (1961: 657), asked whether it is better for nations to ban together in a common currency area, or to maintain monetary policy autonomy and flexible exchange rates, he responded by introducing two competing measures of optimality: a) the capacity to stabilise the component (regional) economies; and 2) the delivery of greater efficiency gains. If we are most interested in securing stable economic conditions, Mundell (1961: 662) advocated small currency areas, and the use of flexible exchange rates across those currency areas (states/regions[24]). However, if our interest is in maximising efficiency, then the optimum currency area should be very large: '...the optimum currency area is the world, regardless of the number of regions of which it is composed.'

Thus, in deciding to join a common currency area, policy makers have to weigh the importance of stabilising their national economies (e.g., secure full employment for their residents) with the desire to maximise the efficiency gains that can be secured by minimising valuation and exchange rate transaction costs associated with money-changing. Eurozone countries have clearly prioritised the needs of money changers over those of securing stable economic conditions for their residents. The distributional effects from these choices should be clear, as I elaborated above: stabilising the national economy benefits labour (especially those employed in the sheltered sectors) and those that rely on the provision of public services; while reducing transaction costs benefits those who rely on money changing (i.e., international investors and those in the exposed or tradables sector).

For Mundell (1961: 662), then, the choice was clear: 'If...the goals of internal stability are to be rigidly pursued, it follows that the greater is the number of separate currency areas in the world, the more successfully will these goals be attained...' In short, if policy makers want to be able to protect citizens from economic insecurity, then they should maintain monetary policy autonomy. On the other hand, if policy makers are more concerned 'with the costs of valuation

---

23. In the US, federal spending represents more than 20 per cent of GDP. The EU budget, by contrast, makes up about 1% of EU GDP, 40 per cent of which is already earmarked for Europe's common agricultural policy. See Stiglitz (2016: 8, 338).

24. For Mundell, an economic region needn't correspond with state boundaries but is defined in terms of factor mobility. More precisely, a region was defined 'in terms of internal factor mobility and external factor immobility' (Ibid.: 661).

and money-changing, not stabilization policy,' (ibid), then it is better to choose exchange rates that are inevitably fixed in a currency union.

Conclusion

This chapter has aimed to outline the political costs of jettisoning a country's monetary policy. In the doing, I have argued for a more balanced evaluation of monetary policy – one that recognises both the political and economic costs/benefits involved. In particular, I have pointed to the significant distributional consequences of various monetary policy decisions.

Because of these distributional effects, we can expect that the political costs of monetary union are inversely related to a state's capacity to conduct an autonomous and effective monetary policy. The following chapters aim to measure the capacity that states have for pursuing an independent monetary policy in the face of a major financial crisis. This is done in two different ways. In the chapter that follows we will see how the policy responses in each case country benefited the most vulnerable groups in society, by looking at those economic indicators that are most relevant for them. The remainder of the book then looks at the responsiveness of national policy decisions to democratic pressures emanating from within each country.

If it can be shown that states are unable to conduct an autonomous or effective monetary policy, then the political costs of jettisoning that policy are small. If, on the other hand, it can be found that some states have been able to sustain a degree of monetary policy autonomy, then I can demonstrate two things: 1) the underlying assumption of much thinking regarding the European monetary project was wrong (that no utility remained in a state's capacity to steer its own monetary policy); and 2) we have an empirical baseline that can be used to measure the loss of political autonomy.

Chapter Three

Debt and Distribution

This chapter provides a comparative snapshot of the financial crisis in four countries, and then contrasts these snapshots against the Euro-area (EA) average. There are many ways to measure the costs of economic crises and our success in fighting them. The first part of this chapter examines a number of headline indicators, such as economic growth, government debt and inflation levels. These indicators can provide useful information about long-term economic trends and potential – and they are often heard on the tongues of economic commentators and investors – but they are not very useful for gauging the human and social costs of the crisis. To gauge these costs, we need to consider whether the authorities have pursued policies that deliver more immediate relief for their citizen constituents. For this reason, the second part of the chapter considers four alternative measures of economic well-being: unemployment, social spending, income inequality and emigration. Together, these two sets of indicators provide us with a fuller understanding of who benefited (or didn't) from the decision to stay within the Eurozone, or to pursue more independent monetary policies.

More than any of the others, this chapter relies on an array of figures and tables. These descriptive statistics are necessary for two reasons: they help to establish the severity and nature of the crisis in all four states under study, and they allow us to see that a state's response to the crisis can have complex effects on different groups within that country. In examining these figures we become aware of how policy makers face two important trade-offs.

On the one hand, they need to decide whether to prioritise the needs of international markets or domestic constituents. This is the main trade-off with regard to political autonomy, as states abandon their capacity to respond to domestic needs when they jettison their monetary policies. On the other hand, policy makers need to balance short-term versus long-term responses to the crisis. Over the long-run, of course, there may not be a conflict between the interests of international and domestic constituents. But it is still too early to measure these potential long-term effects. In the meantime, we *can* measure the shorter-term effects of these policy decisions, and consider whose interests tend to benefit (or not) from those decisions. In the doing we can get a better sense of which policy makers are able to prioritise the interests of their domestic constituents. In the final analysis, readers can gauge for themselves whether the promise of long-term economic gain is worth the substantial short-term costs/misery that domestic constituents are often expected to pay.

Conventional indicators

We begin by gauging the severity of the crisis in our four cases, relative to the EA average. To do this, we examine developments in three of the most common economic indicators: the effect of the crisis on the country's aggregate economy; its government debt level; and its level of inflation. These indicators are often used as shorthand for success/failure when evaluating policy responses to the crisis, and they can be useful in outlining the seriousness (and the underlying nature) of the crisis in each of the cases.

GDP/capita

One of the most common and obvious measures of the crisis is the effect it has had on a country's Gross Domestic Product (GDP). To compare the severity of the crisis across cases, this section employs three related indicators. The first simply compares countries in terms of their per capita GDP, from 2000 to 2014. This indicator provides us with a sense of the general trend over time, and the levels of wealth that separate the four cases. We then turn to a measure of the country's annual change in GDP, in order to compare the depth of the crisis across countries, and to mark the economic nadir in each case. Finally, by measuring and comparing the size of the economic fall, from top to toe, it is possible to rank the depth of the crisis in each state.

Figure 3.1 compares GDP/capita, in a common currency (the euro), since the year 2000. From this figure, three trends are especially noteworthy. The first concerns the relative level of wealth across our four cases. In effect, the sample can be divided in two: there are two relatively wealthy states (Ireland and Iceland) – where GDP per capita is currently equivalent to about €40,000; and two relatively poor states (Hungary and Latvia) – where the GDP/capita level is about a quarter of that in the richer countries (or currently around €10,000). The EA average lies roughly in the middle, at about €30,000 per person in 2014.

Figure 3.1: GDP/capita in four cases, 2000–2014

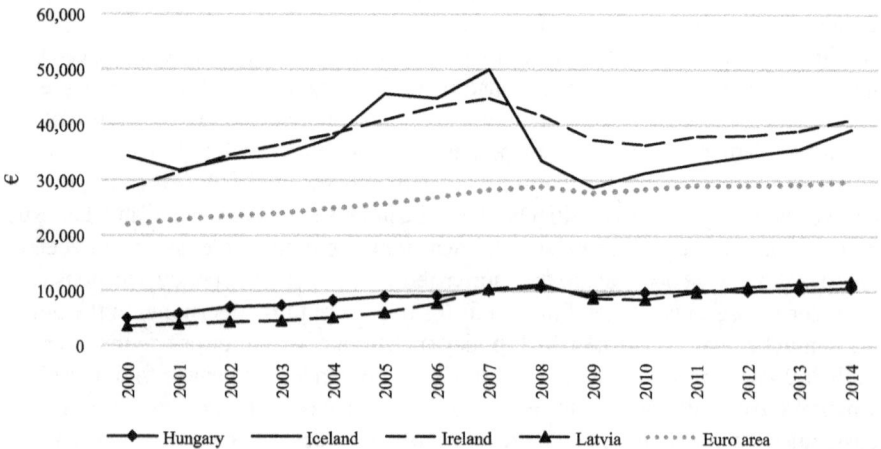

Note: Gross domestic product at market prices. The Euro area (EA) aggregate includes 19 countries.
Source: Eurostat [nama_10_pc].

The second noteworthy trend concerns the relatively smooth and positive trend in the EA-average indicator. The smoothness itself is not surprising, as it results from the aggregation of nineteen (more volatile) national indicators, including (among others) Germany and Greece. But any lessons derived from data, when aggregated at this level, can be very misleading. If policy makers were to use this level of aggregation to gauge the state of Europe's economies (and this *is* the level of aggregation at which Eurozone policy makers at the ECB must focus!), there would be little cause for concern: GDP/capita of the EA-average grew slowly over most of the period, with only a slight dip in 2008 (though it has lumbered under a mostly flat trajectory ever since).

Third, and finally, the Icelandic case seems to be more volatile than the others: its economy experienced a quick and long fall in 2007, before recovering slowly after 2009. This volatility is a result of comparing in euros, and reflects the króna's strong devaluation in response to the crisis (as we will see in Chapter Four). If we compared per-capita growth rates converted into US dollars, then the trends in Iceland and Ireland would have been much more similar (and smoother), while Latvia's trend would become the most volatile.

Because two of the countries in this figure have an independent currency (and hence comparisons require the use of an exchange rate that can be leveraged as a policy instrument), it is easier to compare the effect of the crisis by looking at the annual change in GDP (using their own, national currencies). This comparison is shown in Figure 3.2, and it reveals a very different picture.

Figure 3.2: GDP in four cases, per cent change, 2000–2013

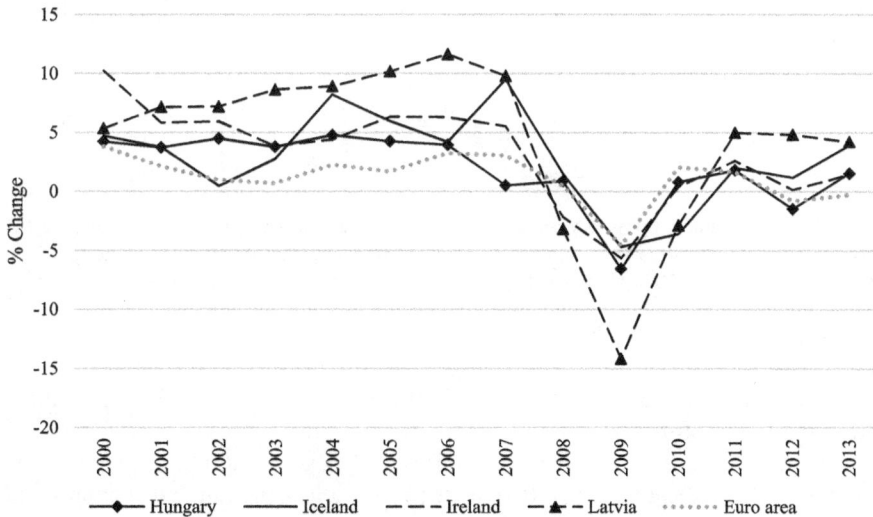

Note: Annual percentages of constant price GDP are year-on-year changes; the base year is country-specific. The Euro area (EA) aggregate includes 19 countries.
Source: IMF (2015a)

From Figure 3.2 it is clear that most countries begin to experience the effects of the crisis in 2007, and that these effects were felt hardest in 2009. In that year, Latvia experienced a remarkable 15 per cent decline in its GDP from the previous year. In the following two years, 2010-2011, all the economies in this study begin to grow again. Several states (including the EA average) experienced another dip in 2012 – and two of the cases again suffered from negative growth (the EA average and Hungary; while Ireland grew by a miserly 0.15 per cent). Finally, none of the states has managed to return to their pre-crisis growth levels, although Latvia (at roughly 5 per cent) has improved more than the others.[1]

From Figure 3.2, then, we can see that the depth of the crisis might be measured by comparing a country's GDP level in 2007 with that in 2009.[2] The results of this simple calculation are shown in Figure 3.3.

Figure 3.3: Per cent change in GDP, EU States and Iceland, 2007–2009

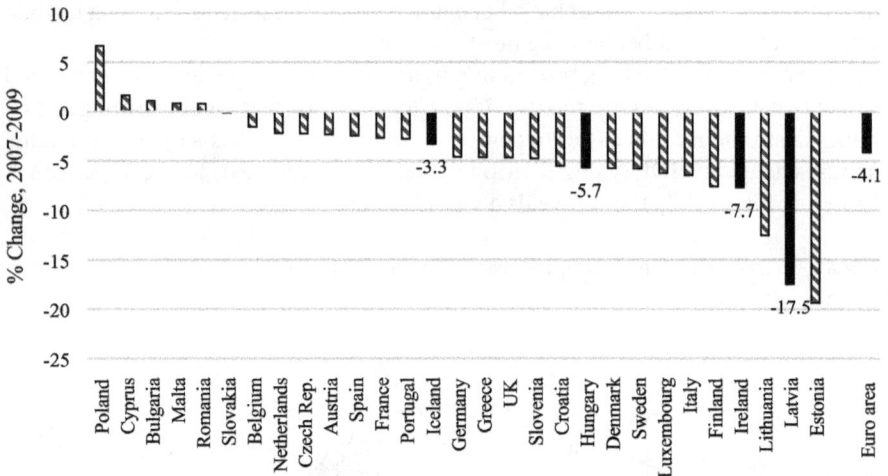

Note: Countries ranked by their change in GDP levels. The four cases under study (and the EA average) are marked solid. This indicator is created by using Eurostat [nama_10_gdp], which relies on an index (2010=100) based on chain-linked volumes, at market prices. The Euro area (EA) aggregate includes 19 countries.
Source: Eurostat [nama_10_gdp]

From Figure 3.3, and given the depth of the crisis depicted in Figure 3.2, it is clear that Latvia suffered the worst crisis – at least with regards to the effect on the country's GDP. Indeed, of the EU countries, only Estonia appears to have fallen further by this indicator. In just two years (2007–2009), the Latvian economy fell

---

1. But, as was seen in Figure 3.1, the aggregate economy in each state has grown, in per capita euro terms, from 2000 to 2014, even if they have not yet returned to their pre-crisis heights (in 2007).

2. This is actually a conservative measure when applied to Latvia, as its economy began to shrink already in 2006. Hence, we are not capturing the full extent of its economic decline.

by a harrowing 17.5 per cent! This is a phenomenal drop in economic activity, especially in light of the fact that Latvia had relatively little debt (*see* below), and its financial sector required relatively less support (c.f. Table 1.1, above). Ireland and Hungary both experienced deep drops in their GDP – worse than the EA average. Iceland, by contrast, seems to have weathered the storm remarkably well: its economy shrank less than the EA average.

Sovereign debt

Contrary to much public commentary, and as clearly demonstrated by Streeck (2014), Europe's sovereign debt burden – for most states – was not the result of economic mismanagement or an overly burdensome welfare state.[3] For most states – and for three of our four cases – sovereign debt was the cost of rescuing financial firms from collapsed markets. To see whether a country's debt was long-standing (e.g., the result of unsustainable social spending), or a more immediate need to shore up a failed industry, Figure 3.4 compares the level of government gross debt, as a percentage of GDP, for the same four countries and the EA average.

Figure 3.4: General government gross debt in four cases, per cent of GDP, 2000–2013

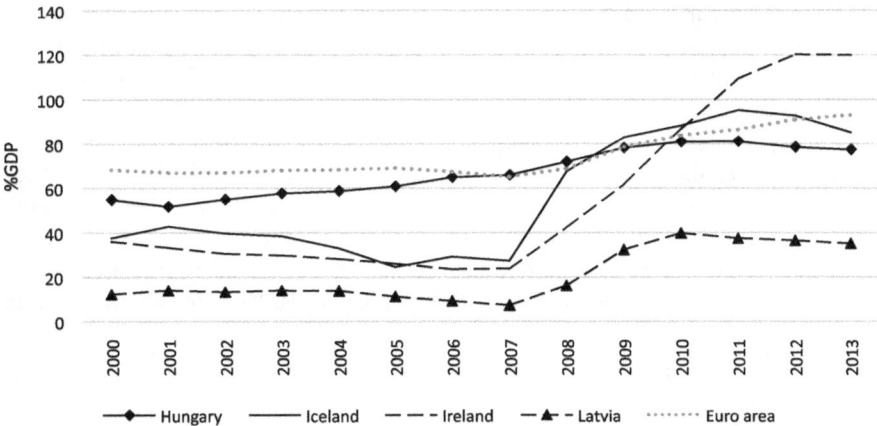

Note: Gross debt consists of all liabilities that require payments of interest and/or principal by the debtor to the creditor at a future date. This includes debt liabilities in the form of SDRs, currency and deposits, debt securities, loans, insurance, pensions and standardised guarantee schemes, and other accounts payable. See original source for more details. The Euro area (EA) aggregate includes 19 countries.
Source: IMF (2015a)

---

3. Of course, this hasn't stopped international lenders from using the debt crisis as an excuse to tie the hands of economic policy makers and/or to limit welfare state expenditures. It would seem that others were heeding the advice of Rahm Emanuel, President-elect Obama's appointed chief of staff in 2008, who (in)famously noted: 'You never want a serious crisis to go to waste. And what I mean by that is an opportunity to do things you think you could not do before' (Emanuel 2009).

Figure 3.4 is revealing in at least four different ways. First, the overall level of debt in the (19 country) EA average is remarkably high over the entire (2000–2013) period. Recall that the EU's Stability and Growth Pact (SGP) requires states to keep their general government debt levels below 60 per cent of GDP.[4] Using the IMF's indicator,[5] the Euro-average debt level surpasses the 60 per cent ceiling for the entire period, and it grew slowly but steadily in response to the crisis (after 2007).

Second, most of our cases were remarkably frugal. Before the crisis, each of the cases was located below the EA average mentioned above, and all but Hungary were well beneath the 60 per cent ceiling. In response to the crisis, only two of the cases (Ireland in 2010; and Iceland in 2009) punctured through that average level (although Hungary's debt level exceeded the EA average, very slightly, in 2008).

Third, in three of the four cases, the debt levels grew very quickly, in response to the crisis. Only in Hungary was the government's debt level relatively high before the crisis, and it remained high throughout the entire period. As we already learned in the introduction, and shall investigate in more detail in Chapter Seven, Hungary did not experience the same sort of financial crisis as the other three cases: Iceland, Ireland and Latvia were all forced to borrow money to bail out their financial sectors; Hungary wasn't. Figure 3.4 reveals that three of the four cases in this study maintained conservative (read balanced) public accounts prior to the crisis, and only got into trouble after responding to the crisis. Hungary's public accounts tell a very different story: here is a state that has long struggled to live within its budget.

Finally, the general trends revealed here are a little different from the change in GDP trends shown in Figure 3.2. In these government debt figures we see that the effects of the crisis (the jump in debt levels) reverberate for some time and produce long-term effects: after increasing, the debt-levels flatten out – at a higher level. Hence, to calculate the severity of the crisis using this measure, it makes more sense to contrast the 2013 and 2007 levels of debt. This is done in Figure 3.5.

---

4.   The Maastricht Treaty (signed 7 February 1992) applies to all EU members and established the Maastricht criteria (often called the convergence criteria). The SGP was adopted in 1997 and applies specifically to those countries participating in the European Monetary Union. Both sets of requirements include a three per cent (of GDP) limit on annual general government budget deficits, and a 60 per cent (of GDP) ceiling on national debt.

5.   As years of haggling have revealed, there is much disagreement about how to actually measure the general government debt level. Ideally, I would prefer to use Eurostat debt indicators, but these do not include Iceland for the entire period. It is for this reason that I employ the IMF indicator.

Figure 3.5: Change in general government debt in EU States and Iceland, per cent of GDP, 2007–2013

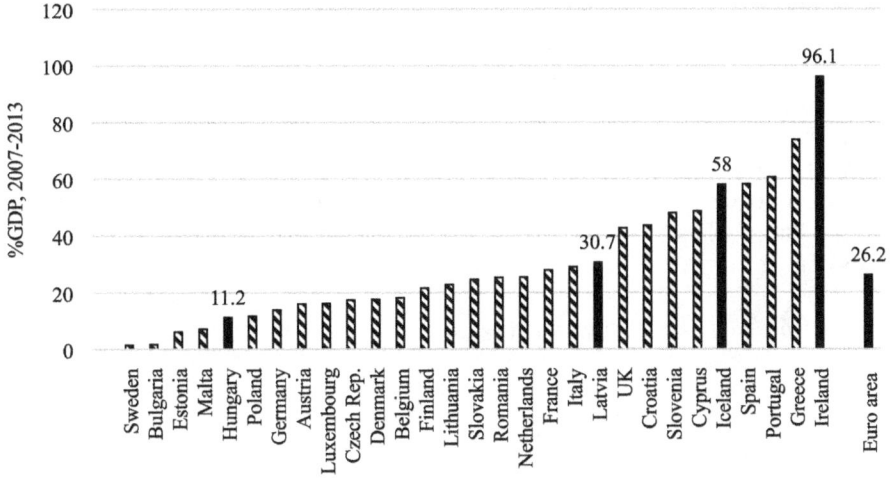

Note: Countries ranked by their change in debt levels. The four cases under study (and the EA average) are marked solid. Icelandic figures are from IMF (2015a). The Euro area (EA) aggregate includes 19 countries.
Source: Eurostat [tsdde410] and IMF (2015a)

This sort of rough indicator does not tell us how the governments spent these borrowed funds – only that they had to borrow. It does, however, demonstrate rather clearly that many European countries increased their debt levels significantly in the wake of the crisis – and three of the four cases in this study find themselves at the deeper end of the debtors' pool. If we use this indicator as a rough surrogate for a government's cost of responding to the crisis, then we can see that the cost of the crisis was highest in Ireland, followed by Greece, Portugal, Spain and Iceland. In three of the four cases in this study (Ireland, Iceland, Latvia), the costs of the crisis were larger than the EA average: they are some of the hardest-hit states in Europe. Hungary, by contrast is clearly different from the other three cases in that the crisis hardly affected its government debt levels during the period in question.

Inflation

The change in a country's price level, or its inflation rate, is another popular indicator for comparing national economic developments (and evaluating the success of government policy). As was made clear in the previous chapter, this is a problematic indicator, in that some groups/interests benefit more from a low inflation environment than do others (and this is especially true with regard to periods of deflation). However, as the SGP requires states to maintain an inflation level below three per cent, and there is broad general consensus on the utility of maintaining stable inflation rates, it is interesting to see how the crisis (and the government's response to that crisis) affected the overall price level in each case.

Figure 3.6 does just that: it takes the year-on-year changes in average consumer prices in the EA, and compares them to developments in the four cases under study. What is especially interesting in this comparison is the fact that, for most of the period (2000–2013), the level of inflation in our four cases was higher than the EA average. This is not to say that the levels of inflation were irresponsibly or dangerously high in these states – as the average EA level of inflation remained very low (around two per cent annually for most of the period). At any rate, for most of the cases, and for most of the period, the level of inflation hovered around two to six per cent. The exception, of course, can be found at the depth of the crisis (2008–2009), when inflation rates briefly spiked (to 15.2 per cent in the case of Latvia!).

Figure 3.6: Inflation rates in four cases, per cent, 2000–2013

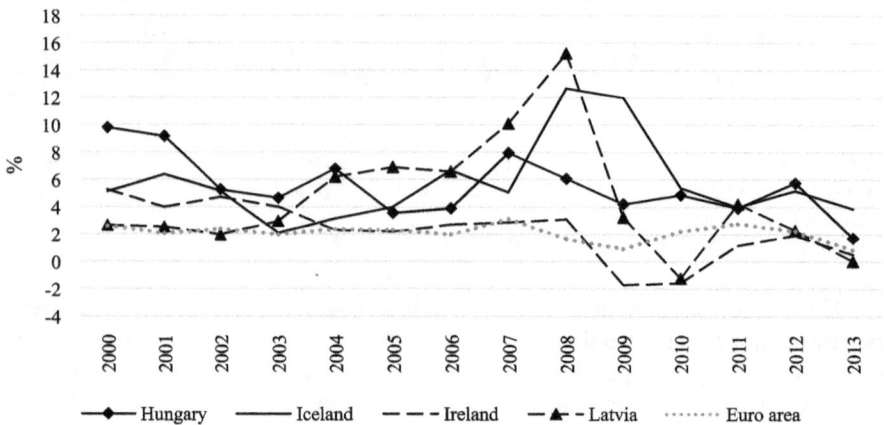

Note: Annual percentages of average consumer prices, year-on-year changes. The Euro area (EA) aggregate includes 19 countries.
Source: IMF (2015a)

The Hungarian case is particularly interesting, as it began the period with a very high level of inflation (9.8 per cent in 2000), but its inflation level was slowly falling before the crisis. Immediately prior to the crisis (in 2007), Hungary experienced a slight jolt in its price level, but the economy quickly returned to its long-term downward trajectory, until 2012 – when it again spiked briefly (this time to 5.7 per cent). By 2013, Hungary's inflation level had fallen to 1.7 per cent (!) – above the EA average, but still quite modest (especially when seen from a historical perspective).

The inflation records of Ireland and Latvia are much more volatile. In Latvia, prices begin to climb long before the crisis, revealing the sort of asset bubble that drove the crisis in many states. In 2008, however, when the Latvian economy imploded, inflation abated and slowed to a crawl. Indeed, the price situation became so dire that the country experienced deflation: its prices (and wages!) were falling in 2010. Ireland also experienced deflation, and its deflationary period was even longer-lasting (2009–2010). It took longer for Irish prices to recover (relative to Latvia's prices) and return to positive terrain – but Ireland's inflation level continued to hover below the EA average. As we shall see in subsequent chapters, this deflation – in both Latvia and Ireland – is evidence of the internal devaluation strategies that Eurozone members were forced to adopt in order to improve their relative competitiveness.

Changes in Latvian prices resemble a roller coaster. Iceland shows a similar, if slightly less volatile, trend. What is most important to note, however, is that Iceland managed to avoid deflation, to the benefit of its workers. In response to the crisis (in 2009, and especially in 2010), Iceland's price level fell significantly, and it has largely returned to its pre-crisis level.

In short, Latvia and Iceland experienced the most volatile price movements in response to the crisis – but these changes were short-lived. All of the countries have been moving in the direction of lower inflation levels, over time, and two of the countries have even fallen into negative territory. There are no signs of runaway inflation in any of the cases.

Distributional indicators

The first section provided an overview of the more market- or investor-oriented indicators that we read about in the daily headlines. These indicators are obviously important for gauging the depth and the nature of the crisis, but they offer only once piece of a much larger puzzle. It is also important to gauge the depth and the effect of the crisis on the lives of those people who live in these countries. As I argued in Chapter Two, one of the ways in which we can evaluate whether policy makers are responding to their constituents' needs is to see if their policies are providing relief to the most vulnerable groups in society. This part of the chapter examines indicators that can reveal such distributional cleavages: how the crisis has affected the average worker (by way of the level of unemployment) and the average citizen (through the effect of the crisis on public spending); the distribution of income within the country (by way of a Gini index); and the level of desperation suffered by those hit hardest by the crisis (as measured by a net migration indicator).

Unemployment

If I were asked to focus on a single indicator for measuring the depth of the crisis, and the government's success in bringing the economy back on track, it would be a country's level of unemployment, over time. This indicator, more than any other, provides insight into how the country's economic fate (and policy response) affects the average citizen. For most people, wages and income from employment are the main means of economic (not to mention psychological) well-being. By examining and comparing changing levels of unemployment, we get a good sense of the difficulties experienced at different stages of the crisis (and the government's responses), across the country cases. After all, even those who were lucky enough to have kept their jobs at the depths of the crisis found their relative bargaining position (vis-à-vis employers) and their level of job security threatened by the growing ranks of the unemployed.

This should be reason enough for policy makers to try and maintain full employment, but the state also has a financial incentive to fight unemployment: when workers lose their jobs, they pay less taxes to the state (decreasing its revenues), and the state – in turn – needs to respond with increased assistance and support for those unemployed (increasing its expenditures). Hence, the best way for a state to minimise its budgetary expenditures (and with it, the state's debt-burden) is to manage its economy in ways that can foster and sustain full employment. Herein lies the biggest paradox of monetary union: in order to secure the fiscal discipline required of monetary union, states have to jettison the one policy that is most likely to deliver that fiscal relief. In short, both the human and public costs of failed markets can be substantial. Examining changes in the unemployment level provides a glimpse of those costs.

How, then, did the crisis affect unemployment levels in Europe? Figure 3.7 displays the unemployment levels, as a percentage of the total labour force, in our four cases and the EA average for most of the 21st century. There are three important characteristics evident in Figure 3.7. First, it would seem that Latvia is the worst place to be a worker in this group of states: the level of unemployment was very high before the crisis (14.3 per cent in 2000), and remains high after the crisis (e.g. 12 per cent in 2013). Worse, Latvia's unemployment record is very volatile: shooting from peaks, to valleys, to peaks again. Conversely, Icelandic workers would seem to be the best off in the sample: they faced an unemployment level, both before and after the crisis, that was always below the other countries in the study. Finally, the EA-average level of unemployment is disturbingly high, and has been growing in recent years.

What is terrifying about this figure (and what escapes our attention when we only focus on growth levels), is how high and persistent unemployment levels remain in Europe. In every case, but Iceland, the level of unemployment is *unacceptably* high. This is clear evidence of failed markets and inadequate policy responses. In the last year of this data series, in 2013, more than ten per cent of the labour force in Ireland, Hungary, Latvia and the EA-average were unable to secure gainful employment. It is a human and political tragedy that so many people are out of work, more than five years after the financial crisis. In short, this figure provides the clearest sign of poor economic management on the part of national and/or European policy makers. Here it would seem that the hands of European policy makers were tied: they were (and are) unable to respond, as their economic ships of state crashed onto the shoals of an economic recession.

When we zoom our focus in to examine the crisis years, we see a pattern that was not unlike what we saw with regard to government debt levels (in Figure 3.4 above): unemployment levels were at their lowest immediately prior to the crisis (in 2007), and then increased in each of the cases over the next three years. For most states, the height of the unemployment crisis hit in 2010, and then began to

Figure 3.7: Unemployment levels in four cases, per cent, 2000–2013

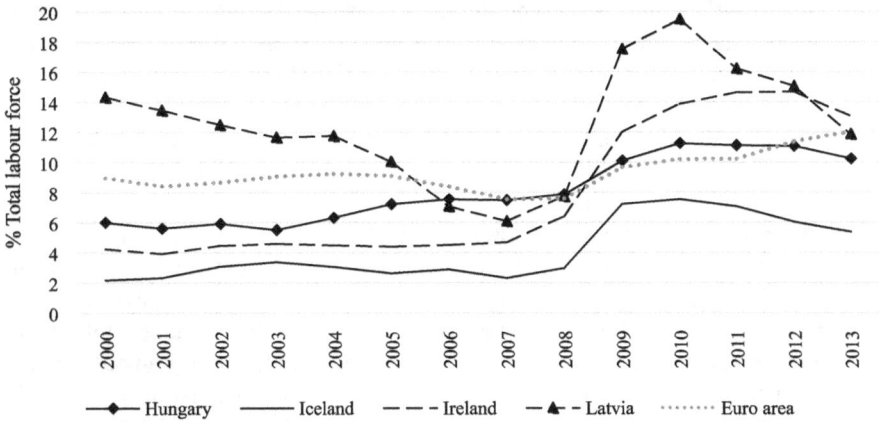

Note: Per cent of total labour force. The Euro area (EA) aggregate includes 19 countries.
Source: IMF (2015a)

Figure 3.8: Increase in unemployment in four cases, 2007–2010

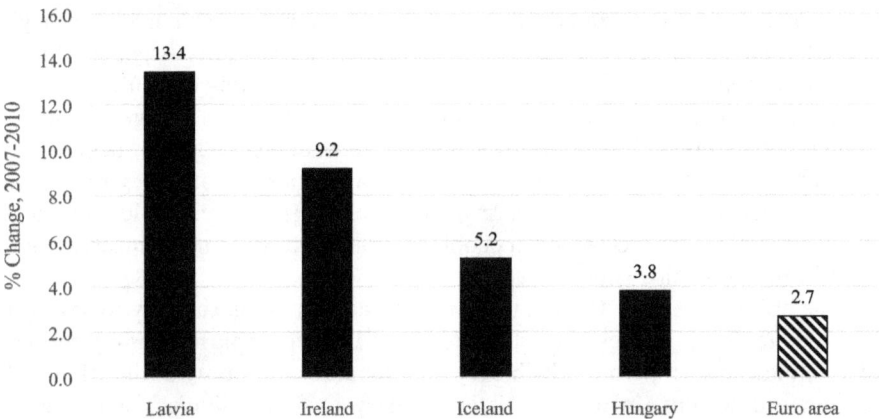

Note: Countries ranked by their change in unemployment levels from 2007 to 2010. The Euro area (EA) aggregate includes 19 countries.
Source: IMF (2015a)

decline slowly thereafter. Ireland is the one exception: its unemployment level continued to grow, slowly, all the way until 2012.

Figure 3.8 provides a snapshot indicator of the enormous costs of the crisis borne by workers, and how it varied across cases.[6] Over the course of three years,

6. As hinted in the previous paragraph, this measure is slightly more conservative when applied to Ireland, as that country's unemployment level continued to grow after 2010. With a more refined measure, the unemployment costs to the Irish economy would be even worse (larger) than displayed in Figure 3.8.

the level of unemployment in Latvia grew by over 13 per cent: from six per cent to 19.5 per cent! (That is not a typo: in 2010, nearly every fifth Latvian was out of work!) Once again, the Latvian case astonishes: the repercussions of the crisis are disproportionately large, given the relatively small size of the country's banking bailout and government debt burden.

The cost of the crisis in Ireland was also enormous, if more understandable – in the sense that Ireland is still digging out from an enormous financial bailout, and bearing a significant debt burden (as a result). Given the enormity of the Icelandic banking collapse (and its size relative to the Icelandic market), we might have expected to see the highest unemployment levels (and jump in unemployment levels) in Iceland. Rather, it seems that Icelandic policy makers have managed to reduce the potential unemployment costs, and made them smaller, relative to expectations (given the depth of its crisis). Once again, Hungary is an outlier: like the EA-average, it experienced a smaller (3.8 per cent) increase in its (already high) unemployment level – reflecting its very different point of departure.

Government spending

Government spending is one of the most important tools that policy makers have in responding rapidly to an economic crisis: this response is channelled through two different conduits. First, the government can inject new (crisis-specific) funds into the economy in an effort to stimulate demand (e.g., starting new infrastructure projects, encouraging the newly unemployed to go to university/college for further training, or simply giving money to the poor). Second, the budgets of democratic governments in developed economies tend to have a number of policy responses that will increase automatically during crisis situations: e.g., unemployment and social protection will kick-in when people lose their jobs and find themselves (and their families) needing support.

The ability of a state to fund these needs depends on its capacity to save (or borrow). In theory, states should try to build budget surpluses during periods of economic growth, from which they can subsequently draw, during times of economic downturn. In practice, it is not easy to find politicians who are so responsible (and far-sighted). In the absence of savings, accumulated deficits end up as government debt – and this accumulated debt can become a significant burden, as we saw in the previous section (and will see more in the chapters that follow). If a state has avoided the accumulation of too much debt when its economy was growing, it can more easily run deficits during periods of crisis to help stimulate the economy for a rapid recovery.

When a state borrows money to cover these accumulated deficits, the price it pays is a reflection of the market's confidence in that state's ability to repay its debts. Hence, if the market believes that a country is pursuing responsible economic policies, and is a trustworthy borrower, then it will offer lower interest rates on its loan to the government (to cover the debt). These long-term interest rates become a good indicator of market confidence, and we shall return to them in Chapter Eight. But Eurozone states struggle with an additional burden, in that they are bound to a rule which limits their deficits to three per cent of GDP (and their government debt levels to 60 per cent of GDP). These rules can be relaxed (or ignored) under extraordinary conditions, but they lurk in the background – informing both governments and market perceptions of appropriate behaviour.

With this brief introduction, let us examine the general governments' structural balances since 2000. This is done in Figure 3.9, where a positive score captures a governments' budget surplus, and a negative score represents a budget deficit. The structural balance takes into account the automatic features mentioned above, in that it records the fiscal balance adjusted for the effects of the economic cycle.[7]

Figure 3.9: General government structural balance in four cases, per cent of GDP, 2000–2013

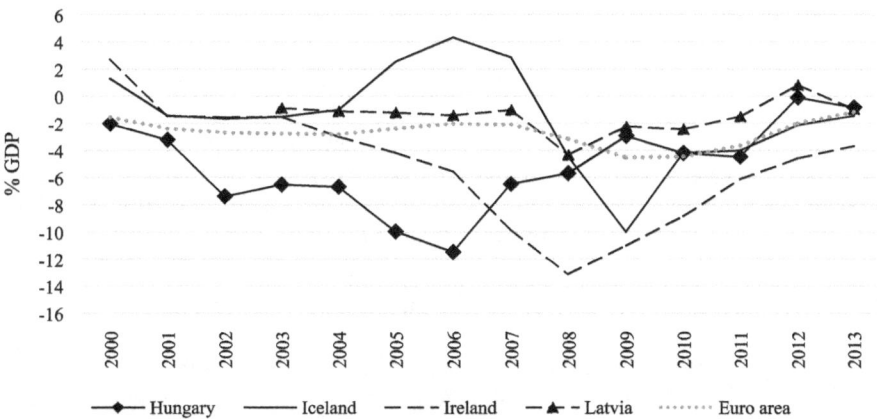

Note: Positive indicators reveal budget surpluses; negative indicators are budget deficits. The structural budget balance refers to the general government cyclically-adjusted balance adjusted for non-structural elements beyond the economic cycle. See the original source for more details. The Euro area (EA) aggregate includes 19 countries.
Source: IMF (2015a).

In Figure 3.9 we see that Iceland is the only case, prior to the crisis, which had built up a budget surplus while the economy was expanding.[8] Every other case, and the EA average, has been running budget deficits over many years. In most cases, these deficits seem to have been manageable, in that the overall level of government debt (except Hungary) is relatively low, as we saw in Figure 3.4.

Let us now consider the budget response to the crisis in each state. In Hungary, the annual budget deficits were large and imposing before the crisis (as we know from the significant size of Hungary's accumulated debt in Figure 3.4), but after 2006, we can see a serious tightening of the Hungarian belt: the deficit decreased

---

7. For a critical discussion of the role that inaccuracies in structural balance indicators played in worsening the crisis in Europe, see Claeys *et al.* (2016).

8. Except for Ireland, in 2000, which also enjoyed a surplus – but this was the only year that Ireland has had a budget surplus in the current millennium.

from 11.5 per cent in 2006, to 5.7 per cent in 2008, and hovered around three and four percent until 2010, before shrinking to almost zero in 2013! In short, Hungary was reining in its deficit in the midst of the crisis – it was not able (or willing) to use the budget for purposes of economic stimulus, but seems to be prioritising the need to pay down its significant levels of debt.

The clearest response to the crisis can be seen in the Icelandic and Irish figures: Iceland's budget balance fell sharply: from a strong (4.3 per cent) surplus in 2006 to a ten per cent deficit in 2009! This suggests that the government was spending lots of money, very quickly, to try to pull its economy out of a tailspin. But after bottoming out in 2008, the government started shrinking that deficit such that it was almost back to balance in 2013. From this indicator it would seem that Iceland has turned the corner and no longer needs to use fiscal stimulus to keep its economy afloat.

Ireland, by contrast, is still producing government deficits in 2013 (-3.7 per cent), and experienced the deepest of the deficits (-13.1 per cent in 2008) in any of our cases. Although Ireland's deficits have been shrinking a little each year, since that time, it still has a long way to go before it can begin to pay off the massive debts we saw earlier in the chapter – especially in light of the sluggish economic growth it was experiencing before 2012 (see Figures 3.1 and 3.2). Still, Ireland is clearing heading in the right direction (albeit slowly).

Policy makers in Latvia seem to be more concerned about their budget balance than they do about their unemployed. Despite a very hard hit to its real economy, as we saw in the previous section, the Latvian authorities have not been willing to expand government spending: their largest deficit was in 2008 (-4.3 per cent), and that was the only year they broke through the three per cent ceiling imposed on it by the SGP.

Now that we've looked at the overall budget balance, we might examine the amount of money that was spent on social protection in response to the crisis. Social protection benefits are government transfers to households (in cash or in kind) to help people deal with a number of different risks and needs, such as disability, sickness, health care, old age, survivors, family/children, unemployment, housing and social exclusion. Some of these protections are not affected by the crisis, and some will increase in response to the crisis. In short, this is a tricky indicator, in that it broadcasts two different signals: 1) the relative wealth of a country (richer countries tend to have more of these protections); but, also, 2) a country's spending response in the face of a crisis (the deeper the crisis, the more a country is expected to spend).[9]

Figure 3.10 compares total social protection expenditures, across all four cases and the EA average. With reference to the first signal, we can see that all of the

---

9. In 2010, the states in Europe with the largest expenditures (as a percentage of GDP) were: Denmark (32.8 per cent); France (32.7); Germany (29.8); Austria (29.6) and the Netherlands (29.3). In other words, all these countries spent more than the cases depicted in Figure 3.10. A wealthy country such as Norway, which suffered less from the crisis, kept is expenditure level rather low (in 2010, 25.1 per cent).

cases exhibit lower levels of social expenditure than the EA average. This means that the wealthier countries (Ireland and especially Iceland) tend to have rather meagre levels of social protection expenditures, relative to their wealth – but more so than their (poorer) case comparisons (Hungary and Latvia). Latvians can expect the least government support, as they have the lowest level of social spending (as a per cent of GDP). This may help to explain why so many Latvians found it necessary to emigrate in response to the crisis (see below). Relative to the other cases, Hungarians and Icelanders enjoy the highest levels of social expenditures, at around 20 per cent of GDP – although Ireland's social protection expenditures increased significantly until 2010, before levelling off. This implies that Hungary, relative to its wealth, is punching above its weight class (i.e., that it is relatively more generous than the others in terms of its social protections expenditures).

Figure 3.10: Total social protection expenditures in four cases, per cent of GDP, 2000–2013

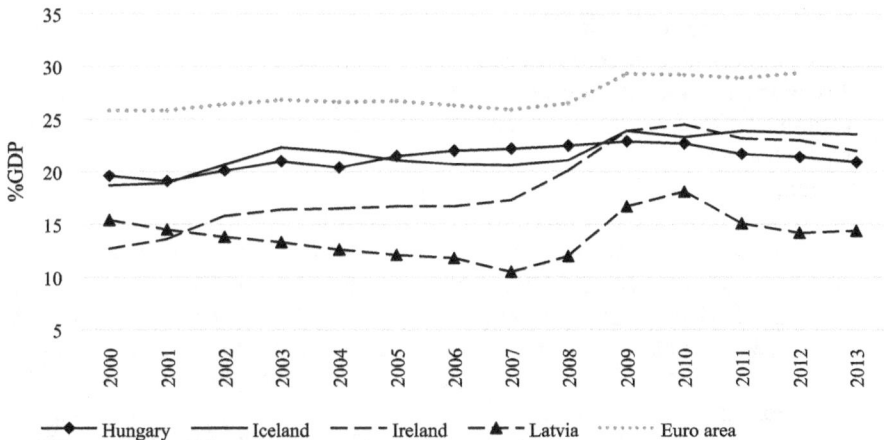

Note: This indicator captures total social protection expenditures, as defined by ESSPROS. The Euro area (EA) aggregate includes 18 countries.
Source: Eurostat [spr_exp_sum]

With respect to the second signal – the crisis response – Ireland and Latvia experienced the largest boosts in social expenditures. This might be read as a sign of failed economic management. Unable to stop the rising levels of unemployment using other policy tools, more Irish and Latvian citizens became dependent upon government support (remember, though, that the level of support is relatively modest in these countries). The Irish response to the crisis stays high, and drops only slightly in subsequent years; whereas Latvia began to spend less after 2010, but still maintains a higher level of spending than it had before the crisis. The EA average also increases noticeably in the wake of the crisis, and these countries maintained that higher level for the remainder of the period (for which we have data). As the expenditure levels in Hungary and Iceland changed remarkably little in the wake of the crisis, we might infer that there was less demand for these sorts of protections.

Income inequality

Any government response to an economic crisis is bound to have distributional consequences. These consequences turn on the decisions made by policy makers, including: 1) who will pay for the costs of crisis (the wealthy or the poor); and 2) who will benefit most – e.g. in the form of financial support and bailouts – from the government's response to the crisis (e.g. bankers or the unemployed)? To put a sharper point on it: when government support is aimed at providing a cushion for investors across Europe, but results in massive unemployment and a rise in sovereign debt levels that squeezes the states' capacity to help the poor and most vulnerable, then the costs of the crisis are paid by those who can afford it least, to the benefit of those who can afford it most.[10]

Evaluating government decisions with respect to their distributional consequences is best dealt with in the country case chapters that follow – where we can climb into the details and complex trade-offs involved. For now, we will only examine a snapshot indicator of those distributional consequences: the change in income inequality over time. In particular, this section considers the effect of the crisis on income inequality, by means of a Gini-index.[11] By seeing if this index changes during (and after) the crisis, we can see the effect that government efforts (or neglect) has had on helping the poorest (or the richest) groups in each state.

Figure 3.11 introduces the income inequality trends for our cases since 2000. What is most surprising, I think, is the fact that the EA average is fairly flat, moving only slightly upward (less equal) in the wake of the crisis. On average, it seems the economic crisis did little to affect the distribution of income within the Euro area. But when we consider the effects in individual countries, we see a much more varied (and volatile) picture. As with the other indicators, we can look first at the different levels of income inequality across our cases, and then consider the trend (in response to the crisis).

The overall level of income inequality in Latvia is significantly higher than in the EA average (and all the other cases), and remains higher throughout the entire period. Irish inequality trends start off higher than the EA average, and tend to track the EA average from about 2008. By contrast, inequality is generally lower in Hungary and Iceland, though the two countries seem to be moving in different directions. By 2013, income inequality in Iceland was significantly lower than the

---

10. As with many of the other policy responses to the crisis, and as I've noted above, there is a clear temporal dimension to this distributional trade off. Those who argue for bailing out the financial sector often do so in the name of helping the very same poor and desperate. In particular, it is hoped that a strengthened financial sector will invest in the sort of productive activity that will eventually create jobs and government revenues (to the benefit of the poor and unemployed). But this relief, if it happens, will occur sometime far off in the future. Our focus now is on the shorter term effects.

11. The Gini index provides a simple indicator of income distribution in a country. In effect, it measures the extent to which the distribution of income among individuals or households within an economy deviates from a perfectly equal distribution. Thus a Gini index of 0 represents perfect equality, while an index of 100 implies perfect inequality.

other cases (at 24); income inequality in Latvia was significantly above the others (at 35.2), while Hungary, Iceland and the EA averages found themselves squeezed in between (28–30).

Figure 3.11: Income inequality in four cases, 2000–2013

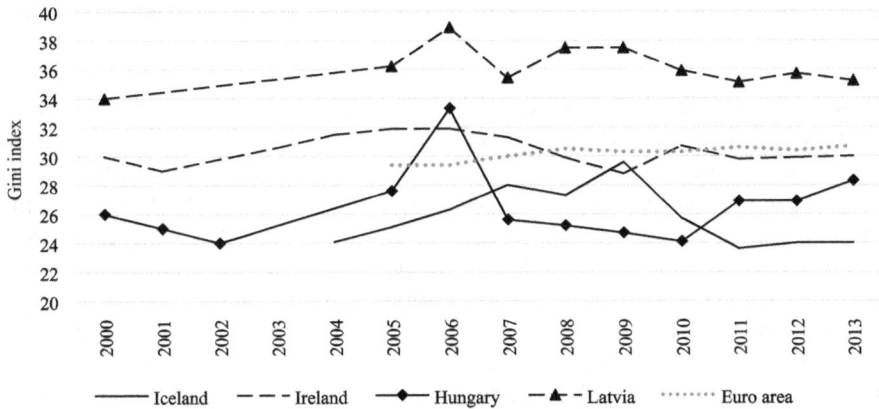

Note: Gini coefficient of equivalised disposable income (original source: SILC). Theoretically, the Gini index can range from 0 (complete equality) to 100 (complete inequality). There are some holes in this data: Iceland lacks data before 2004; Ireland lacks 2002; Hungary lacks 2003 and 2004; Latvia lacks 2001-2004; and the EA-average lacks data before 2005. The Euro area (EA) aggregate includes 19 countries.
Source: Eurostat [ilc_di12]

In terms of national responses to the crisis, there is at least one very surprising result: in Iceland, income inequality was growing strongly before the crisis (in the financial frenzy that was inflating the economy), but then it fell significantly in the wake of the crisis. Only in Iceland, it would seem, have policy makers pursued policies that ended up benefiting the poor and punishing the wealthy when responding to the crisis.

If the Icelandic trend is clear, the trend in Hungary was all over the map: income inequality increased significantly from 2002 to 2006, then dropped precipitously in the following year (2007). Then, for three subsequent years (until 2010), income inequality declined in Hungary. With the new government, in 2010, however, income inequality has begun to grow again, and the inequality levels in Hungary are rapidly approaching those in Ireland and the EA average. In both Ireland and Latvia, there is relatively little response to the crisis – even if the Latvian indicator does seem to hop around prior to the crisis.

Migration

The final distributional indicator, net migration, is the most interesting in that it provides the clearest indicator of the government's ability to provide satisfactory relief for its citizens. In the European Union, where it is possible to move from one state to another in search of employment, emigration can be read as a sign of dissatisfaction. But it is a signal that is sent grudgingly, in that one has to be very desperate to leave friends, family and the familiar: emigration is not a decision made lightly, and most people would prefer to find employment nearer home. But when policy makers are unwilling or unable to buoy their national economies, and public support is cut off due to the state's shrinking resources, then emigration becomes an act of desperation.

Figure 3.12 shows net migration as a share of the national population (per 1,000). The figure can be divided in half, with the top half (positive scores) showing cases where states can attract immigrants, and the bottom half (negative scores) showing cases where states are repelling their citizens as emigrants. As we can clearly see, each of the cases – with the exception of Latvia – was attracting more people than they were deterring before the crisis. Things were going well in these countries, pre-crisis, and their prosperity was attracting immigrants (and returning natives). By contrast, Latvia's population was haemorrhaging over the entire period: more than six people per 1,000 residents were leaving the country each year[12] – even before the crisis hit. For a country with just two million people, this should cause policy makers some concern.

Figure 3.12: Net migration levels in four cases, per 1,000, 2000–2013

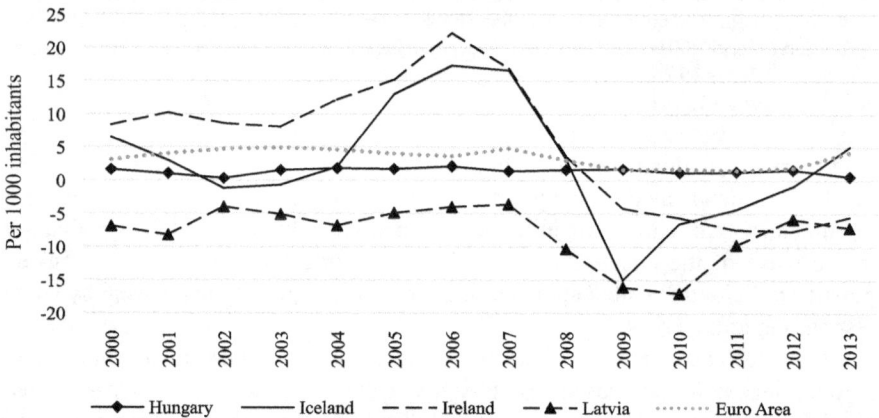

Note: Positive scores indicate net immigration to the country; negative scores indicate net emigration. The indicator is defined as the ratio of net migration (including statistical adjustment) during the year to the average population in that year. The value is expressed per 1000 persons. The net migration plus adjustment is calculated as the difference between the total change and the natural change of the population. The Euro area (EA) aggregate includes 18 countries.
Source: Eurostat [tsdde230]

---

12. This figure comes from Eurostat [migr-emi2]. In Latvia, the rate of emigration per 1,000 residents during this period ranged from 6.8/1000 (in 2002 and 2003) to 18.7/1000 (in 2010). There was only miniscule immigration to Latvia during this period: between 3,000 to 5,000 people per year in 2008–2010 (Eurostat [migr_imm1ctz]).

When the crisis hit, things changed – and they changed quickly: all the countries experienced sizeable drops in their levels of net migration, and almost all of the cases fell into negative territory (with more people leaving than entering their countries). Only Hungary (and the EA average) continued to attract more people than they repelled (positive net migration).

The fall in net migration was most severe in Iceland and Ireland, but also in Latvia. In Iceland, net migration began to fall in 2007, and just two years later the country began to experience high levels of emigration (negative net migration). Only after 2012 was Iceland able to attract people back to the country again. If this large exodus in response to the crisis can be seen as proof of the immense difficulties facing Icelanders at the time, its rapid turn-around can be seen as an indicator of the success that policy makers had in responding to the crisis. Iceland is again attracting, rather than repelling, migrants. Although the number of migrants entering Iceland is lower than before the crisis – the economic situation in the country is no longer forcing its citizens to flee, as it had during the crisis years (from 2007 to 2009).

Ireland is more accustomed to emigrant waves. In this light it may be surprising to see the Irish net migration figures in positive territory, before the crisis. The financial boom that was driving the Irish economy seems to have drawn many Irish home again, with over 20 immigrants per 1,000 residents entering the country in 2006! But from that point forward, the number of immigrants dropped off substantially, and after 2008 Ireland began to send away more workers than it could attract. Since the crisis, people have continued to flee the country, a sure sign of economic (if not also political) desperation. Although Ireland did experience a slight improvement in its net migration level after 2012, it shows the least sign of recovery among all the cases (except Latvia).

While people were fleeing Latvia even before the crisis struck, the situation worsened significantly in 2007, when Latvia's net migration level fell from -3.6 (per 1,000) to -17 in 2010! Since the turn of the millennium, Latvia's overall population has been in a nosedive: it has declined by over 300,000 people (or roughly the size of Iceland's total population!).[13] As in Ireland, there is good reason to interpret this exodus as a sign of desperation, and a rejection of Latvian economic policy (as we shall see later, in Chapter Six).

By contrast, Hungarians are staying put. The country's net migration numbers hardly move, throughout the period, and they shadow those of the EA-average. It would seem that Hungarians are not suffering so much that they are willing to take the desperate measure of moving abroad, away from family and friends, in search of work.

The net migration figures show us people voting with their feet. In these figures we can clearly see that people in Latvia and Ireland are dissatisfied with conditions at home; they lack confidence in their policy makers to rectify the situation, and many citizens seem to be forced to flee their countries in search

13. In 2000 Latvia's population was 2.38 million; in 2013 it had fallen to 2.02 million. See Eurostat [demo_pjan].

of gainful employment abroad. Many thousands of people have chosen to leave their country, rather than hope that the authorities will be able to turn things around in the foreseeable future. In Ireland alone, more than a quarter million people emigrated between 2007 and 2010.[14] Indeed, in both countries, the level of continued emigration, six years after the crisis, can be read as a testimony to failed policy (from the perspective of the migrants, anyway). I can think of no better sign of failed democratic policies than the mass exodus of those citizens who policy makers are supposed to satisfy and represent.

Iceland too suffered significant emigration in response to the crisis. For two years, the drop in net-migration was the steepest in the sample. But it would seem that the Icelandic authorities were able to turn things around relatively quickly: already in 2009, the net-migration figures began to improve, as fewer Icelanders left the country in desperate search of employment elsewhere. Eventually, in 2013, more people began to enter Iceland than were leaving.

In light of the loud criticisms of Hungarian policy in recent years (*see* Chapter Seven), some readers may be surprised that Hungary's net migration numbers stayed relatively flat and positive throughout the entire period. I suspect that this is partly because the Hungarian economy managed to avoid the worst of the crisis, its level of social protection expenditures was relatively high (as seen in Figure 3.10), and that its level of economic hardship has stayed high for a long period – i.e., there was no significant shock that convinced people to leave (as we find in the other cases). If we use net migration as a surrogate for political satisfaction, Hungarians seem relatively satisfied with their government's response to the crisis.

Conclusion

This chapter aimed to provide a statistical overview of the crisis, as applied to the four cases, and compared to the EA average. In doing so, I intended to reveal the nature and depth of the crisis in each case, and the way that the crisis affected their most vulnerable constituents.

I began with the sort of indicators that are most frequently bandied around to interpret the nature of (and response to) the financial crisis: levels of economic growth; sovereign debt; and inflation. For many, economic growth is the end-all of social policy.[15] If we focus on the aggregate EA measure of GDP/capita, a Great Recession is barely noticeable. Per capita GDP in the EA-average grew very slowly but steadily throughout most of the 2000s, with only a slight retreat in 2008–09. However, when we break this aggregate figure down, and look at the experiences of individual countries, we see a very different picture and a great deal of variation. In particular, the experiences of Iceland, Latvia and Ireland were clearly different from that of Hungary.

---

14. Total emigration for the period 2007 to 2010 for the four cases is as follows: Ireland: 261,745; Latvia: 120,367; Hungary 37,939; and Iceland: 28,891. See Eurostat [migr_emi2].

15. As Michel Foucault (2004: 144) noted, with respect to neoliberalism, 'there is only one true and fundamental social policy: economic growth.'

There are no evident winners or losers with regard to overall GDP growth; change in GDP; or inflation. Much of the media talk, about miracle solutions and champion cases, is nothing more than political spin. All of the economies are growing (if slower than before), and none of them show any signs of significant inflation. The latter observation is especially noteworthy, in light of concerns that the use of an autonomous monetary policy might generate undesired, long-term, inflationary pressures. There is no evidence of this pressure in the data. To the contrary, the most volatile inflation rates were found in Latvia – not in the countries that experienced currency depreciations (Hungary and Iceland). The most troubling indicators surveyed in the first section are the very high debt-levels borne by Iceland and Ireland. These countries are still paying the costs of their banking sectors' excesses.

In respect to the individual cases, these figures help us see that the situation in Hungary is very different from the other three cases. The economic crisis affected Hungary, but it did so mostly on the margins: the effect of the crisis is not nearly as evident here as it is in the other cases.

Latvia, on the other hand, was hardest hit by the crisis, and the most vulnerable members of Latvian society have paid the highest price. This price is clearly evident in Latvia's frighteningly high emigration and unemployment figures. Latvia's predicament is odd, if only because the initial crisis was not as deep in Latvia (as it was in, e.g., Ireland and Iceland). As we shall see in Chapter Six, Latvia received foreign support (in the form of the Vienna Initiative) to bailout its banks, and (consequently) its sovereign debt level remained relatively low. Indeed, Latvia had access to a number of policies (e.g., devaluation, increased borrowing and fiscal stimulus) that could have eased the pain imposed on Latvian workers, but policy makers chose not to employ them. To claim, as many do, that Latvia represents an exemplary policy response to the crisis is to ignore two central facts: that the crisis in Latvia should have been mild, relative to other cases, and that Latvians suffered tremendously in pursuit of that policy. Rather, as we shall see below, the Latvian case is an example of a state that is willing to sacrifice the needs of its constituents for the good of the Eurozone.

Ireland's response is even more exemplary of how a monetary union forces its member states to respond. Ireland's financial crisis took a severe bite out of the Irish economy, resulting in a very heavy debt burden for the country. This placed strict limitations on what Irish officials could do to help their constituents/workers. Unlike Latvia, Ireland could not devalue its currency, and its very high debt level made it impossible to stimulate the economy with additional borrowing. In order to pay back its foreign debt, Ireland chose to squeeze wages and prices downward – in an effort to gain international competitiveness. The cost of that policy choice was paid mostly by Irish workers and the Irish poor. Like workers in Latvia, Irish workers fled the country, as the unemployment level skyrocketed.

The Icelandic response couldn't have been more different (relative to that in Latvia or Ireland). At the start of the crisis, the Icelandic situation looked remarkably dire, given the size of its (failed) banking sector, relative to the economy at large. But Iceland managed to turn its economy around much faster than the other cases, and with much less of a burden placed on the more vulnerable groups in Icelandic society. Quite astonishingly, the level of inequality in Iceland actually decreased in Iceland, as the government pursued policies that forced wealthier groups to pay for the damage that their actions inflicted on the rest of the economy. As a result, policy makers were able to minimise the unemployment costs of its (much larger and more damaging) financial crisis, and reverse the outflow of Icelandic workers. As the following chapters will demonstrate, the difference between Latvia, Ireland and Iceland is the difference created by monetary policy autonomy.

This brief overview of various statistical indicators suggests that much of the variance we see in national responses to the crisis can be explained by decisions made by policy makers. The following four chapters dive into these case details.

Chapter Four

Iceland

The modern Icelandic saga is a story of the meteoric rise of a new financial elite, with strong political connections, exploiting the opportunities offered by an under-regulated European financial market. This story is told often in light of Iceland's subsequent success in response to the crisis. *Bloomberg's View* (2012) is typical:

'Few countries blew up more spectacularly than Iceland in the 2008 financial crisis...Since then, Iceland has turned in a pretty impressive performance. It has repaid International Monetary Fund rescue loans ahead of schedule. Growth this year [2012] will be about 2.5 percent, better than most developed economies. Unemployment has fallen by half. In February, Fitch Ratings restored the country's investment-grade status, approvingly citing its "unorthodox crisis policy response."'

While Icelanders obviously suffered from the crisis, and their initial predicament was more precarious than most, Icelandic officials managed to turn things around rather quickly. As we saw in the preceding chapter, Iceland's GDP and employment levels fell less than one might expect (Figures 3.2 and 3.7), and the country's level of inequality actually shrunk in response to the crisis (Figure 3.11). As we shall see, this rapid turn-around was secured with the help of a depreciated currency, and a willingness to ring-fence and protect the domestic banking sector – and Icelanders in general – at the expense of external creditors.

While Iceland's economic lesson is well documented, its political lesson may be more important (if less studied). Iceland's experience (both positive and negative) demonstrates the continued wide scope for monetary policy autonomy in small European states. When policy makers and officials failed (and they failed miserably), they were swiftly kicked out of office. When replaced, a new government responded to the crisis by reasserting political control over the economy, and using that control to secure more just outcomes.

This chapter describes those political benefits. To do so, it is divided into four parts. It begins with a brief introduction to Iceland's rapid embrace of deregulated markets in the 1990s to build up a new financial industry in an economy that was previously dominated by natural resources. The second part of the chapter considers the nature of Iceland's financial crisis and the initial response to that crisis. The third part introduces the political response and fall-out from the crisis. Here we see newly-elected officials responding to political pressures to reassert political authority over markets. The chapter concludes with an overview of recent developments.

Of all the cases in this study, the Icelandic response proves to be the most democratic. Here public dissatisfaction mattered: public officials and shareholders were held accountable for their decisions, and elected officials developed a policy response that protected the most vulnerable Icelanders. The Icelandic response is also the most unique: not only were the institutions of government strong enough to face powerful market interests, and tame them in the name of the public's interest, but officials had the policy tools to secure beneficial outcomes.

Because Iceland was not tightly integrated into European banking and money markets, it maintained a higher degree of policy autonomy, which could be used by democratically-accountable institutions and policy makers. This autonomy can (and was) abused – especially before the crisis hit – but when the abuse was uncovered, there were strong political repercussions. More importantly, this autonomy was used to secure a quick, broad-based economic recovery.

The rise of Viking finance

Politics in Iceland is not the usual Nordic fare. While Nordic governments are often synonymous with social democracy, Iceland has been ruled by a conservative (Independence Party, or IP) government – either alone, or in coalition – for most of the post-war period. The prominence of conservative politics in Iceland reflects the country's traditional reliance on a bounty of natural resources (fish, sheep and – more recently – geothermal energy), and an electoral system which provides substantial over-representation to rural and coastal communities in the Icelandic Parliament (Althingi or *Alþingi*).

These political and economic patterns are linked by powerful family networks to create a strong state-corporate (some would say corrupt) imprint on the Icelandic economy.[1] As new economic interests became more predominant (first those associated with the aluminium sector, in the 1960s, then the privatised financial sector, at the turn of the millennium) they came to leverage the same political linkages, and enjoy the same sort of special status.

The Icelandic economy has always rested on a very narrow base. As a rule of thumb, Iceland's exports can be roughly divided between fish (and fish-related animal products) and industrial goods (related to the fishing industry, but also energy exports, e.g. raw aluminium). To support these export engines, the state played a very active role in the Icelandic economy: owning major industries and fish processing centres, as well as much of the banking sector. Before liberalisation, the largest banks in Iceland were state-owned, and they enjoyed access to cheap lines of credit from the Central Bank of Iceland (or CBI). Though state-owned, leadership positions in the banks were often distributed as political favours: e.g.,

---

1. The family groupings that underlie these political and economic alliances have curiously exotic names (e.g., the Octopus, the Squid and the Locomotives). The Octopus are aligned with the IP; and the Squid with the Progressive Party. See Boyes (2009), Hart-Landsberg (2013) and Wade and Sigurgeirsdottir (2010).

IP-appointees to the state-owned Landsbanki directed loans to IP-controlled businesses (Hart-Landsberg 2013).

This highly-regulated state of affairs came to an end in a flurry of neo-liberalism at the close of the 20th century. While many states were hit by a wave of deregulations during this time, Iceland's experience was marked by two important developments: 1) the political rise of Davíð Oddsson and his fellow-travellers; and 2) the country's 1994 decision to join the European Economic Area (EEA).

Davíð Oddsson became Prime Minister in 1991, and held that position until 2004 (at the end of his reign, Oddsson was Europe's longest-serving Prime Minister). When Oddsson stepped down, his protégé, Geir Haarde (fellow member of the Locomotive group and Finance Minister from 1998 to 2005), took over the reins of government. Then, in October 2005, Oddsson was chosen to chair the governors at the CBI – a position that he held while the eye of a global financial storm passed over Iceland. In both positions, Mr Oddsson held formal responsibility for many of the decisions that brought Iceland to the brink of economic disaster.[2]

Under Oddsson's reign, Iceland moved sharply to the right: many regulations were discarded, private companies and banks were privatised, financial markets were created and encouraged to expand in global markets, corporate tax rates were lowered, the Icelandic stock market was established, and capital controls were abolished (see, e.g., *The Economist* 2001). As his first government (Oddsson I) relied on the small Social Democratic Party for support, there were limits to what the IP could achieve in terms of deregulation. These limits were lifted in 1995, however, when the IP formed a government (Oddsson II) with the Progressive Party (PP), which was better positioned to implement a neo-liberal agenda. This coalition lasted for twelve years, that is until 2007. *See* Table 4.1.

Oddsson's deregulation crusade was facilitated by Iceland's access to a growing European market. This access was secured when Iceland signed the European Economic Area (EEA) agreement in 1994. After considerable debate (in 1992–93), Icelanders decided to join the EEA, but they kept full-EU membership at bay in order to maintain sovereign control over their fishing stocks (Thorhallsson 2002; Ingebritsen 2000). Even though EU membership was a nonstarter[3] for most of Iceland's political elites (including Oddsson and his IP[4]), Iceland's economy became deeply integrated with the rest of Europe's by way of the EEA.

---

2. A jack of all trades, Oddsson was appointed editor-in-chief at *Morgenblaðíð* (the leading Icelandic daily) after leaving the CBI in September 2009, allowing him significant influence over how the crisis is seen in the eyes of Icelanders.

3. In contrast to the other Nordic countries, Icelanders tend to be more enthusiastic about EU membership than their political elites. This probably has something to do with the fact that Iceland's political elites represent economic sectors that employ relatively few people. At any rate, neither the IP, the PP, or the Social Democratic Alliance supported EU membership at the time. In 1994, the Social Democratic Party became the first Icelandic political party to support EU membership in a policy statement.

4. IP's opposition to EU membership draws from several arguments: protecting Iceland's fisheries sector; the need for an autonomous currency and economic policy; the inability of such a small

Table 4.1: Recent governments in Iceland

Government	Prime Minister	From	Until	Coalition Partners
Oddsson I	Oddson, Davíð	30 April 1991	23 April 1995	*IP*, SDP
Oddsson II	Oddson, Davíð	23 April 1995	28 May 1999	*IP*, PP
Oddsson III	Oddson, Davíð	28 May 1999	23 May 2003	*IP*, PP
Ásgrímsson	Ásgrímsson, Halldór	15 Sept 2004	15 June 2006	*PP*
Haarde I	Haarde, Geir	15 June 2006	24 May 2007	*IP*, PP
Haarde II	Haarde, Geir	24 May 2007	1 Feb 2009	*IP*, SDA
Sigurðardóttir I	Sigurðardóttir, Jóhanna	1 Feb 2009	10 May 2009	*SDA*, LGM
Sigurðardóttir II	Sigurðardóttir, Jóhanna	10 May 2009	23 May 2013	*SDA*, LGM
Gunnlaugsson	Gunnlaugsson, Sigmundur Davíð	23 May 2013	7 April 2016	*PP*, IP
Jóhannsson	Jóhannsson, Sigurður Ingi	7 April 2016	10 Jan 2017	*PP*, IP
Benediktsson	Benediktsson, Bjarni	10 Jan 2017	Present	*IP*, LGM, Pirates

Note: In the right-hand column, the coalition party in italics is the Prime Minister's political party. Party acronyms are defined as follows:

IP	Independence Party (Conservative)	*Sjálfstæðisflokkurinn*
PP	Progressive Party (Liberal/Agrarian)	*Framsóknarflokkurinn*
SDP	Social Democratic Party	*Alþýðuflokkurinn*
SDA	Social Democratic Alliance (Centre-Left)	*Samfylkingin*
LGM	Left-Green Movement	*Vinstrihreyfingin – grænt framboð*

In 2000, the Social Democratic Party folded into the Social Democratic Alliance (SDA). The SDA was formed in 1999 as an alliance of Iceland's four left-wing parties: the Social Democrats, the People's Alliance, the Women's List and National Awakening. In 2000, they formally merged under the title 'The Alliance' (*Samfylkingin*). In February 2013 the official name of the party was again changed, to 'The Alliance – Social Democratic Party of Iceland' (*Samfylkingin – Jafnaðarmannaflokkur Íslands*).

In joining the EEA, Iceland was forced to jettison several monetary policy instruments. As Benediktsdottir *et al.* note in their influential *Economic Policy* article, 'This decision to join the EEA affected subsequent developments, inducing Iceland to remove capital controls; allowing Icelandic banks to set up branches

---

state to affect EU decisions (even as a member); and a fear that corporate taxes and regulations would only increase with membership. See, e.g. Thorhallsson (2010: 382).

in EU countries; and paving the way for the banks to borrow from foreign banks because they were, supposedly, subject to EU regulations' (Benediktsdottir *et al.* 2011: 188). Most significantly, the EEA agreement provided Icelandic banks with an opportunity to establish both subsidiaries and branches in all EEA countries – a practice that had been prohibited by law prior to the 1990s (Skaar Viken 2011: 315).

Exposed to Europe's financial markets and its (de)regulated practices, Iceland's banking sectors were privatised, de-regulated and grafted onto a larger European interbank lending market. Bank privatisation began in the late 1990s, and was completed by 2003. First in line was a small investment bank (which, with mergers and acquisitions, eventually became Glitnir). By 2002, the government had sold nearly all of its 70 per cent stake in the two largest commercial banks (Landsbanki and Búnaðarbanki – later Kaupþing, or Kaupthing) (OECD 2003: 88). Behind this drive for privatisation was a realisation of the political and economic gains that could be reaped by influential allies. In this regard, these two large state banks (Landsbanki and Búnaðarbanki) offered the biggest prizes, and were awarded to the two largest political groupings: Landsbanki ended up in the hands of IP supporters; PP supporters landed Kaupthing (Hart-Landsberg 2013).[5]

The privatisation of Iceland's banking sector began in earnest in 1998; by 2003, the total assets of the banking system had climbed to 174 per cent of GDP; by 2007, they had skyrocketed to 744 per cent (Benediktsdottir *et al.* 2011: 185– 86)! In less than a decade, three Icelandic banks (Landsbanki, Kaupthing and Glitnir) grew from being small, public utility organisations to join the ranks of the world's top 300 banks, capturing 85 per cent of Iceland's financial system (Wade and Sigurgeirsdottir 2012: 129). They managed this on the back of a profitable carry trade: borrowing short term, at low interest rates from places like Japan, and then parking that money in Iceland, where the interest rates were much higher. All this was possible in a political atmosphere that was almost devoid of regulation and oversight. On their coattails rode a political elite who bragged about their prowess.

The rapid growth in Iceland's banking sector fuelled an equities and housing bubble, as banks willingly extended credit – thinking they were lending against secure collateral (in the form of inflated real estate prices). Between early 2001 and late 2007, housing prices in Iceland rose by 89 per cent (Schwartz 2011: 297). The rise of the stock market was even more dramatic, as evidenced in Figure 4.1, where the average share price rose annually at about 43.7 per cent between 2003 and 2007 (Benediktsdottir *et al.* 2011: 202).

---

5. See Benediktsdottir *et al.* (2011), Gylfason *et al.* (2010) and Skaar Viken (2011) for more on the various political favours and exchanges that were imbedded in the privatisation of Icelandic banks.

Figure 4.1: The Icelandic stock market, 1992–2016

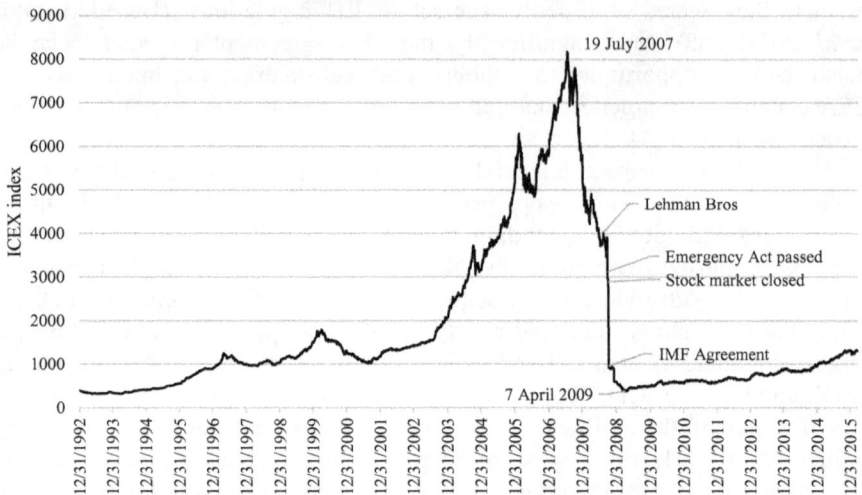

Note: OMX Iceland All Share Index (^ICEX). Daily opening position.
Source: Stooq (2016)

Iceland's banking boom brought with it two serious challenges. The growth itself relied on leveraged borrowing, so that by 2004, Iceland became known as the world's most heavily indebted economy (CBI 2007). But this debt rested in private – not public – hands. This was a problem (and, ironically, Iceland's saving grace), given the country's miniscule size: the level of debt far exceeded the capacity of the state to bail it out. The second challenge is derived from the fact that a very high share of Icelandic debt was carried in foreign currencies.[6] In 2008, household debt in Iceland was estimated to be about 100 per cent of GDP, and 13 per cent of it was carried in foreign currency (and about 80 per cent of all household debt was indexed to inflation). Non-financial business debt was three times larger (300 per cent of GDP), and roughly 70 per cent of bank loans to businesses were in foreign exchange (Benediktsdottir *et al.* 2011: 201). This high exposure to debt in foreign currencies is yet another sign of an under-regulated market, where consumers were lured into very risky loans.

The CBI watched these huge capital inflows and a ballooning current account deficit with growing concern; the country experienced a current account deficit in every year between 2003 and 2009, totalling some €11.8 billion in current prices, or about 160 per cent of GDP in 2009 (Benediktsdottir *et al.* 2011: 200). There were other signs of trouble as well. Already in 2006, a number of cracks had

---

6. The majority of foreign currency loans were actually to holding companies, then to households. The outstanding loans to holding companies were far in excess of one year's GDP at the time of the collapse, when loans to households amounted to one year's GDP (CBI, as referenced by Benediktsdottir *et al.* 2011: 194). The holding companies then invested in stocks, usually domestic (króna-issued) stocks, which rose rapidly with the boom.

appeared in Iceland's façade. In February of that year, Fitch downgraded Iceland's outlook from 'stable' to 'negative' – sparking a minor crisis in confidence. Den Danske Bank (from Denmark) followed suit just a few weeks later. At about the same time, the IMF's (2006) country report warned of difficulties, and in mid-April of 2008, the IMF sent a confidential report to the Haarde government on the need to control its banks. In the meantime, a parade of international economists visited Iceland to warn of impending doom (or, sometimes, to pay tribute to the Icelandic model).[7]

It is this 2006 mini-crisis that encouraged Landsbanki to seek out foreign depositors. Rumours of an upcoming crisis were making it increasingly difficult for Icelandic banks to raise money to fund their asset purchases and to pay down their existing debt (mostly in foreign currencies). To address this problem,[8] Landsbanki created Icesave: an internet-based service that could attract retail deposits by offering more attractive interest rates than the high-street banks. Established first in Britain in October 2006, and in the Netherlands 18 months later (in May 2008 – just months before the meltdown!), Icesave grew rapidly from the attention it received on a number of 'best buy' sites across Europe. Millions of pounds were invested by the likes of Cambridge University; London Metropolitan Police Authority, even the UK Audit Commission – which, ironically enough, is responsible for overseeing local government funds (Wade and Sigurgeirsdottir 2010: 19).

Save the banks!

It took only a fortnight before the collapse of Lehman Brothers brought Iceland's over-extended banks to their knees, and another fortnight of hectic activity before the country realised that it would require economic assistance. Like everywhere else, the first and immediate response to the crisis in Iceland was: save the banks! The biggest banks in Iceland were in dire need of help, but these banks enjoyed strong friends in high places. (As we shall see in subsequent chapters, Iceland was far from unique in this matter.) This section examines the nature of the first, knee-jerk response to that crisis, and the costs it imposed on the Icelandic people.

When Lehman Brothers declared bankruptcy on 15 September 2008, the effect on global money markets was swift. At the time, there was substantial uncertainty about the credit quality of Lehman's assets – all markets knew for sure was that they needed to reduce their exposure to Lehman (and to other institutions holding risky assets). Consequently, global capital markets began to seize up, in the face of rising uncertainty about the scope of worthless assets in the market.

---

7. All of this critical attention left Davíð Oddsson undeterred: 'As far as I can tell,' he said in April 2006, 'the banks are acting responsibly on the good foundations that they have built. It's absurd to talk about a crisis' (quoted in Boyes 2009: 125).

8. Another solution involved so-called 'love letters', in which the banks leveraged up their collateral by circulating each other's debt. See Wade and Sigurgeirsdottir (2010: 19–20).

The problem for Iceland was that its three largest banks depended heavily on those global capital markets, as can be seen in Figure 4.2. In 2008, about two-thirds of the combined balance sheets of the three biggest banks was held in foreign currency. On the liabilities side, the foreign exchange (FX)-denominated share of debt was even higher: almost one-half of financing was in the form of FX deposits and other short-term FX financing. In short, the foreign exchange part of the balance sheet in Iceland's three biggest banks showed a significant maturity mismatch.

Figure 4.2: Source of financing in Iceland's three largest banks (2008)

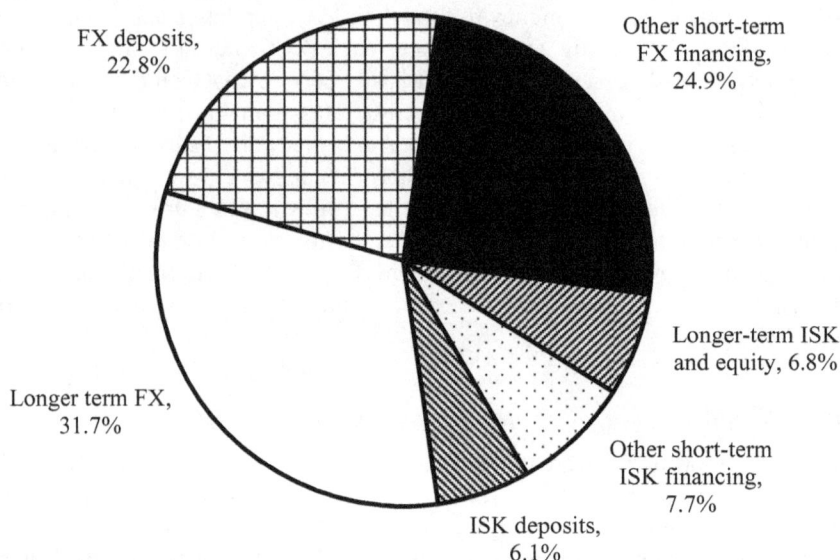

Note: June 2008. FX means foreign exchange; ISK is the Icelandic króna
Source: Guðmundsson (2015: 7)

Glitnir was the weakest of these banks, and was the first to feel the crunch. On 29 September, Glitnir approached the CBI for help with its looming liquidity problem. The governor of the central bank, Davíð Oddsson, responded by offering to buy 75 per cent of Glitnir's shares (for €600 million).[9] Whatever his intent, Oddsson's actions torpedoed the rest of the Icelandic economy. Almost immediately, the market lost confidence in all things Icelandic: the country's credit rating plunged, its banks lost their lines of credit, and runs began on the overseas branches of Icelandic banks (e.g. Icesave).

The first week of October was a nightmare: on 6 October, the Althing was forced to react with an Emergency Act, which authorised the country's Financial

---

9. This plan never was never put into play: Glitnir was placed in receivership by the FME before the purchase plan had been approved by shareholders.

Supervisory Authority (*Fjármálastöðugleikaráð*, or FME) to take over the banks.[10] On the following day, the króna was briefly pegged to a basket of currencies, before allowed to float (and eventually sink). On 7 October, Oddsson went on the evening news to reassure domestic depositors, saying 'We have decided that we are not going to pay the foreign debts of reckless people...we do not intend to pay the debts of the banks that have been a little reckless' (*WSJ* 2008).[11] This, along with other news, triggered Gordon Brown – Britain's Chancellor of the Exchequer at the time – to freeze all of Landsbanki's (Icesave) assets under an anti-terrorism law on the following day (8 October). On 9 October all trading on the OMX Nordic Iceland Exchange was frozen for two days, to prevent further panic from spreading. By the end of the week, Iceland's three biggest banks were bankrupt and in public hands.

The emergency act

In response to the market's reaction to the Glitnir rescue, the Althing passed an Emergency Act, on 6 October, authorising the Financial Supervisory Authority (FME) to take control over financial institutions and provide preferential treatment for borrowers in the event that the banks were to be liquidated.[12] In a separate measure, the retail deposits of Icelandic bank branches were guaranteed in full (PM 2008).

On the next day, 7 October, the FME took control over Landsbanki and Glitnir. On the day after that, they took over Kaupthing. The collapse of these banks threatened to sink the Icelandic economy; but they also would have a significant effect on foreign parties, which were expected to lose an estimated ISK 7,000 billion (roughly €41 billion). As a subsequent finance minister, Steingrímur J. Sigfússon, noted in 2010:

> 'It can be difficult but healthy to recall just how extensive the collapse was in Iceland in terms of the size of the country's economy. The direct consequences of the banking collapse on state finances were enormous. A fiscal surplus of ISK 89 billion in 2007 was replaced by a deficit of ISK 216 billion in 2008, in other words a reversal of over ISK 300 billion. Losses suffered by foreign parties as a result of what happened here have yet to be finally determined, but are not likely to be less than ISK 7000 billion. Figures this high are difficult to comprehend in a country whose GDP is around ISK 1500 billion, or where the value of the catch hauled in by a freezer trawler on a good outing amounts to

---

10. As we shall see, the FME did not have the money to deal with the crisis. But it also lacked qualified staff. In 2006, the FME employed forty-five people, only fourteen of which were economists (Boyes 2009: 122).

11. In the same broadcast, he noted that '[i]f we were tied to the euro, for instance, we would just have to succumb to the laws of Germany and France.'

12. Act No. 125/2008 on the Authority of Treasury Disbursements due to Unusual Financial Market Circumstances, etc.

ISK 100 million and where the total annual healthcare budget is around ISK 100 billion. There have been claims that the collapse of the three Icelandic banks are the seventh-, ninth- and tenth-largest bankruptcies in history. Quite an achievement for such a tiny economy.'

The Icelandic government simply couldn't afford to save the banks and put them into receivership.[13] The FME ring-fenced the Icelandic operations of Landsbanki and Glitnir, to secure continued banking operations for Icelandic families and businesses. The failed banks were then restructured and divided in to a new and an old bank. The Ministry of Finance appointed boards to each of the new banks, and the government injected the necessary capital, which was originally estimated to be about 385 billion krónur: 200 billion in Landsbanki; 110 billion in Glitnir; and 75 billion in Kaupthing (IMF 2008b: 15). The new, state-owned banks took over domestic activities.

In effect, the Emergency Act saved Iceland's domestic banking system by creating new banks – but it did so by carving domestic assets and liabilities out of the old (failed) banks (IMF 2008b: 15). The foreign debt took many forms – on the top was a heap of foreign investors who held bonds issued by these banks. But these debts were secured against a number of Icelandic assets (e.g., mortgages, fishing rights, factories, power plants, future electricity sales, etc.). When the new banks were created, these Icelandic assets went to the new banks, while foreign creditors were only allowed to make claims against the old banks.

This Act sets the stage for much of what happens subsequently, as the Althing was retroactively changing the priority order of claims, in order to save the domestic banking sector. In particular, the Act prioritised deposits and deposit insurance before any other claims on the banks (e.g. bond or shareholders).[14] Deposits in foreign branches were also given priority in the old banks, so that bondholders (including the CBI, Icelandic pension funds and foreigners) would need to wait behind deposit-holders when reimbursements were being distributed.

It was this effort to secure the domestic banking scene that became the source of difficulties for Iceland with respect to Icesave in the UK and Netherlands. On 8 October, in response to rapidly unfolding events, Gordon Brown froze Landsbanki's UK assets under an anti-terrorism law. Icesave was an overseas branch[15] of

---

13. Three months before the crash, the total assets of the banks were $182 billion. This is about 1.8 times the asset of WorldCom before its failure in 2002, and nearly three times the assets of Enron before it failed in 2001. Comparatively speaking Iceland's bank failures were no small potatoes. A global ranking would place Lehman ($691 billion) first and Washington Mutual ($328 billion) second. As separate entities, Kaupthing ($83 billion) would rank fifth, Landsbanki ($50 billion) ninth and Glitnir ($49 billion) tenth (Benediktsdottir *et al.* 2011: 197).

14. Wade and Sigurgeirsdottir (2012: 141) note that even more could be done. By providing unlimited bank deposit guarantees to domestic savers, the Act protected the financial elite. 'Had it limited the guarantee to five million krona ($70,000), it would have protected the entire deposits of 95% of depositors; only the wealthiest 5%, including many politicians, benefited from the unlimited guarantee, which now further constrains public spending.'

15. Icelandic banks pursued different expansion strategies: Landsbanki used overseas branches; Kaupthing used mostly subsidiaries. This difference matters, as branches find themselves under the supervision and insurance of the bank's home country; while subsidiaries fall under

Landsbanki, which means that it fell under Iceland's supervision and insurance system – the Icelandic Depositors' and Investors' Guarantee Fund (DIGF),[16] which operates according to the relevant EU-Directive.[17] The problem was that in 2008, European investors had about \$10.5 billion in Icesave accounts – this was more than half of Iceland's GDP (\$17.5 billion in 2008)! Given the size of these liabilities, relative to Iceland's economy, there was no way that Iceland's monetary authority would be able to rescue Icesave's operations. Worse, the DIGF only had equity of 8.3 billion krónur at the end of 2007, or €90 million at the then going exchange rate (DIGF 2007).

The three governments (Icelandic, Dutch and British) quickly pounded out an agreement to resolve the issue. On 11 October, Iceland agreed to cover the first €20,887 (the deposit insurance amount listed in the EU Directive mentioned above) on Dutch savings accounts in (Landsbanki's) Icesave – using money borrowed from the Dutch government. It was estimated that the total value of Icesave deposits in Netherlands was €1.7 billion (Brogger and Einarsdottir 2008). At same time, Iceland and Britain reached a similar agreement: about 300,000 Iceseave deposits in the UK totalled €5 billion – and they would also be protected by way of a UK loan to the DIGF.

Hence, the Dutch and British governments originally agreed to lend money to the Icelandic government, so that Iceland's deposit insurance program could reimburse Landsbanki's depositors in these two countries. Anybody with elementary mathematic skills could quickly calculate that Iceland's puny economy was insufficient to bail out these foreign depositors. As Gylfason *et al.* (2010: 152) note: 'The audacity is breath-taking: by this strategy, Landsbanki managed to make Iceland's population of 320,000 responsible for the deposits of 400,000 individuals and entities in Britain and the Netherlands, while its owners and managers appropriated the short-term profits.'

Market impact

As politicians worked out a solution for these failed banks, their actions threw Icelandic markets in a tizzy. The most obvious and immediate effect could be seen on the value of the Icelandic króna, as investors began to flee what was looking, more and more, like a sinking ship.

In response to the CBI's willingness to bail out Glitnir Bank, the ISK/€ exchange rate plummeted. Davíð Oddsson, as CBI governor, tried to halt the fall by pegging the króna to a basket of currencies at roughly the pre-crisis rate (131

---

supervision and insurance of the bank's host countries. The complexities and challenges of regulating subsidiaries and branches across EU regulatory space is discussed in World Bank (2012: 153ff). *See also* Chapter Six, below, especially with regard to the Vienna Initiative.

16. In Icelandic: *Tryggingarsjóður*.

17. EU Directive 94/19/EC. In particular, the Directive holds that that the DIGF is responsible for covering €20,887 for each depositor in each financial institution. These are the baseline rules that apply throughout the EU/EEA, of which Iceland is a part. Skaar Viken (2011: 319) notes that there is an apparent contradiction between the EU deposit regulations and EEA regulations that forbid government bail-outs.

krónur/€). There is much speculation and little certainty as to why he did this,[18] but the central bank clearly lacked the reserves to defend the peg, while billions of krónur fled the country. The reserves were drained in a matter of hours, and the currency continued to depreciate in value, as seen in Figure 4.3.

Figure 4.3: Króna/€ exchange rate, 2000–2016

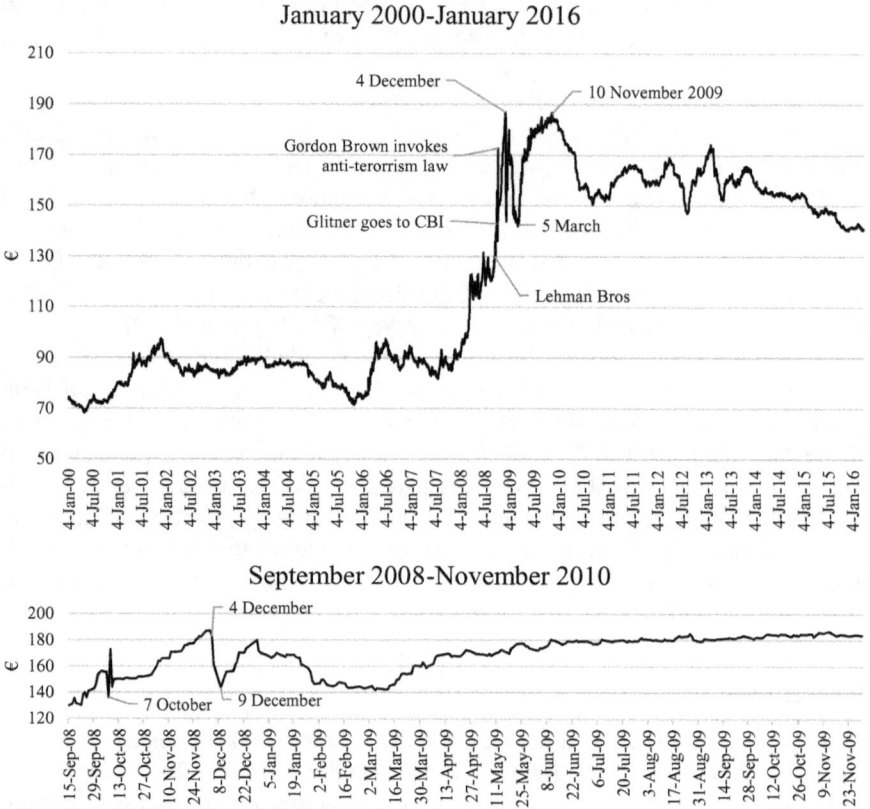

Note: Daily fixing, mid-rate. A rise in the € cost constitutes a depreciation in the value of the króna (i.e., when the curve goes up, the króna depreciates vis-à-vis the euro; when it goes down, it appreciates).
Source: CBI (2016)

On Wednesday night, 8 October – the same day that Gordon Brown invoked the anti-terrorism law – the CBI abandoned the peg, and the króna was allowed

18. Apparently, Oddsson did not consult his chief economist at the central bank, nor anyone else – except his protégé, Prime Minister Haarde. Wade and Sigurgeirsdottir (2010: 21–22) speculate on two different motives for the brief and temporary fix: 1) that Oddsson wanted to stabilise the exchange rate long enough for the Icelandic elite to dump their krónur and spirit out their capital; or 2) there was some political infighting between competing interests, and the delay was used to ensure that Kaupthing Bank would go down with the others (Kaupthing had strong links to the PP; while Landsbanki had close ties to Oddsson and the IP). As the authors note: 'These are murky waters' (note 26).

to fall to 172. This constituted a 33 per cent drop since the demise of Lehman Brothers (from €130 to €172). By 4 December, the daily mid-range value of the króna would fall even farther, to 183.7. In November of 2008, in its assessment of the situation, the IMF (2008b: 9) estimated that the nominal exchange rate of the ISK fell by over 65 per cent on a trade-weighted basis since the beginning of the year (i.e. over 11 months). In response to this fall, the authorities chose to implement a foreign exchange auction, which was held daily, beginning on 15 October.[19]

As we saw above, in Figure 4.1, the stock-market reaction was just as volatile. On Thursday, 9 October, all trading on OMX Nordic Iceland Exchange was frozen for two days, to prevent further panic from spreading. The market closure was extended through Monday 13 October, and the market reopened on 14 October. The main index (OMX Iceland 15), had fallen 77 per cent since the closure (from 3,044.6 to 678.4) – in large part because the three largest banks formed about 73 per cent of the value of that index.

International support

The decision to recapitalise the banks and bail out their depositors was fairly easy; finding the money to pay for it was another matter. On 24 October, Iceland turned to the IMF. The resulting IMF programme had three main goals: to stabilise the exchange rate; to provide fiscal sustainability; and to reconstruct the finance sector (IMF 2008b). With the depreciation already a *fait accompli*, the IMF approved stringent foreign exchange controls to stop any additional capital flight, and supported the government's decision to rescue the domestic banking sector.

As a significant depreciation had already occurred, and the banking crisis was being dealt with under the framework of the Emergency Act, the IMF's effort centred on securing comprehensive capital controls and the money necessary to pay for the bank-support project. The argument for capital controls was one of temporary necessity. In the face of this enormous crisis, many foreign investors were anxious to unwind their króna positions, and domestic depositors and investors were also looking to flee a currency that was rapidly sinking in value. Recognising these pressures (and the CBI's dwindling reserves), Iceland was encouraged to maintain its capital controls,[20] and forfeit any ambition at maintaining a fixed exchange rate regime (IMF 2008b:11).

The capital controls helped to stabilise the exchange rate in a situation where the currency had fallen by more than 50 per cent in 2008. At the time of the crisis,

---

19. For more details on this auction, see IMF (2008b: 6).

20. The capital controls regime came about in two waves: early in the crisis, in response to the failures of the three banks, the CBI introduced temporary guidelines on modifications in currency outflow (CBI 2008a). The CBI and Minister for Business Affairs then agreed to replace these temporary measures with a new set of currency regulations on 28 November (CBI 2008b). These regulations took the form of a Parliamentary amendment to Act no. 87/1992 on Foreign Exchange. The Act gave the CBI temporary authorisation to set rules limiting international capital movements, with the aim of restricting the outflow of foreign currency, for instance, by imposing obligations to repatriate foreign currency.

the controls locked in an estimated €4.2 billion in carry traders' position, or 41 per cent of Iceland's 2008 GDP (Danielsson and Krisjánsdóttir 2015). This money was anxious to leave, and authorities feared the consequences on the Icelandic economy: they needed to stem the outflow of capital to stabilise the exchange rate and to return monetary policy to some degree of normalcy. In short, as a subsequent governor of the central bank noted, 'In this situation, the capital controls gave monetary policy more scope to focus on the domestic economy...' (Guðmundsson 2015: 3). As an additional bonus, the controls would make it easier for the government to finance (domestically) what would promise to be a large fiscal deficit. Because Iceland's more wealthy taxpayers could not flee with their money, capital controls made it easier to generate tax revenues.

The second important issue was the need for financial support. Once the banking crisis hit, Iceland needed to move quickly to try and stabilise its exchange rate and to secure the necessary funds for re-capitalising its banking system. Financial support was needed to cover three main[21] costs:

- the need to compensate insured foreign depositors at failed Icelandic banks (estimated to reach 47 per cent of GDP);
- the need to re-capitalise the new banks (estimated to be 26 per cent of GDP); and
- the need to re-capitalise the CBI (estimated to reach ten per cent of GDP).

Together, then, it was tentatively estimated that the gross fiscal costs of bank restructuring would amount to 83 per cent of Iceland's GDP! And the largest chunk of these costs were directed at paying off foreign depositors (IMF 2008b: 7).

The IMF arrived in October 2008 to prepare a crisis management programme (IMF 2008b). This programme offered a conditional loan of $2.1 billion (€1.58 billion) to help stabilise the króna; and the Nordic central banks were persuaded to pledge another $2.5 billion, again with conditions. Poland and the Faeroe Islands also chipped in to help support the króna. Most importantly, the IMF made its money conditional on British and Dutch demands to bail-out Icesave depositors.[22] On 16 November, the government announced it was willing to comply to the EU Deposit Guarantee Scheme, and – three days later, on 19 November – the IMF Board approved the loan. The IMF programme ended officially on 31 August, 2011 – although Iceland's last remaining capital controls were not lifted before the spring of 2017.

---

21. The IMF (2008b: 7) also estimated that rising interest rates would bring additional costs, and these were roughly estimated to add another 5.4 per cent of GDP to the 2009 fiscal budget.

22. This point is made by Wade and Sigurgeirsdottir (2010: 22–3) and is commonly held. But the explicit conditions of the formal agreement do not make any reference to the British and Dutch demands (IMF 2008b).

Reaction and repercussions

By the middle of November 2008, most of the groundwork for Iceland's response to the crisis was in place. All that was lacking was a sense of remorse on the part of the responsible actors. The sitting government, especially the IP, was well known for its close personal links to Iceland's financial elite, and for sponsoring the deregulation frenzy that had fuelled its rise. Icelandic voters expected their government to take responsibility for the crisis, and punish the wrong-doers. But after hammering together a bank resolution and aid package, the sitting IP-SDA government continued to act as if nothing had happened. For the remainder of 2008, not a single politician or political party took responsibility for the decisions and mistakes that led to the crisis. Although the Prime Minister had assembled a committee to investigate the causes of the crisis in November, it was not seen as particularly serious, or effective: by December it had only issued a single press release.

Public suspicion and frustration grew along with the government's inaction, propelling an indigenous protest movement. Every Saturday, Icelanders gathered in front of the Althing, banging together pots and pans, linking arms in a circle around the parliament building, pelting the building with food, and demanding the government's resignation. Their frustration was clearly audible in a popular slogan, later printed on placards and t-shirts: '*Helvítis fokking fokk*'.[23]

Dissatisfied with the status quo, and with the pace of political reform, the protestors demanded the government's resignation, the removal of important financial leaders, and called for new elections. At their peak it was estimated that more than seven thousand people showed up to the rallies, demanding reforms and accountability (Boyes 2009: 195).[24] This 'pots and pans' revolution crescendoed until reaching its climax on 20 April, becoming Iceland's largest protest movement since the country joined NATO in 1949.

After a long Christmas respite, the protests took on a sharper and more demanding tone. When the Althing re-convened on 22 January – after the Christmas break – the Prime Minister provided his first detailed account of what the government had been doing since the crisis in October. The report was vague; its prescription offered too little, too late; and the volume of protest was turned up yet another notch.

On the following day, 23 January 2009, the protestors could claim their first political casualty. Geir Haarde announced that he would step down as Prime Minister for reasons of health, and that he would not run for re-election: an interim government would rule until new parliamentary elections could be held later in

---

23. Or 'What the Fuckety Fucking Fuck!', as translated by Boyes (2009: 190).

24. 7,000 people on the street, in a town with 100,000 inhabitants, represents a sizeable share of Reykjavik's population protesting out in the cold!

the spring.[25] Two days later (25 January), the Banking and Commerce Minister, Björgvin G. Sigurðsson, fired the head of the FME and then promptly resigned himself.

With the IP out of the picture, the President then turned to Gísladóttir and Steingrímur J. Sigfússon (of the Left-Green Movement, or LGM) to create a new government. Their coalition would fall five seats short of a majority in parliament, but the PP could be relied upon to support the coalition (without actually joining the government). Neither of these party leaders became the new prime minister,[26] however, as the position went to the SDA's Jóhanna Sigurðardóttir, then the Minister of Social Affairs and Social Security.

In the April 2009 elections, a new red-red (SDA-LGM) coalition won a narrow majority. But the election delivered a significant blow to the IP, which suffered the worst election result in its history: winning just 23.7 per cent of the votes – a loss of 13 percentage points (Hardarson and Kristinsson 2010: 1015). This reduced the IP's number of parliamentary seats to just 16, despite the advantages provided to it by the electoral system (as hinted above). This constituted the IP's worse electoral results since its formation in 1929.

The incoming government represented a significant shift to the left in Icelandic politics, proclaiming itself to be 'a Nordic Welfare Government' (Ólafsson 2011a: 40), and promising a return to egalitarianism and support for the weakest elements in Icelandic society. They also offered greater emphasis on ethics and accountability in government, and a revision of the Constitution. Despite growing public pressure, the new government was not (at first) willing to renege on the terms of the original IMF agreement (signed by the previous government).

Politics above markets

In order to access the IMF loan, the new government needed to resolve its differences with the Netherlands and the UK over the Icesave debt issue. At the heart of this matter was whether Iceland's elected officials were to follow the vocal demands of their constituents, or the powerful demands of private creditors. The result was three different parliamentary acts, authorising the government to conclude agreements with the UK and the Netherlands, as briefly outlined in Table 4.2.

---

25. In a brief attempt to hold onto power, Haarde held emergency talks with Ingibjörg Sólrún Gísladóttir (head of the SDA, Haarde's coalition party) to discuss saving the government. The effort failed: Gísladóttir's party demanded that Oddsson be replaced as CBI governor, but Haarde was unwilling to go that far – he preferred to let his government collapse over firing his old mentor.

26. Like Haarde, Gísladóttir was also unwell, undergoing treatment for a benign brain tumour since September 2008.

Table 4.2: Icesave acts

No.	Act	Content	Fate
I	Act 96/2009	Act would have Iceland pay the UK and the Netherlands more than $5 billion lost in Icelandic deposit accounts over an eight-year period (2016–2024). In the first round (June) the bill was opposed: it passed after amendments were added that set a ceiling on payments, based on the country's GDP, to protect Iceland's sovereignty. Date: 28 August 2009	• Approved in the Althing (34 votes to 15, with 14 abstentions) • Signed by President Grímsson • Enacted 2 September 2009 • Rejected by UK and Netherlands
II	Act 1/2010	Amends 96/2009 to meet British and Dutch concerns, but includes a change to usual credit priority order (that varied from Icelandic law). This would significantly increase Iceland's liabilities. Repayment stretched over 14 years. Date: 30 December 2009	• Narrowly passes in the Althing (33 votes to 30) • President Grímsson refuses to sign (5 January 2010) • The Althing unanimously agrees to a referendum (8 January 2010) • 93% of voters oppose the bill on 6 March (2010) referendum
III	Act 13/2011	Renegotiated deal with new terms and conditions for repayment. Repayment terms now extended to thirty years, with lower interest rates. Removed demand that priority claims be placed on an equal footing; payment terms included minimum and ceiling provisions.	• Passes the Althing (44 to 16) on 16 February 2011 • President Grímsson refuses to sign (20 February 2011) • Rejected by 58.9% of voters on 9 April (2011) referendum.

Sources: Alþingi (2009a and 2009b); PM (2009, 2010 and 2011); and Sigurdardóttir (2011)

Each of the Icesave agreements specify how, and on what terms, the UK and the Netherlands were to reclaim the €4 billion they had already spent in bailing out Icesave depositors at home. At issue was whether Icelandic taxpayers should be forced to pay the debts of failed Icelandic banks abroad, in the context of a systemic financial crisis.[27] The problem was that Iceland's DIGF had insufficient funds to cover these demands, and the UK and the Netherlands wanted the people of Iceland to cover the difference. The Icelandic government contended that the relevant EU Directive (94/19/EU) 'imposes no obligation of result on the State to use its own resources in order to guarantee the pay-out of a deposit-guarantee scheme in the event that "all else fails"', and even if it did—'Iceland was prevented from doing so by force majeure' (MFA nd).

---

27. The Icelandic government recognised that the DIGF was obliged to cover these deposits, by way of Directive 94/19/EC – but the DIGF was unable, as its funds were limited. See MFA (nd).

The first (and quickly revised) Icesave Act radically redefined the nature of Iceland's responsibility with regard to the private debt obligations of its banks. This Act (No. 96/2009) asserted the primacy of Iceland's political sovereignty over its sundry economic obligations:[28]

1. '[t]here will be no attachment of assets that are critical for Iceland to carry out its obligations as a sovereign state in a satisfactory manner' (article 2.2); and

2. '...there will be a cap on payments of respectively 4% of cumulative GDP growth with regard to the UK and 2% of cumulative growth with regard to the Netherlands' (i.e., payments shall not exceed six per cent of the cumulative GDP growth) (article 3).

In this text, and in the political acrobatics surrounding it, we see a democratically-accountable body demanding of its foreign creditors the right to protect its own critical assets, and to limit the size of payments on its debt obligations such that they could not undermine the economic well-being of the country. No other state in Europe was willing (or able) to make similar demands. Here we see the clearest evidence of the capacity of an independent state to stand up to powerful financial interests – both at home and abroad.

This first proposed solution, perhaps not surprisingly, was rejected by the Netherlands and the UK, who then offered better terms in return. The Althing then pieced together a second Act (1/2010) that included an inflated interest rate – i.e., a substantial mark-up on the UK and the Netherland's financing costs (Baldursson 2011: 3). Although this repayment scheme made it through the Althing (narrowly), it met very stiff opposition in the court of public opinion. Consequently, the country's President, Ólafur Ragnar Grímsson, sided with the protestors and refused to sign the Act into law. When the plan was vetted in a public referendum (the country's first since 1944), 93 per cent of the voters opposed the debt-repayment plan – only 1.9 per cent of the voters gave their support (Statistics Iceland 2010).

The Althing rushed back to the drawing board. Although the third Icesave Act (Act 13/2011) improved Iceland's terms and conditions, it still faced strong public resistance. Once again, the Act found support in the Althing (this time with a strong majority), but the President (again) sought the people's explicit backing: any agreement would place an onerous burden on the Icelandic people, and he felt that it was only right that *they* made the final decision. The second referendum was also defeated, this time by a narrower margin (58.9 per cent).

These bills were controversial, and generated much political heat, as Icelanders debated among themselves whether it was appropriate for taxpayers to bear the burden of bad decisions made by a pampered few. As President Sigurdardóttir wrote in a 2011 *Guardian* editorial: 'People ask themselves: why do we, as taxpayers, have to shoulder the burden of problems caused by the behaviour of

---

28. Alþingi (2009a). See also Alþingi (2009b).

irresponsible bankers? Taxes should be used for public services, for the welfare of ordinary citizens, but not because of huge losses of financial institutions.'

Frustrated with the inability of the Icelandic government to deliver a satisfactory solution, the EFTA Surveillance Authority lodged a formal complaint with the EFTA Court on 14 December 2011. The Court's decision, on 28 January 2013, held that Iceland was under no obligation to compensate the two governments, since the regulations on cross-border deposit insurance did not apply in the face of a 'systemic bank failure of the magnitude experienced in Iceland' (EFTA Surveillance Authority 2011).

As this case is frequently misunderstood, I should elaborate on what was at stake. This case was *not* about whether depositors in the UK and the Netherlands would be, or should be, protected. In the intervening period it had become clear that the Landsbanki estate would likely have enough outlays to bail out the depositors.[29] Indeed, Iceland had already paid more than 90 per cent of the minimum deposit guaranteed, required by EEA membership, using money raised from selling Landsbanki assets (Myles 2013). Rather, this case was about whether a sovereign state should be held responsible for the decisions made by private companies, and whether the UK and the Netherlands could jump to the front of the creditors' que. Even the *Financial Times* (2013) recognised the justice of the Icelandic position, and used it to push for banking reforms in Europe:

'This is a victory for law and economic sense. The ruling makes clear that EU law does not require taxpayers to bail out private banks, the mistake that proved so disastrous for Ireland yet still claims pride of place in European banking policy doctrine. It also implicitly shows that if Iceland's deposit insurance scheme was inadequate under EU standards, so is that of every EU country.'

The decision facing Icelanders in each of the referendums, as well as their elected politicians in the Althing, was whether the voice of the people could stand up to the power of money. As the President of Iceland would later note: 'To me it was self-evident that democracy had to prevail, even if all the governments of Europe, and powerful interests in my own country, favoured the financial stakeholders. When our nations come to such crossroads, politics in its classical sense must carry the day' (Grímsson 2012: 274). The Icelandic people prioritised the values of democracy over those of the market. The more difficult question that remains is: Why didn't other states prioritise in a similar fashion?

---

29. Iceland's government contends that 'The Icesave depositors in the UK have received full repayments and the Netherlands depositors have received compensation of EUR 100 000 or well in excess of the EUR 20 000…Certain Landsbanki wholesale depositors in the UK, such as certain charities, endowments and local governments, did not receive any such payments as they were not covered by the UK deposit guarantee scheme. However, due to partial payments commenced by the Estate of Landsbanki in December 2011 these depositors have already received payments amounting to approximately 50% of the total claim, well in excess of the EUR 20 000 minimum' (MFA nd).

Economic management

There are three main costs to the government associated with this sort of financial tsunami: bailing out the banks, re-floating the economy that sunk as a result, and providing life boats for the broader citizenry. In Iceland, these costs were minimised by limiting the public's financial responsibility, and demanding that the risk-takers themselves bear a larger share of the burden. By choosing this strategy, Iceland managed to recapitalise its banks with only a small increase (3.8 per cent of GDP) in government net debt (OECD 2011a: 51).

Even though the government was able to limit its financial responsibilities with regard to the liabilities of its banks, the costs of rebuilding the Icelandic economy were enormous. Worse, these costs were likely to fall on the country's most vulnerable citizens, in the form of increased unemployment and reduced social spending. To minimise these costs, the new government needed to kick-start the national economy (thereby increasing government revenues), and shrink its expenditures in a way that would do least harm to those that could ill afford it.

It is difficult to pay down one's debt with a shrinking income. Any debt repayment strategy needs to first consider how to maximise income – or, for a country, to stimulate economic growth. The new government's engine of economic growth did *not* come from reducing the power (and wages) of its workforce (as we find in the Irish and Latvian cases to follow), but from stimulating exports and domestic demand. The Icelandic response to the crisis proved to be remarkably effective.

Because it still enjoyed its own currency, the króna, the international currency market generated the sort of price adjustment necessary to re-boot the Icelandic economy. In other words, as international demand for the króna fell, so did its value. This steep depreciation of the króna (*see* Figure 4.3) transferred the country's burden of adjustment across a broader spectrum of the population, spurred exports and economic growth, and allowed Iceland to sustain higher levels of public spending. In the doing, however, it reduced the real purchasing power of the general public (due to subsequent, if slight, inflation) – so other measures were needed to protect those at the bottom of the income ladder (see below).

The most significant effect of the depreciation can be seen in the price of Icelandic exports and imports. Almost immediately, Icelandic exporters enjoyed increased international competitiveness as the króna's nominal exchange rate fell by some 45 per cent, and the capital restrictions kept inflation (and the flight from króna investments) under control. When possible, Icelanders began to replace imports with (now cheaper) domestically-produced goods, and Icelandic exports enjoyed a significant (and almost immediate) boost in competitiveness. This is clearly seen in Figure 4.4, where we see exports overtake imports in 2008, and the country has enjoyed a net trade surplus ever since (see also Benediktsdottir *et al.* 2011: 205). This surplus fuelled an expansion of jobs, economic growth and revenues to pay down the debt.

Figure 4.4: Trade in goods and services, Iceland, 2000–2014

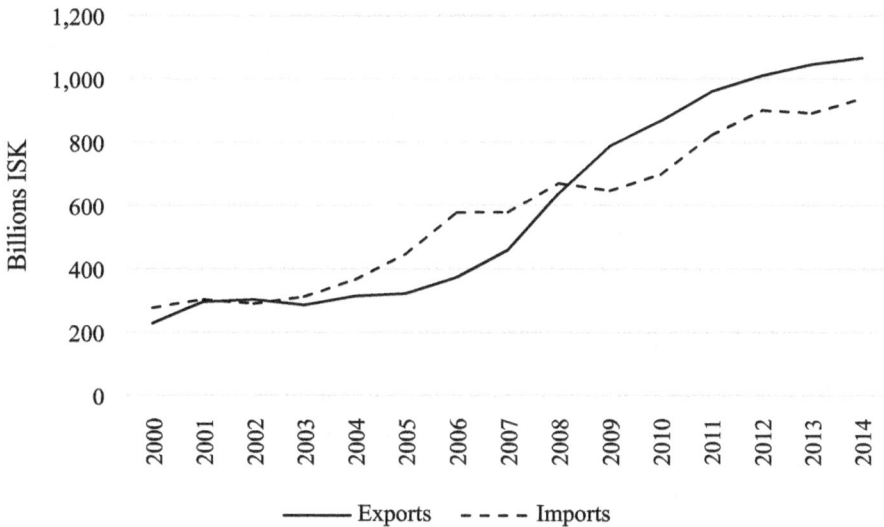

Sources: OECD (2016a and b)

Almost immediately, the depreciation made Iceland more competitive, such that the unemployment effects of its crisis were much smaller than in other places. Rather than try and save their way to redemption, or to squeeze competitiveness out of reduced wages (and spending power at home), the Icelandic authorities relied on foreign demand (in the form of exports) to grow their way out of the crisis – and the cheaper ISK provided the necessary price platform to do so. As we have already seen in Figure 3.7, Iceland experienced only a modest (five per cent) drop in employment from 2007 to 2010, especially compared to what happened in Latvia (17 per cent drop) and Ireland (13 per cent). This is not to say that Icelanders did not have to pay a substantial price – they did, and that cost is evident in e.g., massive emigration (*see* Figure 3.12) – but Iceland used its monetary autonomy to change the game quickly and effectively, to the benefit of Icelanders. This export-driven growth, on the back of a depreciated currency, helped buoy employment and family incomes, while reducing demand for social services. All this helped to increase government revenues and to minimise social expenditures.

The new government also promised to protect vulnerable Icelanders from the massive budget cuts that the crisis brought into play. It did this with a two-pronged policy. The first prong is the most obvious: it aimed to reduce cuts to welfare expenditures more than the cuts to other expenditure areas. The second prong provided debt-relief to the many households that had taken out foreign loans, and now found themselves suffering as the result of the currency depreciation.

Even though the government was under severe fiscal pressure, it decided to strengthen key social programs. For example, the government increased unemployment benefits in 2007–2010, and lengthened the period during which workers could receive unemployment benefits (from three to four years). It also boosted, significantly, the means-tested social assistance allowance, in addition to lifting the minimum pension benefit and minimum wage – while general wages remained largely unchanged.[30]

Iceland was clearly living beyond its means, and the Icelandic standard of living would need to be cut. By targeting the expenditures carefully, this necessary cut was felt disproportionately by higher income households. We have already seen evidence of this in the last chapter (Figure 3.11), where Iceland was the only case in which income inequality actually shrunk in response to the crisis. Overall, from the period between 2008 and 2010, household disposal incomes fell, on average, by 5.5 per cent in Iceland – as can be seen in Figure 4.5. But the lowest income deciles were protected from that fall, and actually enjoyed improvements in their disposable earnings over this time (whereas the richest ten per cent were hit with an astonishing 26.3 per cent drop in their earnings). The reason for this is that the government's social expenditures for the weakest groups were protected, while the tax burden was distributed such that the richest groups paid a larger share (as is also shown in Figure 4.5).

Figure 4.5: Change in earnings and tax burdens, Iceland, 2008–2010

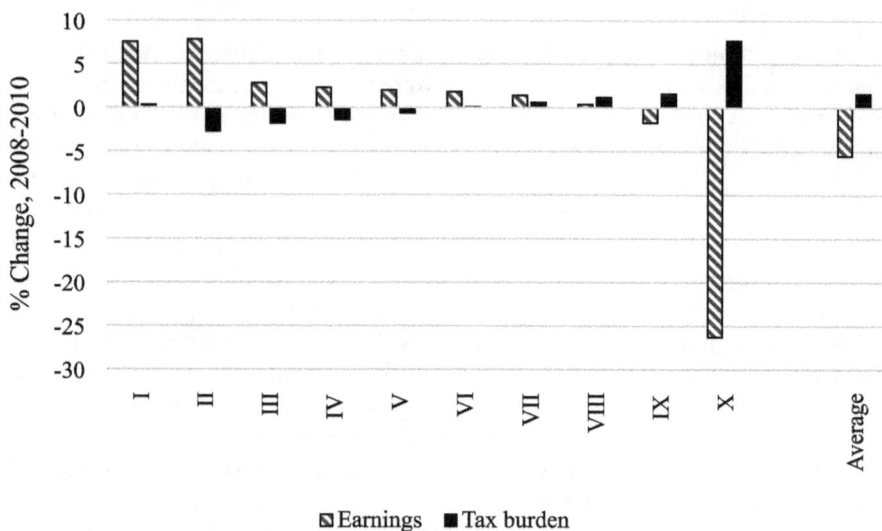

Note: Changes in families' disposable earnings and net effective tax burden from 2008 to 2010 in per cent, by income deciles, from the lowest income group (I) to the highest (X). Ólafsson (2011b: 24) speculates that the reason why the tax rates increased on the lowest decile is that this includes elderly pensioners who have savings in banks, and received a higher tax rate on interest income.
Source: Ólafsson (2011b: 23–4)

---

30. Ólafsson (2011b: 2, 13–14); see also Ólafsson (2011a and 2012).

Figure 4.5 clearly shows two important, and inverse patterns – both of which are derived from the government's targeted policies. In the immediate wake of the crisis (2008–2010), the tax burden in Iceland shifted from the lowest income groups to those that could afford it most: to the highest income decile. At the same time, the distribution of family disposable earnings shifted in the opposite direction: the poorest families received the biggest boost in earnings; the richest families received the biggest cut! Here too we find evidence of the government prioritising justice over markets.

While the currency depreciation was useful for kick-starting Iceland's export industries, it also increased inflation modestly, which reduced the purchasing power of wages for those Icelanders who still had a job. As a consequence, real wages fell by over 12 per cent in the 2008–2009 period, before improving markedly in 2010 and 2011 (Ólafsson 2011b: 9). To protect these workers, the government needed to reduce the biggest drain on their shrinking (real) pay check: consumer debt.

The government used targeted household debt restricting policies to help ease the burden on the most vulnerable groups. According to the IMF (2012a: 106), Iceland quickly moved 'to ensure that families did not lose their homes owing to temporary problems and to prevent a spike in foreclosures leading to a housing market meltdown.' Those measures included:

'a moratorium on foreclosures, a temporary suspension of debt service for exchange-rate- and CPI-indexed loans, and rescheduling (payment smoothing) of those loans. About half the households with eligible loans took advantage of payment smoothing, which reduced current debt service payments by 15 to 20 percent and 30 to 40 percent for CPI-indexed and foreign-exchange-indexed loans, respectively' (ibid.).

Additional debt relief was secured by subsidising the interest costs of housing loans. As a result, the government ended up paying about 35 per cent of the interest cost of Icelandic mortgages, and up to 45 per cent for the lowest income groups (Ólafsson 2012: 2).

The main challenge lay in the fact that a surprisingly large number of mortgages had been taken out in foreign currencies. The currency depreciation (and subsequent inflation) had made these nearly impossible to pay off. In order to help the households burdened with these debts, and to free up domestic demand in a context where real wages were falling, the Supreme Court and government stepped in to protect consumers who had been lured into a risky lending market in foreign exchange.

In particular, the Icelandic Supreme Court declared FX-indexed loans (i.e. loans paid out and collected in Icelandic krónur, but indexed to foreign currencies) to be illegal (OECD 2011a: 21). This rescued many consumers and businesses, and shifted the burden back to the banks that had marketed and profited from such risky mortgages. The first ruling (in June 2010) applied only to the motor vehicle loans of households. The Althing later (December 2010) extended this benefit to residential mortgage loans. Finally, in June 2011, the Supreme Court extended it even further, to include corporate loans. These loans were converted to domestic currency loans, whereby the outstanding principles of the loans were reduced considerably, and the interest rates were also recalculated (retroactively as well) using the lowest non-indexed interest rate published by the CBI (Darvas 2011: 6).

In doing this, the government was trying to soften the economic downside from the currency depreciation, and help stimulate domestic demand as a means to further fuel economic growth. Rather than forcing workers to pay for the mistakes of bankers (by squeezing wages and social expenditures in an austerity drive), Iceland's new government shifted more of the burden over to those who had benefited the most from the financial frenzy – and who were most responsible for the crisis. Icelanders also experienced austerity – but it was an austerity that was more broadly shared than in any of the other cases. In the doing, the government's response was evaluated favourably by both the IMF and Icelandic voters, at least until 2013 (Hardarson and Kristinsson 2014: 155).

Accountability

Because the Icelandic authorities maintained control over many of the relevant policy instruments, they could be held accountable for the mistakes that were made. This oversight capacity is surely strengthened by the very small and closed nature of Icelandic society. But because the authority in Iceland to make decisions regarding capital controls or bank bail-outs was *not* shared with the EU, there was no doubting who was ultimately responsible for the actions (or inactions) taken. More to the point: as policy makers wielded effective and independent policy instruments, changing policy makers could deliver a real change in policy.

This, I think, is very significant. In the wake of the crisis it was easy to find elections across Europe being used to hold elected officials accountable for the crisis (or for developing ineffective responses to the crisis, once it hit). But in most cases, incoming officials were unable to change the country's course of action, because they lacked the capacity to do so. These elections clearly revealed the limits to political power in the face of international markets. Nowhere is this clearer than in the case of Ireland, as we shall see in Chapter Five. In Iceland, by contrast, the sitting government was kicked out of office, and a new government was able to set a radically different policy course. This is not just a matter of a change in political parties (e.g. from Conservatives to Social Democrats) at the helm of government[31] – this is a matter of people demanding real change in policies, and actually getting it.

The flipside of autonomy is accountability. Here too, the Icelandic case is exemplary. In no other case was the government's investigation of wrongdoing more transparent and thorough. The new, Sigurðardóttir (I), government was bent on replacing Oddsson as CBI governor (indeed, it might be said that Haarde's government fell on this point). But Oddsson was unwilling to step down: he had

---

31. As we have already seen: the hands of Iceland's Social Democrats were also dirty, as the SDA had shared power in the Haarde II government, when the crisis struck.

a fixed term as bank governor – and thought that a (leftist) prime minister was overstepping her constitutional authority.[32] But as public demonstrations became more vocal, then gathered outside the CBI building, Oddsson was forced to resign in February 2009, along with the rest of the central bank's governing leadership and that of the Financial Supervisory Authority. I cannot think of another state where the governor(s) of the central bank were held fully accountable for their mistakes.

As far as I know, Iceland is also the only country in the world to attempt to impeach, and eventually launch legal proceedings against, a politician for his/her involvement in the financial crisis. On 28 September 2010, a majority in the Althing voted to indict the former Prime Minister, Geir Haarde, on changes of negligence in office. He eventually stood trial and, on 23 April 2013, was found guilty on one of four charges. This was a minor charge (failure to hold cabinet meetings on important state matters), so Haarde was released without punishment (BBC News 2012). Haarde's indictment came from a Special Investigative Commission (SIC) report that was delivered to the Althing on 12 April 2010. This report accused the former Prime Minster, along with his Finance Minister (Árni M. Mathiesen) and Minister of Business Affairs (Björgvin G. Sigurdsson) of negligence.

To root-out negligence and wrong-doing, two important investigatory bodies were launched by the Althing towards the close of 2010. The SIC was established by Act No. 142/2008 on 12 December 2008, to investigate the collapse of Iceland's three main banks. The Committee included three prominent members,[33] and its final report was exhaustingly thorough, weighing in at a strapping 2,600 pages, nine volumes and eight kilograms (SIC 2010)!

In addition to the CBI governors and the Prime Minister, many other important actors have also been investigated and punished. This work is largely the result of the Office of the Special Prosecutor (OSP). The Althing established the OSP on 10 December 2008 (two days prior to the SIC), and tasked it with investigating suspected criminal conduct leading up to, in connection with, or in the wake of, the banking crisis. Three months later, Ólafur Þór Hauksson was appointed as Special Prosecutor.[34] His office has brought the arrests (and convictions) of several business leaders, including members of the different banks' senior management teams.

Last, but not least, the crisis in Iceland – and especially the massive protests it provoked (uncommon in Iceland before the financial crisis) – propelled a

---

32. Apparently, Oddsson even hung up on the Prime Minister's phone call (he subsequently claimed it had been a bad line). See Boyes (2009: 197–8).

33. Supreme Court Judge, Mr Páll Hreinsson, Parliamentary Ombudsman of Iceland, Mr Tryggvi Gunnarsson, and Mrs Sigríður Benediktsdóttir Ph.D., lecturer and associate chair at Yale University.

34. In 2011, the OSP had 216 people officially classified as suspects and 470 suspects and witnesses had been brought in for questioning. According to the Minister for Internal Affairs, the OSP was conducting about eighty different cases at that time (IceNews 2011). In 2016, the OSP was formally shut down, and any remaining projects were moved to the new office of the District Prosecutor.

re-examination of Iceland's outdated constitution. The crisis had clearly revealed how the existing constitution was unable to prevent the sort of cronyism that can easily sink an economy. When the new SDA-LGM coalition came to power – the first majority government that didn't include the IP or PP – it opened up an opportunity for radical constitutional reform.

By 2012, the Icelandic constitution was profoundly revised by a remarkably novel, crowd-sourced, process.[35] This process, and its end product, generated a thorough re-examination of the nature of politics in Iceland, and a healthy discussion about what Icelanders expected from their government. In late 2012, in a non-binding referendum, 67 per cent of the population supported the new constitution (although voter turnout was only 49 per cent). Since then, however, the new constitution has been put on hold.

Recent developments

The new, SDA-LGM, government grew increasingly unpopular. When it started in government, in February 2009, it enjoyed a 65 per cent approval rating. By 2012, however, its approval rating had dropped to anywhere between 28 and 35 per cent (Hardarson and Kristinsson 2013: 101). There are many theories as to why its popularity fell, including internal divisions within the government coalition, its support of EU membership, and the unpopularity of its support for the Icesave Acts (see, e.g., Hardarson and Kristinsson 2014), but the end result was a return to power of the two dominant parties of modern Icelandic politics: the IP and the PP. The 2013 parliamentary elections seemed to signal that most Icelanders were willing to put the crisis behind them: they allowed the old gatekeepers back to their post.[36]

Before losing power, the SDA-led government pushed hard for Iceland to join the EU. During the 2009 election campaign, when the SDA was swept into government, the future prime minster, Jóhanna Sigurðardóttir, was quoted as saying: 'If we apply immediately for EU membership we will be able to adopt the euro within four years' (quoted in Totaro 2009). With the SDA in government (on 16 July 2009), Iceland applied to join the EU, and formal negotiations were on-going in the middle of the crisis (having begun in late July 2010). But by September 2013, it became increasingly evident that Icelanders were not interested in jettisoning their currency and joining the EU, and Iceland's government suspended its application.

---

35. See the documentary film, 'Blueberry Soup', for a study of how the crisis propelled this new constitution in Iceland. Available at: http://www.wilmaswishes.com/index.html

36. At the time of this writing, this may be changing, and old wounds may be re-opening. On 5 April 2016, the head of the PP, and sitting Prime Minister, Sigmundur Davíð Gunnlaugsson, was forced to resign when leaked files from the 'Panama Papers' showed that his wife owned an offshore firm in a tax haven, with significant claims on the country's collapsed banks. Sigurður Ingi Jóhannsson replaced him as Prime Minister until new elections were held in October 2016. The IP's Bjarni Benediktsson became PM in January of 2017.

But deciding not to join the EU does not mean that Icelanders want to return to business as before. Indeed, Iceland is looking for new ways to extend its monetary policy autonomy. What is especially interesting is the willingness of the (then) Prime Minster Gunnlauggson to commission a major report on the monetary system, and to consider a radical change in the way that money is created in Iceland. Issued by the Chair of the Althing's Committee for Economic Affairs and Trade (and PP politician), Frosti Sigurjonsson, this report argued that the existing fractional reserve system of banking 'may have been a long term contributing factor to various monetary problems in Iceland...' (Sigurjonsson 2015: 10), and that a revolutionary change in the control of credit was needed to limit the greed and power of private banks. To do this, the report argues for the adoption of a Sovereign Monetary System, where 'only the central bank, owned by the state, may create money as coin, notes or electronic money. Private commercial banks would be prevented from creating money' (Ibid).

This is radical stuff, and it may not come to fruition. But in Iceland, politicians are actually struggling with how to balance the needs of democratic control and free markets. While in most other countries (and the EU), the financial crisis has brought substantial banking reforms, these reforms are designed to strengthen the position of commercial banks (and to ensure that they can continue creating money). In Iceland, by contrast, officials are considering a novel system that would do just the opposite: it would get rid of the fractional reserve system, and reserve for the state the right to create money (and the revenues that this right can generate). This is not a novel reform – it was first proposed by the University of Chicago's Irving Fischer during the 1930s Great Depression. But this reform was not able to gain any traction in the United States, given the power and influence of the commercial banking sector. In Iceland, after the crisis wiped out its nascent financial elite, such a reform has more hope of seeing the light of day.

Conclusion

Iceland's experience is almost universally embraced because it showed that it was possible to prioritise the interests of people over those of bankers and the finance industry. This chapter has endeavoured to show that Icelandic officials were better equipped to pursue popular policies because they maintained their own currency and an independent monetary policy.

It is clear that Iceland had more options than other countries because it could maintain control over its currency, and with it, monetary policy. Iceland simply wouldn't have enjoyed the same rapid or broad-based transformation in the absence of a currency depreciation, the implementation of capital controls and the ability to exert more political influence over the central bank (not to mention the debts of its domestic banking sector). As we saw in the Althing's debt-repayment legislation (Icesave Act I), the Icelanders took political sovereignty seriously, and were willing (and able) to isolate and defend it from international creditors. These are the clear political benefits of monetary policy autonomy.

In addition, Iceland benefited from not being backed by the European Central Bank (ECB). I suspect that Icelandic elites would have followed the path chosen by elites elsewhere, if given the chance: they would have preferred to rescue their financial brethren, and force Icelandic taxpayers to bail them out. Given the country's small size, however, the absence of any viable lender of last resort meant there was little doubt that Iceland could *not* bail out its irresponsible banks. While it did not seem so at the time, the people of Iceland were lucky that the ECB was unwilling (or not required) to stand ready to assist – doing so would have cost future generations dearly (see the Irish response, below).

Contrary to more common lessons about the nature of the crisis (and national responses), Iceland secured its room for movement because its banking sector was *too big to be saved*. In this context, political agitation could secure real change. In the right hands, an autonomous monetary policy (in the form of a devaluation, capital controls and the undisputed authority to let its banks collapse) proved key to Iceland's robust recovery. Staying outside of the European Union, and outside of the monetary union, Icelanders could band together to bring down a bankrupt government, turn their backs on enormous political and economic pressure emanating from abroad and redirect their economy on a new, *productive*, export-based footing. In Iceland, the financial genie was put back in its bottle again.

It is too easy to exaggerate the positive, and to overlook the negative, elements to the Icelandic response. The crisis has cost Icelanders dearly, and many of those who benefited most from the financial bubble have managed to avoid paying their due share of the clean-up bill. I do not mean to imply that Iceland's response was the sole result of its ability to devalue its currency (or any particular institutional feature, for that matter). This multifaceted response reflects deeper components of the Icelandic political character. Preferences and expectations about proper political behaviour differ from country to country, and these mores are not easy to transplant in foreign soils.

But this is the whole point of democratic policy autonomy – states can and do differ in their economic make-up and policy preferences. To manage the domestic economy in a way that benefits it citizens, we need to preserve those instruments that allow us to hold policy makers accountable, and deliver the desired (popular) outcomes.

Chapter Five

Ireland

Even though there are significant differences, the crisis in Ireland is remarkably similar to what we saw in Iceland. In both countries, poor regulation and a speculative frenzy inflated asset bubbles that eventually burst, pushing banks into bankruptcy. In both countries, busted banks turned to the state for help when they lost access to international short-term loans. After their asset bubbles burst, and the underlying value of their holdings fell, these banks became insolvent and in desperate need of recapitalisation. Given the size of the bail-outs required, each state was forced to consider international assistance, enormous loans and drastic policy responses (to pay down those loans). Last, but not least, citizens in both countries suffered greatly because of the greed, corruption and cronyism of their political and economic elites.

But there are also important differences that separate these two cases. For one thing, the size of the banking crisis in Iceland, relative to the size of the home economy, was significantly larger and more threatening than it was in Ireland. As a percentage of GDP, Ireland's bank recapitalisation requirements were relatively modest, compared to Iceland's (c.f. Table 1.1). This makes the second important difference all the more surprising: the Irish crisis proved to be much deeper and costlier, in both economic and social terms (as we saw in Chapter Three). This chapter examines how Ireland transformed from Celtic Tiger to ward of the Troika. As with the previous chapter, we begin with a brief description of how Ireland found itself in economic crisis, then introduce the Irish response to that crisis and consider the political reaction and repercussions. When this is done, we can clearly see how Ireland's options were shaped by its membership in the EMU. In contrasting the Irish and Icelandic cases, then, we find that Ireland's options in struggling with the crisis were limited by its full integration into a nascent monetary union in Europe.

The rise of a Celtic Tiger

For the first decade of the 21st century, Ireland was the darling of free-marketers. This small country, on the margins of Europe, managed to transform itself quickly from rags to apparent riches. It did so by attracting foreign investment with a corporate-friendly tax rate, easy access to the European market, and a laissez-faire approach to regulation and oversight.[1] Ireland's impressive economic

---

1.   Even before the crisis, Dublin had earned a reputation 'as something of the Wild West of European finance' (Lavery and O'Brien 2005).

transformation was frequently compared with those of the Asian Tigers, and a new – Celtic – Tiger became a model for emulation, both within the EU and beyond (see, e.g., O'Toole 2010b: chapter 1).

Ireland's rapid economic growth was fuelled by its ability to attract foreign investors wanting to conduct business in Europe. This European kick-start was the result of a longer-term strategy to wrestle the Irish economy away from the United Kingdom, by fully integrating it with the rest of Europe, under the auspices of the European Economic Community (EEC, subsequently the EU). Hence, the origins of the Celtic Tiger can be traced back to 1973 (when Ireland joined the EEC) and to 1979 (when it joined the EMS). Joining the first club helped to coax the Irish economy from its close economic and financial links with the UK; joining the latter allowed Ireland to break the one-to-one parity that existed between the Irish pound and British sterling.

By the late 1980s, Ireland was able to attract US Multinational Corporations (MNCs) that were looking to access a growing market in Europe (while fearing the creation of a Fortress Europe that would keep them at bay). As Ireland signed the Maastricht Treaty in 1992, and joined ten other members to establish the euro (in January 1999), foreign investors saw a country fully committed to the European project. These MNCs were attracted to Ireland's flexible, English-speaking workforce, and – perhaps more importantly – its low corporate tax rate (originally zero per cent tax on profits of manufactured exports (!), then 10 per cent, later raised to 12.5 per cent – where it stands today), generous capital grants, investment depreciation allowances, tax exemptions for R&D and the like.

This economic transformation was accompanied by a substantial shift to the right in Irish politics, beginning when Fianna Fáil (FF) and the Progressive Democrats (PD) came together in 1997 to share power under the leadership of the irrepressible Bertie Ahern (*see* Table 5.1). Ahern would remain in the position of Taoiseach (Prime Minister) until 2008, and his party would stay in power until 2011, when it was blamed for the crisis and removed from office in an upset election.

While impressive when in bloom, Ireland's real growth (and economic miracle) was relatively short lived, stretching roughly from 1995 to 2001. During this time, the Irish enjoyed a sharp rise in both worker productivity and manufacturing exports. By the turn of the millennium, however, both these trends were beginning to wane. Between 2000 and 2004, for example, Ireland shed about 30,000 manufacturing jobs: from about 250,000 to 220,000 (CSO 2016a).

At the same time, membership in the Eurozone was making it increasingly difficult for Ireland to maintain the competitiveness that had fuelled its exports. In the first years of the new millennium, Irish inflation rates were consistently higher than the European average (*see* Figure 3.6); this undermined the country's competitiveness and inflated an ominous property bubble. As Donovan and Murphy (2014: 94) noted in their analysis of the crisis: 'If Ireland had not been

Table 5.1: Recent governments in Ireland

Government	Taoiseach (PM)	Tánaiste (Deputy)	From	Until	Coalition Partners
Ahern I	Bertie Ahern	Mary Harney	26 June 1997	6 June 2002	*FF*, PD
Ahern II	Bertie Ahern	Mary Harney	6 June 2002	14 June 2007	*FF*, PD
Ahern III	Bertie Ahern	Brian Cowen	14 June 2007	7 May 2008	*FF*, GP
Cowen I	Brian Cowen	Mary Coughlan	7 May 2008	9 March 2011	*FF*, GP
Kenny I	Enda Kenny	Eamon Gilmore (2011–14); Joan Burton (2014–16)	9 March 2011	10 March 2016	*FG*, LP
Kenny II	Enda Kenny	Frances Fitzgerald	6 May 2016	Present	*FG*, Independents

Note: In the right-hand column, the coalition party in italics is the Taoiseach's political party. Party acronyms are defined as follows:

FF	*Fianna Fáil*	The Republican Party (centre-right)
PD	Progressive Democrats	*An Páirtí Daonlathach* (conservative, neo-liberal)
GP	Green Party	*Comhaontas Glas* (centre-left)
FG	*Fine Gael*	Tribe of the Irish (centre-right, Christian democrat)
LP	Labour Party	*Páirtí an Lucht Oibre* (centre-left, social democrat)

a member of the euro area, the appropriate response in the case of "overheating" and the risk of a bubble emerging would have been to tighten monetary policy significantly. Such an option was of course unavailable.'

Property prices exploded, as can be seen in Figure 5.1, and the blast propelled a vicious economic cycle. Rising property prices encouraged even more people to borrow and invest in property. By 2006, every seventh worker in Ireland was employed in the construction sector, and that sector constituted almost 24 per cent of Ireland's GDP (O'Toole 2010b: 22–23, 120). Although the need to deflate this property bubble was clearly evident to many outside observers,[2] the authorities seemed blind to the threat that it posed.

In Figure 5.1 we can see a slight hesitation in the market around 2001. This brief respite offered an opportune moment for a policy correction. But instead of dampening the speculative activity, and stabilising the construction industry, an FF-led government decided to substitute one source of growth with another. In trying to replace the growth once generated by FDI, the government opted for a strategy that the National Competitive Council would subsequently call: 'growth derived from asset price inflation, fuelled by a combination of low interest rates,

---

2. The most vocal of these was probably Morgan Kelly, professor of economics at University College Dublin, and frequent commentator at the *Irish Times*. See, e.g., Kelly (2006 and 2007).

Figure 5.1: Average new house prices, Ireland, 1975–2014

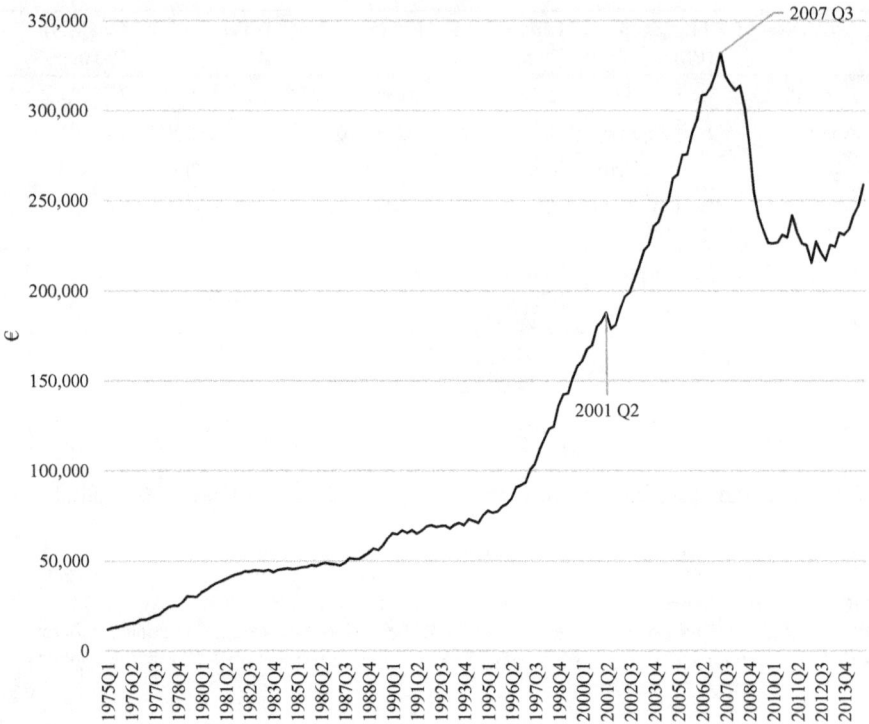

Source: CSO (2016b)

reckless spending and speculation' (NCC 2009: 8). In particular, the government introduced several property-based tax incentives and a reduction in the stamp duty to entice further property development. The predictable result was more building, higher land prices, and the continued diversion of productive investment into speculative property development.

'The state ended up subsidising—to the tune of around €2 billion in all—the building of houses whose purpose was to provide shelter, not for real people, but for the taxes of their builders. The tax costs to the state of the various "renewal" schemes amounted to a staggering 43 per cent of the cost of the actual developments. Instead of providing real houses for people who desperately needed them, €2 billion of public money was squandered on putting up empty shells in places where no one wanted to live' (O'Toole 2010b: 119).

The banks were only too happy to oblige with this new plan; they increased lending to property developers and builders. To fund these loans, Irish banks did like everybody else (*see* the Iceland and Latvian chapters): they borrowed, short-term, from abroad. As a consequence, the banks' loan-to-deposit ratios soared.[3] As in the other two countries, Irish banks came to depend on foreign wholesale borrowing and short-term subordinated debt. As in Latvia, these loans were pumped into a housing and construction bubble that was about to pop. At the height of the boom, the assets of the domestic banks amounted to five times Ireland's GDP – and property made up almost 30 per cent of those loans in 2006 (IMF 2010b). In short, the balance sheets of Ireland's banks were in no position to deal with the global financial crisis when it hit; and the Irish economy had little hope of bailing them out.

This is the first ingredient of what would become Ireland's financial crisis. In Ireland, three inter-related crises mixed together to create a potent cocktail that knocked Ireland's economy off its feet.

The *property crisis*, just described, was a classic asset bubble – that popped. Property values in Ireland were massively overvalued, driven by market hysteria, and financed by a bloated and greedy banking system. Betting myopically on the property and construction markets, instead of pursuing a more responsible and diversified portfolio, Irish banks accessed international wholesale funding in apparently limitless amounts, at very low interest rates, in a context with very little regulation. Although the banks were raking in money when times were good, this left them in an extremely precarious position once property values began to fall.

As in Iceland, the banks' over-reliance on foreign short-term borrowing became a problem when international lending markets seized up. Quite simply: the money stopped coming, creating a *bank crisis*. When the property bubble burst, and housing prices began to fall, Irish banks found themselves in a terrible squeeze. What first appeared as a liquidity crisis revealed itself to be a full-blown solvency crisis. The state found it necessary to step in, if Ireland was to keep its indigenous financial sector afloat.

The property and bank crises resulted in a *fiscal crisis* for the Irish authorities. On the one hand, the state had become overly dependent on property-related revenues (due to the incentives mentioned above). Consequently, an important source of state revenue fell along with prices in the property market. On the other hand, the bank crisis required the state to divert an ever-increasing amount of money to recapitalise the banks and to service its expanding debt burden. The result was a growing gap in the Irish government's finances, as shown in Figure 5.2. Although revenues decreased slightly, expenditures exploded in response to the property and banking crises (until 2010).

---

3. Nyberg (2011: 39) calculated that the gap between the banks' lending and their retail deposits rose from €26 billion in 2002 to €129 billion by 2008. This gap was filled by wholesale funding, mostly from abroad.

Figure 5.2: General government finances, Ireland, 2000–2014

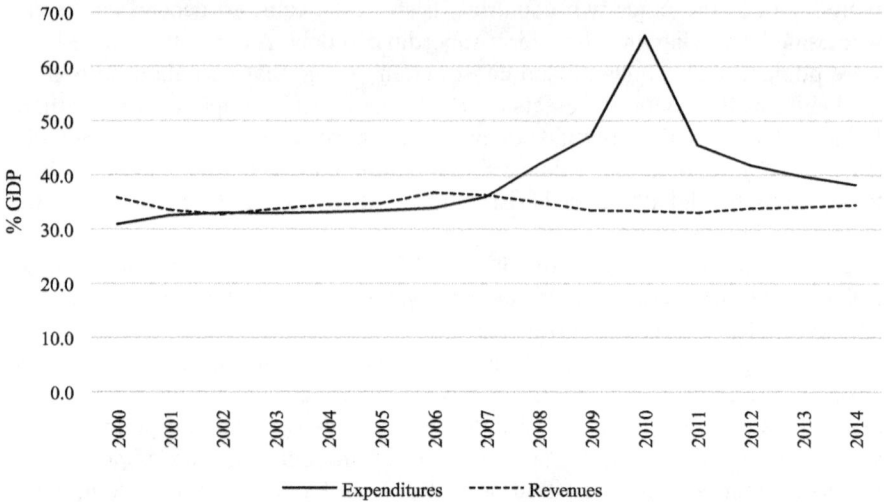

Source: Eurostat [gov_10a_main]

These three crises – property, bank and fiscal – came together to create a spiral of economic decline that is the Irish financial crisis. When the property bubble burst, it left a sizeable hole in the government's finances and exposed the extent of risk-taking and mismanagement in Irish banks. In rescuing the banks (and all their creditors), the government's finances were squeezed on both ends: they lost an important source of revenue with the collapse of the property bubble, and their expenditures grew precipitously – in order to bail out the banks and to support a population suffering under the Great Recession. After 2007, and especially 2008, the number of unemployed in Ireland skyrocketed (as we saw in Figure 3.7). As Ireland's economic reputation took a dive, along with its credit rating, the resulting increase in borrowing costs made it impossible to continue business as before.

Busted

As in Iceland, the threat to the Irish banking system was almost immediately evident in the wake of Lehman Brothers' collapse: there was a €130 billion gap between what the banks had lent out (mostly to property developers), and the deposits taken in – and this gap was being bridged by borrowing on international markets.

Even if Ireland's financial regulators did not seem overly bothered,[4] markets began to worry about the state of Irish banks. Triggered by the near collapse of

---

4.   In late September 2008, the Financial Regulator reported to the Finance Minister that there was no cause for significant concern about the Irish banking system (Donovan and Murphy 2014:

Bear Stearns, share prices for Irish banks fell sharply on 17 March 2008 (the so-called St Patrick's Day Massacre). Although all of the major banks in Ireland were in trouble, Anglo Irish's position was especially vulnerable: its share price dropped 23 per cent at one point during the St Patrick Day's Massacre, before ending the day at 15 per cent down (Donovan and Murphy 2014: 186).

Anglo's liquidity was drying up. After first trying (unsuccessfully) to secure more foreign funding, the bank tried to cobble together a domestic rescue package. On 18 September the bank met with Ireland's Minister for Finance, Brian Lenihan, to discuss a possible merger with Irish Nationwide Building Society (INBS). When this (rather fanciful) plan didn't bear fruit (INBS was also on the ropes), Anglo approached Irish Life and Permanent – and was again rejected. Desperate, Anglo turned to the Bank of Ireland and Allied Irish Banks (AIB) to secure emergency liquidity support. Once again, they were rejected (Donovan and Murphy 2014: 192).

By the end of the month, Anglo and its brethren had run out of time and money. On 29 September, the ISEQ index of Irish shares suffered its largest ever one-day hit: falling by 13 per cent (RTÉ News 2008). Banking stocks were hit particularly hard. Shares in Anglo Irish, already down to one-third of what they were a year earlier (due in part to the St Patty's Day Massacre), fell 46 per cent; while shares in AIB – Ireland's largest bank – fell by nearly 17 per cent (Spain 2008; RTÉ News 2008). In response to the market crash, Taoiseach Brian Cowen, his Finance Minister, Brian Lenihan, and the heads of Irish banks met overnight to hammer out the details of what would become a massive guarantee: the Government Bank Guarantee Scheme, or the Credit Institutions (Financial Support) Bill 2008.

Unlike any of the other cases in this study, the Irish authorities first tried to solve this problem on their own – without recourse to international assistance. They (mistakenly) believed that Ireland was large enough and rich enough to bail out its own banks. In doing so, their initial (albeit implicit) objective was that 'no Irish bank can be allowed to fail' (see Honohan 2010: 119–20; Nyberg 2011: 78). To secure that objective, they offered a remarkably generous, blanket guarantee that protected *all* depositors and creditors (both junior and senior alike) in Irish banks. On the day after the market crashed, 30 September 2008, Lenihan introduced the package: a quick (two-year) bailout, valued at €365 billion, or more than 2.5 times Ireland's GDP (Honohan 2010: 19). The government planned to pay for this bailout by cutting public sector wages, social welfare and capital spending. In short, the people of Ireland promised to pay for the brazen mistakes made by the country's financial elites.

---

82). Indeed, just three months before the government was forced to provide an unconditional guarantee for Irish banks (end of June 2008), the CBOI published its *2007 Annual Report*, where Governor John Hurley wrote 'Irish banks have negligible exposure to the sub-prime sector and they remain relatively healthy by the standard measures of capital, profitability and asset quality. This has been confirmed by the stress testing exercise we have carried out with the banks' (Hurley 2007: 9).

This decision seemed, at first, uncontroversial. A majority in parliament were in favour of the guarantee (124 TDs[5]), while only 18 TDs opposed. Fine Gael, Sinn Féin and the Independent Party supported the government's decision; only the Labour Party was opposed (Kirby 2012: 259; Gilmore 2016: 15). Indeed, the man most responsible for the guarantee, Brian Lenihan subsequently (and infamously) bragged about how the Irish bank bailout would be 'the cheapest in the world' (Carswell 2008).

To get a sense of how large this guarantee was, we can compare it to the controversial TARP (Toxic Asset Relief Program) bailout plan presented to US President George Bush (that received only grudging approval by Congress). The TARP provided $700 billion to bailout a financial sector that serves about 300 million people. Ireland has a population of around 4.6 million people, yet the country offered a guarantee worth about $520 billion (€365 billion, at the going exchange rate). While each American was being asked to fork out $2,333 to rescue their bankers; every person in Ireland was expected to pay (on average) $113,044!

The Irish guarantee was unique in that it was a home-grown effort (at least at first), and that it provided a blanket guarantee, protecting both depositors and creditors alike. Rather than force bank creditors to bear the biggest burden – as was done in Iceland – the Irish government wanted to protect them from harm. Clearly, the government hoped to return to business as quickly as possible (with no proposed change in management, or accountability measures). Although the government was fronting a great deal of money, and this money would be secured by cutting government expenditures that benefit the general population, it asking nothing in return from an industry that had already proven itself incompetent and corrupt.[6] Only the Labour Party leader, Eamon Gilmore, seemed to be concerned about this at the time:

'I can see what is in this guarantee for the banks and their shareholders, some of whom have already made gains today on the strength of it. I can see what is in it for the six bank chief executives who between them earn €13 million a year. However, I cannot see what is in it for the people or the taxpayers who may yet have to foot the bill. If the Taoiseach is proposing to hand over the deeds of the country to bail out the banks, what are we getting in return?' (Gilmore 2016: 15).

The blanket guarantee of 2008

While there is not enough space to explore any of the details of the 2008 guarantee, we can consider the nature of the bailout, and its consequences for both the finance industry and Irish taxpayers. Ireland had six damaged banks, and the government

---

5.   TD is the equivalent of MP, or Member of Parliament. TD (*Teachta Dála*, or 'Deputy to the *Dáil*') is a member of *Dáil Éireann*, the lower house of the *Oireachtas* (the Irish Parliament).

6.   The scale of corruption became even clearer when audio tapes were released by the *Irish Independent* newspaper, on which Irish bankers demonstrated a remarkable arrogance and contempt for regulators, elected officials, and the taxpayers who would eventually bail them out. See Lyons and Sheridan (2014).

promised all of them its support. The blanket guarantee originally promised up to €400 billion in support, but it was soon evident that nobody knew the actual extent of the problem.

The guarantee was remarkably broad: it covered all Irish deposits[7] (including corporate and interbank), bonds, senior debt and certain subordinated debt. Almost immediately, the authorities recapitalised two of the banks (Anglo Irish and Bank of Ireland), and they eventually took over Anglo in January 2009. This recapitalisation effort came at a cost of over €30 billion, and in the form of promissory notes – amounting to €3.1 billion every year over a ten-year period. In other words, the state needed to make a sizeable cash payment every year for the following ten years, with the next payment due in in 2012 (Gilmore 2016: 107)! The authorities also created a so-called 'bad bank', the National Asset Management Agency (NAMA), to take the banks' toxic assets off their books. NAMA used taxpayer money to buy the bank's bad assets, at above book value, and then sold NAMA shares back to the banks. The banks, then, used these shares as collateral to get liquidity from the ECB (Blyth 2013: 235–6).

In April 2010, the total cost of the bank bailouts was estimated to be around €73 billion – an enormous bill for a country that has less than five million people.

'As a taxpayer, what does a bailout bill of €70 billion mean? It means that every cent of income tax that you pay for the next two to three years will go to repay Anglo's losses, every cent for the following two years will go on AIB, and every cent for the next year and a half on the others. In other words, the Irish State is insolvent: its liabilities far exceed any realistic means of repaying them' (Kelly 2010).

€73 billion constituted roughly 44 per cent of Ireland's 2010 GDP. Of that €73 billion, roughly €40 billion went to pay for NAMA, €7 billion went to AIB and Bank of Ireland, and an estimated €26 billion went to Anglo Irish, EBS (Ireland's largest building society) and INBS (Oliver 2010). Worse yet, in April 2010, Eurostat insisted that the whole 10-year recapitalisation programme be accounted for in one budget. As a result, Ireland's official budget deficit in 2010 was jacked up to 32 per cent of GDP (Dineen 2012). This constitutes the peak in expenditures in Figure 5.2.

As painful as they were, these actions were insufficient to restore confidence. Ireland's reputation (and sources of funding) continued to deteriorate when it became obvious that the financial situation of the banks was worse than first disclosed. Credit Default Swap (CDS)[8] rates on Irish government debt increased markedly; and Ireland's ten-year bond yields went from four per cent in 2006 to 14.55 per cent in July 2011, as Ireland's bonds were consigned to 'junk' status

---

7.   It should be noted that ordinary deposits were already covered (up to €100,000) under a European-wide scheme.

8.   CDSs offer a rough measure of the market's estimation of the cost of insuring against default by the government (or corporate entity).

(Gilmore 2016: 23). Without access to funding markets, and with Irish depositors taking flight (in the absence of capital controls), the Irish banking system turned to the ECB's financing facilities and to CBOI Emergency Liquidity Assistance (OECD 2011b: 70). As risk spreads surged, Ireland was priced out of the sovereign bond market and was forced to turn to the international community to secure support for its economic adjustment programme.

The Troika bailout

Ireland was forced to seek external financing in late 2010, and found it in a rich collection of friends: the European Commission, the ECB and the IMF (hence Troika). Ireland's Troika bailout was introduced on 21 November 2010, and approved by the ECOFIN Council and the IMF Board in the same month (see IMF 2010a and EC 2011). The end result was a controversial €85 billion package, designed to last for three years (2011–2013). In it, up to €50 billion was earmarked for fiscal needs and €35 billion was targeted for banking support measures (EC 2011: 5). Of the total €85 billion, €17.5 billion was to be provided by Ireland itself, to cover the fiscal deficit, the costs of bank recapitalisation and the debt-maturities (OECD 2011b: 12). The Irish component would be paid for with an austere four-year plan, entitled *The National Recovery Plan 2011-2014* (GoI 2010), which relied mostly on cuts in public spending, along with some tax increases.

Ireland's Troika bailout had three main goals: restoring stability to the banking system; regaining market access for the government and kick-starting economic recovery (Coakley 2015). Given its design, the first two objectives were easier to secure than the third. Even though Ireland had nowhere else to turn to secure needed funds, the Troika package was very controversial. First of all, the agreement placed Ireland on a very short political leash: all of its budget decisions needed to be cleared with the Troika; Ireland's fiscal performance would be subject to quarterly reviews; and Troika personnel would be placed in core government departments to oversee developments. Second, the government was required to dip into its National Pension Reserve Fund to recapitalise the banks. Third, the interest rates charged to Ireland were much higher than expected, and borderline exploitative: 'The ECB was borrowing at 1.75 per cent on the open market, and lending on to Ireland at around 3 per cent, making a tidy 1.25 per cent mark-up on our misery' (Gilmore 2016: 104). Finally, of course, the *National Recovery Plan 2011-2014* included deep fiscal cuts (€15 billion between 2011 and 2014), most of which would come by way of spending cuts – while €5 billion would be derived from raising taxes (IMF 2010c), in hopes of reducing the government's budget deficit to three per cent of GDP by 2014. While Ireland's government expenditures would need to be cut in a dramatic fashion (witness Figure 5.2, after 2011), there was absolutely no willingness on the part of the Irish authorities, to lower their infamously low (12.5 per cent) corporate income tax rate. Any attempt to change that rate, in the absence of capital controls, would threaten massive capital flight and reduced FDI.

In December 2013, Ireland successfully completed the Troika's financial assistance programme, with most of its policy conditions having been met. From that point on – five years after the original bailout – Ireland could begin to see a light at the end of its tunnel. Ireland was finally able to finance itself again, without outside assistance. Still, the country remains bound by the programme's strict austerity measures, and subjected to post-programme surveillance (PPS) – and it will be so until 75 per cent of its debts have been paid off (barring any early repayments, Ireland's PPS will last until 2031).

The overall effects on the Irish economy were predictably austere.[9] Ireland's GDP fell by almost eight per cent between 2007 and 2009 (Figure 3.3) and its debt-level skyrocketed to 120 per cent of GDP (Figure 3.4). While the program was successful in reducing the government deficit to below the magic three per cent level in 2015, it did so by imposing widespread budget cuts: the country reduced its number of public servants by 25,000 (down from 307,000); cut the pay of new entrants to the public service by ten per cent; cut public service pensions by up to 12 per cent; and cut spending on health, education and social welfare. It was even proposed that the country's minimum wage be cut by €1 an hour – although the new government managed to reverse this in May 2011 (Kirby 2012: 253).

As unemployment rose, so too did the level of income inequality – if only slightly (Figure 3.11). But the wealthiest tier in Irish society still managed to do well during the downturn. The *Allianz Global Wealth Report* showed that the Irish share of global financial assets had grown by over seven per cent a year from 2008 to 2009 (Steck *et al*. 2010: 81); while a report on Ireland's 300 richest individuals published by the *Sunday Independent* revealed that their collective wealth had increased by €6.7 billion between 2010 and 2011, to a total of €57 billion (Webb 2011); and the number of Irish billionaires increased from six in 2006, to 9 in 2010, and to 11 in 2011 (Kirby 2012: 264). For most everyone else, however, the Great Recession cut deeply: more and more workers lost faith in the Irish economy and emigrated abroad (Figure 3.12).

Politics as usual

There can be little doubt that the path chosen by the Irish authorities was a costly one, but did it enjoy politically legitimacy? To what extent were the decisions affected by public opinion or outside pressure, and did the responsible parties bear any of the blame/costs for their apparent misdeeds? To answer these questions, this section is divided into three parts. The first part considers the electoral consequences of the crisis, and the Irish government's response; the second part examines one of the most controversial elements in that response – the decision to protect senior bondholders; and the third part looks at the official Irish investigation into what went wrong, and who was to be held accountable.

---

9.   For more on the politics of austerity in Ireland, see Hardiman and Regan (2013).

Votes count, resources matter[10]

At one level, it is difficult to gauge the scope of political dissatisfaction with the government's policies, as the Irish do not seem to get terribly worked up about these things. As Eoin O'Malley asserted in his 2013 round-up of Irish politics: 'If anything, Ireland has been remarkable for the lack of public protests that are observed in other European countries' (O'Malley 2013: 107). This absence of protest is especially remarkable when one recognises that the pain inflicted by these bailouts was more severe in Ireland than it was in, say, Iceland. How should we account for this lack of voice?

Lenihan implied that we might interpret Irish quiescence as a sort of stoic consent: 'The steps taken have impressed our partners in Europe, who are amazed at our capacity to take pain. In France, you would have riots if you tried to do this' (quoted in Lucey 2009). While there can be little doubt that the Irish people have been exposed to a great deal of pain, their 'capacity to take pain' can have a myriad of explanations. One likely alternative is that the Irish have become increasingly apathetic and dissatisfied with the political process surrounding the crisis. Indeed, Eurobarometer polls reveal a startling rise in the level of dissatisfaction with the way democracy works in Ireland, as shown in Figure 5.3. Compared to the EU-average, the Irish were – before 2007 – relatively satisfied with how their democracy worked. But in the wake of the blanket guarantee and the Troika bailout, the level of Irish dissatisfaction approached EU-average levels. This trend peaks in 2013, when the Troika bailout formally ends, and receded significantly in 2014. But it remains very high, relative to its pre-crisis level.

As Irish perceptions of their democratic system have deteriorated, so too has their trust in the national parliament, the *Oireachtas*. Before the crisis, Irish respondents tended to trust their parliament more than the citizens of other EU states, as shown in Figure 5.4. From 2008 – the year of the blanket guarantee – the level of distrust rose significantly, and it has remained higher than the EU-average ever since.

Perhaps the best indicator for the degree of political frustration that the Irish are experiencing can be found in the increased number of Irish emigrants (as witnessed in Figure 3.12). It seems that the Irish level of desperation is so high, and the hope for a future fix so low, that workers are fleeing the country in despair. Between 2007 and 2012, the number of registered emigrants from Ireland almost doubled, from 48,040 to 89,436 (Eurostat [migr_emi2]). In other words, for every 1,000 people in Ireland in 2012, almost twenty people left for greener pastures.

As seen in Figures 5.3 and 5.4, Irish levels of distrust and dissatisfaction have surpassed the levels long experienced in most EU countries (EU-average). While this degree of political frustration can reflect the overall state of the economy (not just political inefficacy), my underlying point is that elected officials in a

---

10. This is obviously a play on Stein Rokkan's famous slogan about the trade-offs between electoral democracy and corporatist interest mediation (Rokkan 1966: 105).

Figure 5.3: Dissatisfaction with democracy at home, Ireland and EU-average, 2004–2014

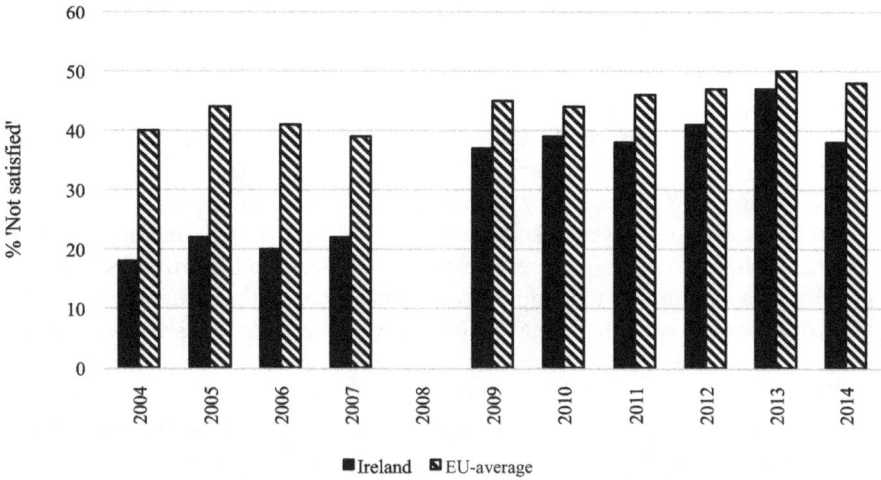

■Ireland ◩EU-average

Note: Total share of those who responded 'Not Satisfied' to the following question: 'On the whole, are you very satisfied, fairly satisfied, not very satisfied or not at all satisfied with the way democracy works in (OUR COUNTRY)?' The actual question number varies from year to year, but the question text remains the same in each survey. The question did not seem to appear in 2008. Contact author for more detailed information about the source.
Source: Eurobarometer [EB62-EB82]

Figure 5.4: Distrust of national parliament, Ireland and EU-average, 2004–2014

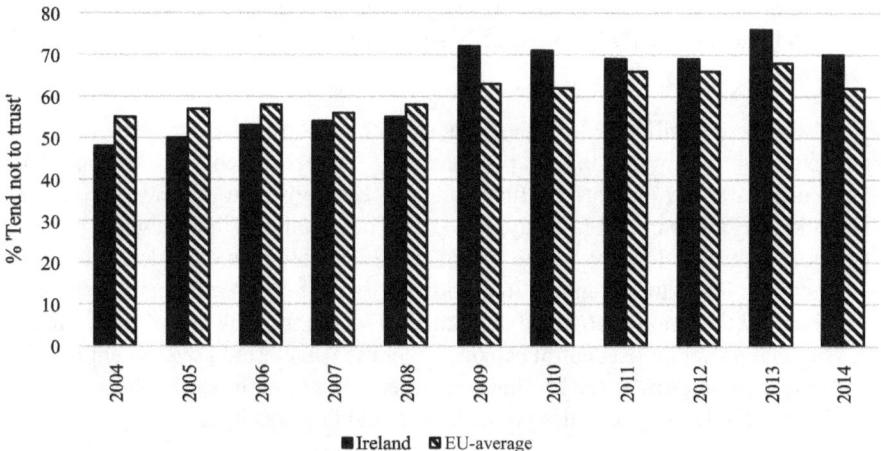

■Ireland ◩EU-average

Note: Share who answered 'Tend not to trust' to the following question: 'I would like to ask you a question about how much trust you have in certain institutions…Please tell me if you tend to trust or tend not to trust the (NATIONALITY) parliament.' The actual question number varies from year to year, but the question text remains the same in each survey. Contact author for more detailed information about the source.
Source: Eurobarometer [EB62-EB82]

democracy are responsible for managing the economy in a way that benefits their constituents. A failed economy reflects failed policies.

Whatever the source of this frustration and distrust, a sense of political indignation seems to have risen in response to the November 2010 Troika bailout, which was broadly seen as a betrayal of Irish sovereignty and appeasement in the face of foreign capital interests.

The Irish people learned about the Troika bailout on 18 November 2008, from their Central Bank Governor (Patrick Honohan) in a radio interview from Frankfurt on RTÉ's *Morning Ireland* program. This, in itself, is rather remarkable. And odd. Given the issues at stake, and the political costs involved, one might expect that the Taoiseach, or his Finance Minister, would want to take responsibility for announcing a bailout plan that imposed a significant constraint on Irish sovereignty. But '[i]t appears that neither the Minister of Finance nor the Taoiseach were made aware in advance of the Governor's statement to be made the following morning [in the interview]' (Donovan and Murphy 2014: 242, fn. 29). Indeed, some FF ministers had appeared on television less than a week before Honohan's interview, pleading ignorance of any plan for a bailout (Gilmore 2016: 38).

Honohan was in Frankfurt as part of a team negotiating a bailout from the Troika. His attendance was required by the two very different roles he was destined to play: as Governor of the Central Bank of Ireland (CBOI) and (critically) as a member of the ECB's Governing Council. This double (and conflicting) role makes it difficult to know where Honohan's loyalties lay when negotiating (and announcing) the deal: were they with the Irish people, or with the ECB?[11]

'...he [Honohan] also plays for the opposing team a member of the council of the European Central Bank, whose decision he is bound to carry out...rarely has a finance minister been so deftly sliced off at the ankles by his central bank governor' (Kelly 2011).

Given these conflicting loyalties, it is strange that '[i]t was Governor Honohan who ended up informing the Irish people of this unprecedented event that involved the ceding of a major part of financial and economic sovereignty to external institutions' (Donovan and Murphy, 2014: 2). These authors (ibid) suggest that this 'was a telling testimony as to the extent to which politicians had lost credibility with both the international institutions and the Irish public.' While this may be true, Honohan's actions may also be an indication of where the real seat of power lies in Ireland: that an appointed central banker, rather than an elected government official, holds the most important cards. This was especially true in Ireland, whose Finance Minister had to learn economics on the fly (his training was in law), and where:

'A weak, demoralised rump administration, served by the same Department of Finance that oversaw the gestation of the crisis, went into bat against the big

---

11. When asked if he had consulted the government on the radio interview that announced the Troika bailout, Honohan said 'No, I operate an independent role here' (O'Brien 2011).

powers of global finance…A government that was spooked and stampeded by the small-time bullies of the Irish banks was never going to be able to stand up to the International Monetary Fund (IMF) and the European Central Bank (ECB)' (O'Toole 2010a).

Regardless of the messenger, Irish tempers were ignited by the public announcement of the Troika bailout. On the day after Honohan's announcement, a lead article in the *Irish Times* (2010) equated it with an assault on Irish sovereignty:

'It may seem strange to some that the Irish Times would ask whether this is what the men of 1916 died for: a bailout from the German chancellor with a few shillings of sympathy from the British chancellor on the side…Having obtained our political independence from Britain to be the master of our own affairs, *we have now surrendered our sovereignty to the European Commission, the European Central Bank and the International Monetary Fund*' (emphasis added).

Just one week later, on 27 November 2010, the Irish stopped being silent: almost one hundred thousand people marched through the streets of Dublin, carrying banners and placards quoting James Connolly and other heroes of Irish Independence (MacArthur 2011: 44).

The Irish public had noticed that an important component of their sovereignty had been taken from them, and they spoke out clearly. As this realisation occurred at the very time that Ireland was preparing its election for the 31st Dáil (to be held on 25 February 2011), the Troika bailout became political fodder in the election campaign. The public's broad disdain for the bailout was translated into a steady decline in support for the governing FF-GP coalition.

Consistently opposed to the bailout, the Labour Party (LP) hoped to turn the election into a referendum on the bailout package. While campaigning, Labour's leader proclaimed: 'The first choice that Irish voters are going to have to make in this election is whether our budgets are decided in Frankfurt, or whether they are decided by the democratically-elected government of the Irish people.' If elected into government, Gilmore promised that a Labour government would renegotiate the terms of the Troika bailout, summarising the voters' choice in stark terms: 'It's Frankfurt's way or Labour's way' (Gilmore, 2011).[12]

The resulting (February 2011) election was a milestone. Fine Gael (FG) and the LP formed a coalition government (with the largest majority in Irish electoral history), while FF was reduced to a shadow of its former self—losing 58 of its 78 seats in parliament (Kirby 2012: 251). Even though the incoming FG-LP coalition enjoyed a solid majority, and campaigned on the need to renegotiate the

---

12. Two other (smaller) parties also opposed the bailout, but in even more forceful terms. Sinn Féin advocated a unilateral renunciation of the package and immediate closure of the banks (without bondholder compensation). The Socialist Party wanted to take Troika funds that were earmarked for the bank bailout and divert them to create jobs and infrastructure. See Kirby (2011: 5 and 7).

agreement, Ireland ended up stuck with Frankfurt's way: the new government was unable to get any of its most important concessions, including their desire to burn senior bondholders (McGee 2011; O'Malley 2013: 106; Gilmore 2016: 111–12).[13] Eventually, the new government came to accept the framework for the national recovery plan, as it was tied to the Memorandum of Understanding on which the Troika funding depended.

As in Iceland, the crisis in Ireland also prompted a lively debate about the need for extensive reforms of the electoral and political system, and these reforms became an important part of the February 2011 general election campaign. This too is an indicator of the scope of political frustration and dissatisfaction in the country. The LP proposed a convention to draft a new constitution, with wide-ranging reforms of the political system, within twelve months of taking office. The *Irish Times* (2011) editorialised that these changes would lead to 'seismic changes in our system of constitutional democracy' (see Kirby 2011: 6). The reforms being discussed were aimed at creating greater parliamentary oversight over executive decision making and greater public transparency, even though there was no discussion about the content of economic or social policy (Kirby 2012: 261).[14]

It is important to note that the election cannot and should not be read as a blanket rejection of Ireland's support for membership in either the EU or the Eurozone. In the following year, 2012, the Irish were given an opportunity to vote on whether to ratify the Treaty on Stability, Coordination and Governance in Economic and Monetary Union (better known as the 'fiscal compact'). This treaty aims to prevent countries (like Ireland) from running 'structural' budget deficits in the future. The referendum was supported by all the major parties in Ireland, and much of the campaign discourse revolved around the potential risk (and associated cost) to Ireland should they oppose the fiscal compact (O'Malley 2013: 109). Only Sinn Féin and the Socialist Party opposed the treaty, calling it 'the Austerity Treaty'. On 31 May, the referendum was carried by a comfortable 60/40 margin, with 50.6 per cent of the eligible votes cast. Indeed, Irish support for the euro remains strong, even during and after the crisis hit, as shown in Figure 5.5. While 30–40 per cent of respondents across the EU voice opposition to the euro,[15] the

---

13. In his memoirs, Gilmore contends that the LP was rewarded for joining the government – it was able to renegotiate the interest rate, limit privatisation and restore the minimum wage. But the LP was unable to get the ECB to budge on how to handle the senior bondholders: 'Although as a government we were determined to burn the senior bondholders in Anglo, the European Central Bank would not permit it, and as the ECB was the source of the liquidity funding for all our banks, we were not in a very strong position to argue' (Gilmore 2016: 61, 111).

14. This constitutional convention didn't happen within the proposed 12-month time span. However, in July of 2012 the parliament passed a resolution that created a citizens' assembly (the Convention on the Constitution) whose purpose was to review the Irish Constitution, including its electoral system. The Constitutional Convention met between December 2012 and the end of March 2014 and considered a variety of issues, including two issues that were eventually put to referendum: legalising same-sex marriage (accepted) and reducing the age of eligibility for the president (rejected).

15. Given relatively high levels of uncertainty, the supporting figures for the euro in the EU-average range in the 50–60 per cent range.

level of Irish opposition has always been much lower. In 2009, Irish opposition to the euro began to rise slowly, and it spiked in 2013 – but it never broached the 25 per cent mark and began to retreat immediately thereafter (in 2014).

Figure 5.5: Opposition to euro, Ireland and EU-average, 2004–2014

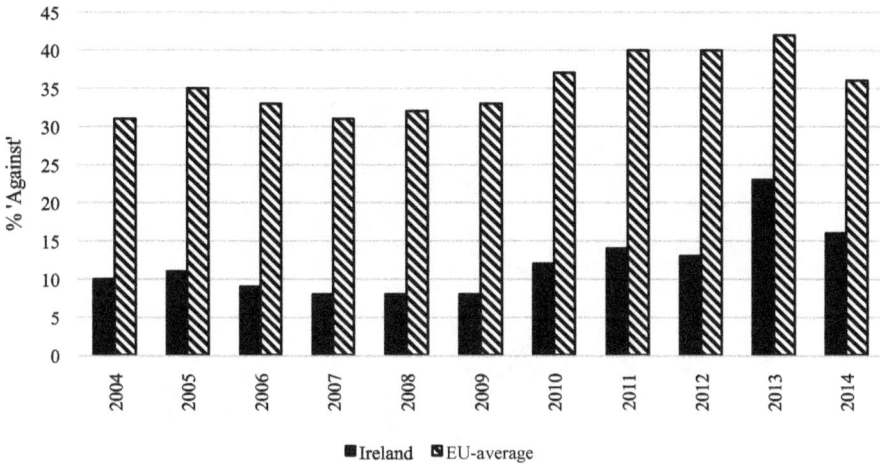

■ Ireland　◨ EU-average

Note: Share of 'Against' responses to the following question: 'Please tell me whether you are for or against a European Monetary Union with one single currency, the euro?' The actual question number varies from year to year, but the question text remains the same in each survey. Contact author for more detailed information about the source.
Source: Eurobarometer [EB62-EB82]

As in Iceland, the Irish went to the polls to choose a different path forward. They had no intent to drop out of the Eurozone, but they did hope to punish the bankers who had caused the crisis and to minimise its cost on the public purse. Voters in all shapes and sizes sought policy options that could get the Irish economy back on track again. Indeed, the Labour Party made this option the cornerstone of its election campaign. But in Ireland, the election results hardly mattered and they had only a nominal effect on Irish policy with respect to the crisis. While the parties in government changed, the most egregious components of the Troika bailout remained in place. Some of this political inefficacy might be explained by the fact that Labour was forced to share power with its more conservative coalition partner, Fine Gael. But a more likely explanation lies in the fact, broadly acknowledged during the election campaign, that Ireland really didn't enjoy any freedom to re-negotiate the deal. Its political hands had already been tied by the central bankers sitting in Frankfurt.

Friends in high places

One of the most interesting, unique and costly aspects of the Irish response to the crisis was the willingness of authorities to provide a blanket guarantee to the people who had profited most from the banks' excesses, and to go to such great fiscal lengths to protect them. This was also one of the most controversial aspects of the Troika bailout – and one that the LP in government fought hard to rescind (albeit unsuccessfully). The decision to protect creditors is important for at least two reasons: it appears as unjust (i.e. that those who were responsible for the mess were not held accountable), and because the protections provided were very costly for the Irish people. If Ireland had forced bank creditors to saddle more of these losses, the state's debt burden could have been substantially reduced.[16] As can be seen in Figure 5.6, there were over €124 billion in senior unsecured debts lying in the banks covered by the guarantee (33 per cent of all liabilities).

Figure 5.6: Covered banks in Ireland, 2008

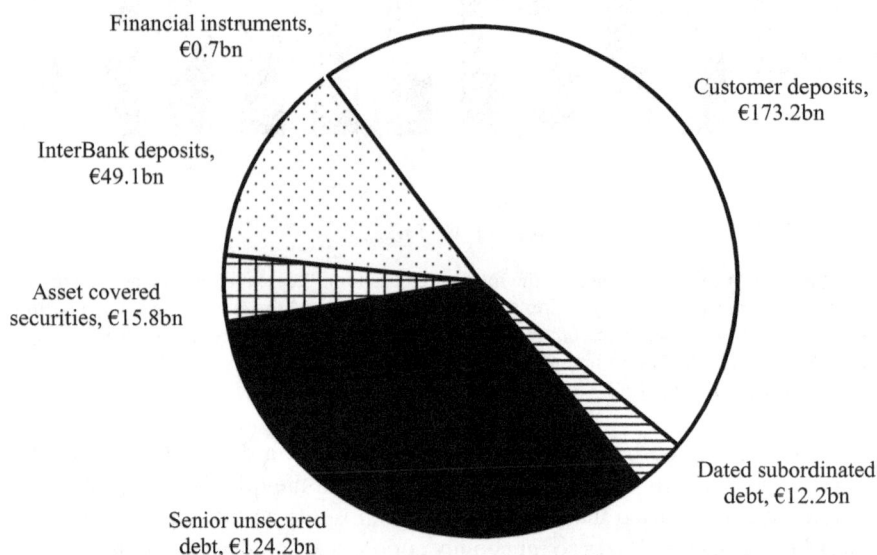

Financial instruments, €0.7bn

Customer deposits, €173.2bn

InterBank deposits, €49.1bn

Asset covered securities, €15.8bn

Dated subordinated debt, €12.2bn

Senior unsecured debt, €124.2bn

Note: Liabilities guaranteed by the Irish state on 30 September 2008.
Source: Nyberg (2011: 77)

The Irish recovery plan rested on a massive bailout to the benefit of bank bondholders. The Taoiseach (Cowen) and his Finance Minister (Lenihan) both argued that depositors and (senior) bondholders had equally protected status under Irish law, thus impeding any differential treatment (Cowen 2012: 8). But no legal opinion from the country's Attorney General at that time has been made public to collaborate this claim (Donovan and Murphy 2014: 206). By contrast, the

---

16. It is important to recognise that not all creditors escaped the crisis unscathed. Cowen (2012: 7) notes there were about €20 billion of junior banks bonds outstanding in September 2008, and that these were eventually discounted, on average by between 80–90 per cent (they matured after the guarantee). The same point was made by Honohan (2012: 12), who contends that shareholder write-downs for the six banks covered by the guarantee exceeded €29 billion.

economist, Morgan Kelly (2010) argued that Ireland had every right to terminate the guarantee on the grounds that three of the banks had withheld material information about their solvency, in violation of the 1971 Central Bank Act. Indeed, Kelly suggested that Ireland could have changed course, and terminated the bank guarantee, as late as September 2010. In that month, €55 billion of bank bonds (held mostly by UK, German and French banks) matured and had to be repaid by Ireland (using money mostly borrowed from the ECB). When this money was paid back, there was little point in asking the bondholders to help foot the bill (it had already been paid!).

With hindsight, it seems that protecting bondholders was less a question of legality, and more a question of political will. If we assume that Ireland enjoyed some legal leeway, what might account for the government's willingness to foot the entire bill? Clearly, policy makers had been misinformed about the seriousness of the bank's situation, and they probably didn't think that the full guarantee would be required. But even if they were aware of the scope of the problem, they may have chosen to protect senior bank creditors on ideological grounds: i.e. they worried that Ireland would ruin its reputation for being a business-friendly host for FDI. Lenihan seems to have suggested as much in a 2010 statement: 'There is simply no way this country, whose banks are so dependent on international investors, can unilaterally renege on senior bondholders against the wishes of our own European partners and the European institutions. That course of action has never been an option during the crisis' (Lenihan 2010).

But pursuing this strategy begs another set of questions. Why would a country want to subsidise a sector that has proven itself to be greedy, risky, ineffective and (quite possibly) criminal? Wouldn't it be better to rebuild the country's broken reputation on a more solid footing? One plausible answer is the corrupt ties that bind political and economic elites in Ireland. We shall turn to this explanation shortly. Another plausible explanation for Ireland's embrace of the bankers is the pressure emanating from the ECB and sundry banking interests across the European Union. As Donovan and Murphy (2014: 214) point out, the decision to protect senior bank creditors '…reflects pressures from the ECB and elsewhere owing to fear about contagion (within both Ireland and the euro area) and, relatedly, the creation of unacceptable precedents. Irish consideration of the burning of bondholders option undoubtedly has also had to take into account the willingness of the ECB to continue to provide low cost funding to Irish banks.'

Indeed, commentators on the Irish case are almost always pointing to the need to bend to the ECB's will, or the fear of what Morgan Kelley (2010) calls an 'unpleasant showdown with the European Central Bank'. This sort of anxiety was clearly evident when former Taoiseach Cowen described the need to repay the senior bondholders: 'At no stage during the crisis would the European authorities, especially the European Central Bank, have countenanced the dishonouring of senior bank bonds. The euro area policy of "No bank failures and no burning of senior bank creditors" has been a constant during the crisis. And as a member of the euro area, Ireland must play by the rules' (Cowen 2012: 8).

This sort of pressure from the ECB is all the more evident after Ireland turned to the Troika for help. As Kelly (2010) would have it 'During September [2010], the Irish Republic quietly ceased to exist as an autonomous fiscal entity, and became a ward of the European Central Bank.' This squeeze is partly because poor economic management had placed Ireland in a position of servitude, and partly because the Troika wanted to protect the underlying creditors (e.g. French, German and UK banks). But it may also have been that the ECB was tired of bailing out Irish banks.[17] This seems to be the message sent in 2010, when ECB President Jean-Claude Trichet wrote to Lenihan, threatening to withdraw emergency funding for Ireland's banks unless the country signed up to the international bailout.[18]

Whatever the impetus, the bailout stank of corruption, as everybody involved – but the Irish taxpayer – had something to gain:

'The German and French banks whose solvency is the overriding concern of the ECB get their money back. Senior Irish policymakers get to roll over and have their tummies tickled by their European overlords and be told what good sports they have been. And best of all, apart from some token departures of executives too old and rich to care less, the senior management of the banks that caused this crisis continue to enjoy their richly earned rewards. The only difficulty is that the Government's open-ended commitment to cover the bank losses far exceeds the fiscal capacity of the Irish State' (Kelly 2010).

Reports from the Troika negotiations paint a picture of the Irish authorities being frustrated and forced to take decisions that were aimed more at protecting the Eurozone than in helping the Irish people. These reports suggest that the ECB was adamant about the need to stop any possible source of contagion. Jorg Asmussen, State secretary at the German Finance Ministry (who attended the 16 November meeting in Frankfurt), was quoted as saying: 'It was made very clear to the Irish finance minister that it is not just about Ireland. The functioning of the currency union was at stake' (O'Brien 2011). In an April 2011 interview, Lenihan confirmed that the ECB precipitated the Irish rescue package and that the Bank did so as Irish banks grew more dependent on its short-term liquidity funding. Lenihan believed that neither the IMF nor the European Commission was overly concerned with the Irish situation – but that the ECB was forcing the issue. The

---

17. Before the Troika bailout, the ECB was providing massive liquidity support to Ireland's failed banks in an effort to keep them afloat. These banks had come to rely on ECB credit (both standard credit and Emergency Lending Assistance, or ELA). In effect, ELA funding worked to bail out the bondholders, as maturing bonds were repaid (Eichengreen 2015: 6). By early 2011, the ECB's willingness to push Ireland into the Troika bailout signals a desire for a new mechanism to relieve it of this burden (Murphy 2010).

18. See Kelpie (2014). The original exchange of letters can be found at: http://www.ecb.europa.eu/press/html/irish-letters.en.html.

ECB leadership pressed their view 'with great vigour': that quickly 'putting the fiscal house in order' would resolve the banking problem (O'Brien 2011).[19]

> '...it would appear that the European Central Bank exerted pressure to insist that no measures should be introduced to require burden-sharing by the private sector (or at least not until the permanent European debt resolution facility came into effect in 2013). The consequence was that the total liabilities for the domestic banks were in effect to be borne by the taxpayers. The story of the Irish fiscal adjustment, the size of the deficit, the scale of the debt, follows from this decision' (Dellepiane and Hardiman 2012: 12).

Irish accountability

Before being voted out of office, the FF-GP government commissioned four different reports on the crisis: Regling and Watson (2010); Honohan (2010); Wright (2010) and Nyberg (2011). With these reports, the people of Ireland might hope to discover what went wrong, and who would be held accountable for the costly mistakes. The authors of the report, however, were given a much narrower mandate. As a consequence, the reports had little real political impact.

The first problem was a lack of distance and/or disinterest. These reports were commissioned and authored by people with vested interests in the industry. Three of the reports (Regling and Watson 2010; Honohan 2010; and Wright 2010) were commissioned by Lenihan's Ministry for Finance; the fourth (Nyberg 2011) was commissioned by the Government's Statutory Commission of Investigation into the Banking Sector in Ireland. To make matters worse, the reports were authored by people with strong connections to the financial sector. For example, Regling was the CEO of the European Financial Stability Facility; while Honohan was the new central bank governor.

By design, the reports did not address or evaluate the roles played by elected officials, or aim for political impact. All the reports were based on secret (non-public) inquiries, and were focused on identifying the failures in specific institutions, namely the CBOI, the Financial Regulator, the Finance Department and the banks (taken as a group). Both the Honohan and Nyberg reports note the relative absence of official records, and the use of anonymity to protect those involved (in the name of confidentiality restrictions). Donovan and Murphy (2014:

---

19. After the election, in June 2011, the new Minister for Finance, Michael Noonan, announced in Washington that he'd won IMF support to impose substantial losses on senior bondholders in the two banks (Anglo Irish and INBS), who'd been especially reckless. He noted that he still needed to win ECB support for this move – but his announcement unnerved the financial markets. This forced him to make an immediate clarification – that no moves were being contemplated against bondholders at other Irish banks. ECB sources made it clear that the Bank was not going to change its opposition to such a move (Kirby 2012: 260–1). Noonan was especially upset by this, as his party had worked so hard to sell the Lisbon Treaty to the Irish people, just a few years earlier (Brennan 2010).

198–99), for their part, point out that Oireachtas committees do not enjoy the liberty to conduct investigatory hearing or to compel witnesses to attend hearings and give evidence (absent a constitutional modification).

The Regling and Watson (2010) report deals with macro-economic developments internationally and in Ireland, as well as monetary and fiscal policy in the period before the crisis. It totals forty-nine pages, with its appendix. The Wright (2010) report focuses on the performance of the Finance Ministry, with an eye at making changes for the future. This report is a little longer (seventy-eight pages), but includes more appendixes. The other two reports were more thorough and lengthy. The Nyberg (2011) report was commissioned to consider why so many Irish institutions, both public and private, had acted imprudently, while the Honohan Report was produced by the Governor of the CBOI (although he did not hold that position when the first bailout occurred) and focused on the role of the authorities (the Financial Regulator and the CBOI) with regard to regulatory and financial stability policy (prior to the crisis). The Nyberg report totalled 155 pages, including appendixes, and the Honohan Report counted 177 pages in total. Each of these four reports, even when combined, are a mere shadow of the SIC (2010) report in Iceland, which weighed in at 2,600 pages.

Compared to the Icelandic reviews, these four reports constitute a disappointment: they are astonishingly brief, remarkably forgiving – at times even uncritical – and they were conducted before the more controversial Troika bailout took place. While acknowledging serious errors, mismanagement and insufficient regulation – as well as the need for subsequent investigations – these reports were relatively superficial, and contained little or no political sting (see, e.g., Finn 2011: 21). Each report noted the need to understand the failures in management and operation, the existence of a sort of herd behaviour and an ineffective regulatory apparatus. Ireland, it seems, suffered from a brief and unfortunate lapse of group thinking.

For almost two years after the original crisis, there was little attempt to correct (or even investigate) the mistakes that had brought about the crisis. Most of the people responsible for the crisis remained in positions of power.[20] Business continued as before: in December 2010 it was learned that the Minister for Justice was to receive a €325,000 'golden handshake' on top of his more than €100,000 yearly pension; the exorbitant pensions and perks allocated to the Teachta Dálas (members of the lower house of Irish parliament) remained in place; and Allied Irish was reported to have handed out €60 million in executive bonuses during 2009–11, during a period of public austerity (MacArthur 2011: 44). Finally, in July 2012, three former Anglo officials (including the ex-Chairman, Sean FitzPatrick), were charged with criminal breaches of company law with respect to a questionable

---

20. See, e.g., Brennan (2010); MacArthur (2011: 44); and Kirby (2012: 264). The one exception is Patrick Neary, the chief executive officer of the Financial Regulator, who was pressed to retire in January 2009. The term of the CBOI governor during the crisis, John Hurley, was scheduled to end in March of 2008, but his term of office was temporarily extended (until the end of September) to assist in stabilising the financial system.

transaction in the so-called Maple 10 affair (Donovan and Murphy 2014: 188). This appears to be the limit of public accountability for a crisis that placed almost 300,000 people out of work (in 2012).

Worse, few people in Ireland were willing to trust the government's handling of the crisis, given the close and public relationship between Fianna Fáil and the country's financial elite. Under Ahern's leadership, the FF (and Irish politics, in general) was seen as corrupt, and the public was increasingly aware of (and concerned about) its strong connections to the banking, real estate and construction sectors:[21]

> '...the Fianna Fáil tent at Galway's annual horse-racing festival, which was stocked with an agreeably vulgar cast of characters from the Irish construction sector, eager to sign another cheque for their political benefactors. With the sordid relationship between Fianna Fáil and the banking-construction nexus so well documented, few are included to take its handling of the crisis at face value' (Finn 2011: 21).

This perception was widespread, both abroad and at home: *The Economist* (2010) magazine noted that 'the tight-knit world of Dublin's political and financial elite does not encourage challenges to consensual thinking.' Even the CBOI governor, Patrick Honohan (2010: 9), writes of an 'unduly deferential' approach to banks by regulators.

In Ireland, there was no proper clean-up after the crisis. Very few of the people responsible for the crisis were held accountable – whether they profited in government or while employed by the banks. One likely reason for this is the difficulty in establishing where, exactly, regulatory responsibility lay (e.g. in Brussels, Frankfurt or in Dublin).

The role of monetary policy

The Irish people suffered greatly from the crisis, and the source of this suffering can be traced back to two issues. The first issue is the nature of the particular rescue packages that were offered, and the costs associated with these. The second issue concerns the depth of the recession that resulted, and the difficulties that authorities had in kick-starting the Irish economy. In both issues, Irish policy makers were handicapped by their membership in the Eurozone.

To estimate the extent to which Ireland's crisis can be traced back to its membership in the Eurozone, we need to entertain a counterfactual: what could Ireland have done differently, if it still had its own currency? This counterfactual can be conjured up by contrasting the Irish and Icelandic cases.

---

21. Of all the disclosed donations to the FF between 1997 and 2007, 40 per cent are said to have come from builders and property owners (Finn 2011: 20).

Bailout packages

As already noted, the most significant difference separating the Irish and Icelandic response to their banking crises is the unwillingness of the Irish authorities to let their banks go under (and saddle the bondholders with the resulting losses). Here it seems abundantly clear that the opportunities available to the Irish authorities were limited by the needs of the broader European community, to which they belonged. More to the point, the ECB was adamant about protecting the senior bondholders at Irish banks and in making the Irish people pay for the bill.

Because Ireland was part of the Eurozone, it had access to a lender of last resort: the ECB. The ECB's deep pockets made it feasible to consider and pay for a bailout of the banks – even if such a bailout would place an enormous burden on the Irish people. In Iceland, by contrast, the lack of a sufficiently large central bank meant that a bailout was untenable, even impossible. In this instance, Iceland benefited from being too small to bail, while Ireland could tap into larger sums of money (with which to throw at the banks).

This access to financing delivered three fateful consequences. First, as I hinted above, it meant that the Irish authorities had an option to bailout the banks, where this option was not available in the Icelandic case. Second, the decision-making body of the ECB includes member state central bank governors for those countries that had invested in these failed banks: they had a direct financial interest in ensuring their own banks did not collapse, along with the Irish. It was better for the ECB leadership to have the Irish people pay these bills than deal with the economic challenges of failed banks in their own backyards. Finally, as the ECB continued to provide liquidity to these failed banks, it found itself helping to bankroll Ireland's bondholder bailout. By early 2011, Ireland needed about 20 per cent of the ECB's total lending in order to prop up its banking sector – totalling €140 billion (Murphy 2010). Over the long run, this was not a tenable solution for the ECB; it began to press Ireland to find alternative solutions, and the Troika bailout was just that sort of solution.

Each of these consequences reflected the interests of broader European investors and institutions, more than they did the will of the Irish people. While it is not unreasonable to expect creditors to impose stringent constraints on their borrowers to ensure their repayment (this is, after all, what creditors do), the Icelandic case demonstrates that sovereign states have more room to wiggle (should they choose to do so). More popular and just outcomes are possible when a country still enjoys some wiggling room.

Throughout the negotiations over the Troika bailout, the Irish people and their representatives were told that they needed to consider the broader consequences of their decision. Irish independence, it was said, would threaten the stability of Europe in a wave of contagion; at stake were Europe's financial markets and the Eurozone itself. After all, if Irish officials were to listen to its voters rather than the ECB, what would stop Greece, Spain, Portugal or Italy from following suit?

Economic mismanagement

The second difficult issue is derived from the lack of tools available to bring the Irish economy out of recession. Indeed, a significant part of the blame for why Ireland ended up in its desperate situation could be placed at the footsteps of monetary union, and the absence of an appropriate monetary policy.

In sharing a common monetary policy with the rest of Europe, the Irish authorities stood defenceless in the face of large inflows of capital.[22] As in Iceland, a large, laxly regulated European financial market was awash with mobile capital, with few or any bulkheads to contain it. This capital enjoyed the freedom of mobility provided by Europe's common market, and was attracted to the low interest rates on offer in Ireland (an entirely inappropriate monetary policy for Irish conditions at the time) and the absence of any foreign exchange risk.

This point is made explicit in the Regling and Watson (2010: 24) report, when they note that EMU membership 'certainly reinforced vulnerabilities in the economy'. Inappropriately low interest rates 'contributed to the credit boom, the strong increase in household debt, the property bubble and the general overheating of the economy. The removal of exchange rate risk facilitated foreign funding, including for the growing current account deficits. This financing ease meant that Ireland's boom could continue for longer than without EMU membership, and the asset bubble could become bigger.'[23]

But the authors are quick to affirm that being a member of a larger monetary union

> 'helped Ireland to survive better the global financial crisis. Without EMU, European currency markets would have been in turmoil in 2008-9. Funding problems for the banking sector would have become much bigger. Firms and household would have borrowed more in foreign currency, and would have been exposed to balance sheet risks. …None of the interlocutors in Ireland, with whom the authors of this report talked, questioned that EMU membership for Ireland has been, on balance, highly beneficial' (Regling and Watson 2010: 25).

---

22. This is not exactly true. There are several things that Ireland (or other Eurozone states) could have done to try and slow the massive capital flows and brake economic growth. For example, taxation policy could have been used to redirect income from consumption to saving, property taxes could have been increased to slow the expansion of the non-tradable sector, and taxes on imported goods (e.g., vehicles) could have been used to temper demand for imports. But the countries in this study were either unaware or unwilling to use them. At any rate these measures are not as effective as devaluation or capital controls in stopping the flows – but they can be used to throw some sand in the machinery.

23. See also Eichengreen (2015: 1): 'It is tempting to argue that the structure and, indeed, the very existence of the European Union and the Eurozone helped set the stage for the crisis—that conditions in Ireland could not have developed as they did in the absence of these entities.' But Eichengreen later notes how other countries, such as Iceland, also developed severe financial difficulties without being full members of either European club.

In the same way that a European-wide monetary policy was clearly inappropriate for Irish conditions prior to the crisis, and even contributed to the financial frenzy, the constraints of a shared monetary policy limited Ireland's response to the crisis. These limitations were of three sorts.

First of all, Ireland was not able to impose *capital controls* to stop the financial haemorrhaging once it started. As in Iceland, bank depositors and footloose capital were fleeing Irish accounts like rats from a sinking ship. Without capital controls the authorities were powerless to stop it (at least in the short run). This pushed them deeper into debt (and into the arms of the ECB). Unlike in Iceland, however, this policy tool was seldom discussed as an option in the Irish context. This is, in part, due to fear for the impact it might have on future FDI to Ireland, and in part because it was not allowed in the Eurozone (at least not until later, when Cyprus was granted permission to do so).

The second problem with sharing a common currency is the inability to set appropriate *interest rates*. Just as low interest rates helped to get Ireland into this mess, inappropriately high interest rates (in both 2008 and 2011) undermined the Irish recovery efforts (Eichengreen 2015: 11). Absent capital controls, and with the ECB's policy aimed at conditions across the Eurozone (not at the specific economic needs of any particular country), Ireland had to struggle against an interest rate policy that was contrary to its own economic needs.

The third constraint is clearly the largest: Ireland did not have recourse to a *currency depreciation*. To climb out of its recession, Ireland needed to find an alternative means to stimulate economic growth and international competitiveness. But the decision to bail out the banks created an enormous burden of debt that required servicing. Worse, the conditions placed on it by lenders (especially in the Troika bailout) required significant cuts in social spending, which undermined domestic demand. In effect, Ireland was stuck in an austerity trap and had little means to stimulate the necessary economic growth. While Ireland was experiencing its deepest economic crisis since the Great Depression, the Troika bailout required it to return to a balanced budget (more precisely, a deficit of less than three per cent of GDP) by 2014.

In Iceland, the reader will recall, an economic turn-around was sparked by a currency depreciation that almost immediately changed that country's terms of trade: exports grew and imports fell, as Icelanders began to buy more domestic goods, supporting local demand.

While this generated a slight increase in inflation, it also sparked widespread economic growth and confidence in the Icelandic economy. As part of a monetary union, Ireland did not enjoy this sort of option – it would have to increase international competitiveness by shrinking wages and prices.

'In addition to the large debt service obligation assumed by the public sector, Ireland's adjustment burden was exacerbated by the hard exchange rate peg and stagnation in export demand from trading partners that were also beset by the great recession. The situation was further aggravated by the procyclical fiscal contraction adopted under the adjustment programme (as in several other

EU countries), which degenerated into a vicious race to the bottom' (Kopits 2014: 137).

Predictably, there was little effect on the Irish trading balance, as seen in Figure 5.7. For the entire 21st century, Ireland has enjoyed a strong export surplus, due mostly to its ability to attract FDI (the products and services of which are subsequently exported to other EU member states).[24] When the crisis hit, exports continued to hold their position, and hovered around the same level, but it took five years (2009–2014!) before the country was able to regain the sort of competitive footing necessary to increases exports. At the same time, the imports continued to grow from 2009 on.

Figure 5.7: Irish exports and imports, 2000–2015

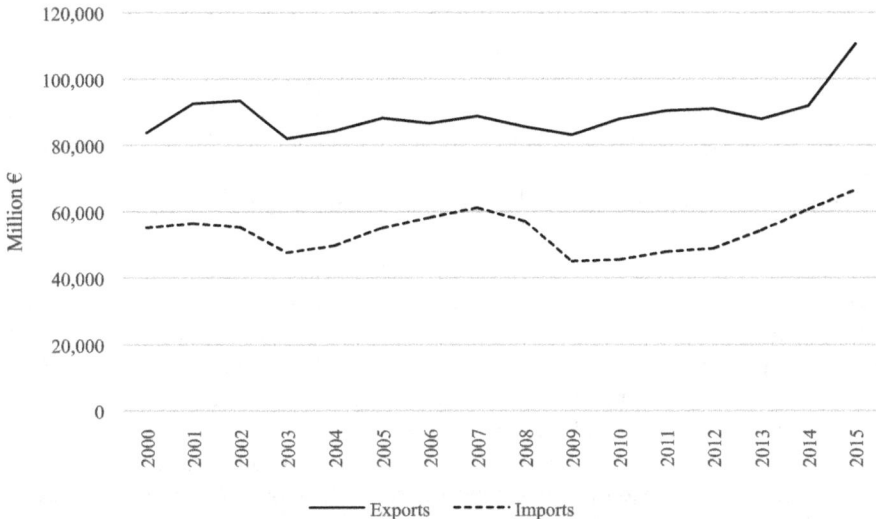

Note: Trade to all countries of the world, millions of €.
Source: Eurostat [ext_lt_intertrd]

Slowly, eventually, the Irish economy began to recover – but it did so by undertaking a very painful and slow-working adjustment, paid mostly by the weakest elements in Irish society (those most likely to lose their jobs, those who were forced to emigrate, or those who rely on government support). As labour markets tightened and the ranks of the poor and unemployed swelled, the average

24. These export figures can be misleading if used as a surrogate for economic or employment growth. For one thing, US companies are responsible for almost 90 per cent of Ireland's exports, but with relatively few jobs as a result (Regan 2014: 27). In addition, after 2014, there was a change made in the way that the National Accounts are calculated in Ireland. 'As a result of these changes, goods owned by an Irish entity that are manufactured in and shipped from a foreign country are now recorded as Irish exports' (CBOI 2014: 7).

annual wage in Ireland was frozen at its 2008 levels, or around €50,000 (OECD 2016b).

In Ireland, the constraints of a common monetary policy were evident in both the run-up to the crisis, during the crisis itself, and in its aftermath. Unable to control domestic interest rates, capital flows, the foreign value of its currency, or even how to deal with its own banks, the Irish authorities found themselves bound to a floundering ship, whose tiller was in the hands of others.

Recent developments

Ireland's response to the crisis was very effective in meeting the sort of performance criteria set by the Troika and often bantered around by economic analysts and commentators. Ireland's budget deficit was reduced in full haste, its banks have been recapitalised and the austerity drive has improved Ireland's cost competitiveness. In Figure 5.7 we could already see these signs of a new Irish economy rising. This impressive growth in exports was achieved as Ireland became the fastest growing economy in Europe (4.8 per cent in 2014). And, after a series of very tight budgets, Ireland's budget deficit met the SGP criteria in 2016, by coming in at less than three per cent of GDP.

While this economic growth is surely welcome, it is far too early to call the Irish response a success. For one thing, the recovery was remarkably slow if one recognises the crisis began in 2008 (rather than in 2010, when the Troika stepped in). For another, it is probably inaccurate to suggest that the growth and export surge is driven by Ireland's austerity policies. Indeed, several political economists have questioned the role that austerity has played in bringing about Ireland's economic transformation, pointing instead to the role of a weaker euro, and foreign investments in the high-skill, high-wage sectors: e.g. in biotech, pharmaceuticals and IT services (see, e.g., Legrain 2016; Regan 2014). But this is not the place to engage in a debate about the causes of Ireland's apparent success in meeting its performance criteria. My point, all along, has been to argue that these sorts of criteria are entirely insufficient for gauging the real effects of policy decisions.

If we look at broader measure of success, the Irish case loses much of its lustre. The government's response to the crisis had inflicted serious damage on the political legitimacy of, and trust in, the country's parliamentary democracy; it has increased economic inequality; and delayed the country's economic recovery (hence prolonging the significant human and social cost associated with a delayed recovery). Even at the time of this writing, in March 2016 – eight years after the original crisis broke – about 8.6 per cent of the Irish workforce (or 188,000 people) remains out of work (CSO 2016c). In addition, over the past year (April 2014–April 2015), 80,900 emigrants were forced to leave their country in search of opportunities abroad (CSO 2015). All of this is happening in an economy now celebrated as a 'Celtic Comeback'.[25]

---

25. This is a reference to the 15 October 2012 cover of *Time* magazine, which featured the sitting Taoiseach, Enda Kenny.

Conclusion

The Irish response to the crisis was heavily influenced by its membership in the Eurozone. This influence was especially strong in determining the more unique and troubling aspects of Ireland's policies: its enormous cost; its delayed recovery; and its willingness to defend the banks. Without access to capital controls, a depreciating exchange rate, suitable interest rate policies and the even the freedom to punish its banks, the Irish crisis placed a heavy burden on workers and government recipients who had little or nothing to do with the crisis. In this regard, the Irish response couldn't be any more different than the Icelandic.

From a political perspective, what is most disconcerting about the Irish response is how it revealed the impotence of Ireland's democratic institutions in addressing the crisis. This impotence is most clearly evident in the inability of a newly elected government, whose electoral platform rested on renegotiating the Troika bailout terms, to change government policy. But we can also see it in the constant reminder that Irish officials needed to conduct policy with an eye at protecting the entire Eurozone, rather than respond to the explicit preferences of their constituents.

Ireland was clearly hurt by its lack of an autonomous monetary policy, but I do not mean to suggest that Ireland was completely without choices, or that all of its problems can be traced to membership in the Eurozone. Sometimes the choices taken reflect the interest of Irish elites, who firmly believed that the country's economic future lies in attracting foreign investors (and would do anything to keep that money coming). Consequently, policy makers wished to avoid any discussion of increasing Ireland's low corporate tax rate, or forcing bank shareholders to pay for the damage they caused. At other times, Ireland's choices were made for them by others – but these constraints came from being heavily indebted, rather than it being a member of the Eurozone.

Rather, I am arguing that Ireland's decisions lacked democratic legitimacy. Ireland's choices were driven by the needs of the Eurozone, more than those of the Irish people. When finally given an opportunity to voice their opinion on how the crisis was being handled (in the 2011 elections), the Irish discovered that electoral pressure could not deliver any significant change in policy or in Ireland's relationship to its lenders. These are the clear political costs of monetary union in Europe.

Chapter Six

Latvia

At first glance, Latvia comes across as a policy replica of Ireland, only smaller. Latvian officials followed the Irish lead by marketing their country as a safe and lucrative (read low cost) investment environment for footloose capital hoping to enter the European Union. To secure these objectives, they joined the EU in 2004, firmly linked their currency (the lat, or LVL) to the euro, and set their sights on joining the Eurozone.

Latvia's pre-crisis conditions were also similar to Ireland's. Europe's aggregate monetary policy proved entirely inappropriate: even as the Latvian economy overheated, cheap money continued to pour in, generating strong inflationary pressures (including a boom in housing prices). As elsewhere, a burst bubble brought down an important bank, and politicians raced to its aid. The cost of bailing out this bank came in the form of public debt, and the harsh fiscal austerity measures used to pay it down. In response, the Latvian economy dive-bombed.

But the Latvian example is different from Ireland's, in that Latvia enjoyed greater policy latitude, even if it chose not to use it. Because Latvia was not yet part of the Eurozone, it still enjoyed a national currency, and with it the opportunities that an autonomous monetary policy can provide. Latvia's authorities had a choice: they could have followed Iceland's route out of the recession (e.g. downplaying the threats of contagion; devaluing their currency; imposing capital controls; letting their banks go-under; or even trying to hold their relevant authorities accountable). Indeed, a gaggle of international experts and organisations encouraged the Latvian authorities to exploit those advantages of monetary policy autonomy. But Latvian officials chose a more austere path: they were drawn to the promise of the long-term gains offered by full euro membership, and jettisoned their monetary policy autonomy. In the doing, they decided that workers at home, rather than foreign creditors, should pay the costs of bank failure.

Rise of a Baltic Tiger: prelude to crisis

Latvia has come a long way, both economically and politically, since re-gaining its independence. The country's transition to a market economy produced at least two painful economic retractions (1991 and 1993) and an early bout of run-a-way inflation – in 1992 the inflation rate was 958.7 per cent (IMF 1998: 127)! In an attempt to provide a more stable economic environment and attract foreign commerce and investment, the Latvian authorities linked the lat to the IMF's Special Drawing Right (SDR) basket of currencies.

To place its economy on a more competitive footing, Latvia embraced a series of structural reforms: e.g., privatising land and enterprises, strengthening property rights, deregulating the financial sector, civil service reforms, etc. To encourage trade liberalisation, Latvia joined the WTO in 1999 and the EU in 2004; the latter was also important for securing additional sources of funding (e.g. the Cohesive Fund, the European Social Fund and the European Regional Development Fund). On 1 January 2005, the lat was pegged to the euro (at 1.42 €/LVL), and later that year (2 May) Latvia joined Europe's Exchange Rate Mechanism (ERM II). The harvest from these sundry policy decisions was a phenomenal rise in Latvian GDP, as seen in Figure 6.1.

Figure 6.1: Latvian GDP, 1990–2013

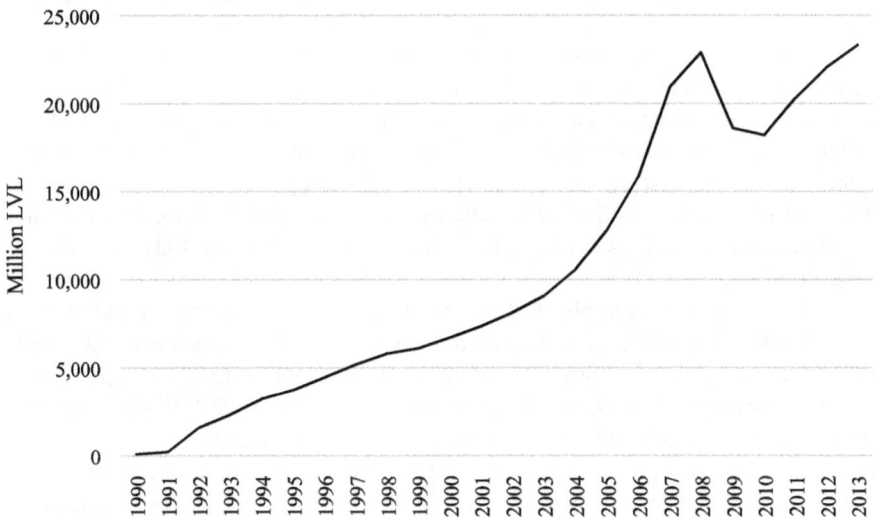

Note: Current GDP at market prices, millions of lats
Source: Eurostat [nama_gdp_c]

Latvia's economic approach was heavily influenced by a collection of elites, trained at Georgetown University (Viksnins 2008).[1] Believing that Latvia's economic future lay in attracting more speculative financial flows, rather than trying to rebuild Latvia's industrial or agricultural footing, this group lobbied for a strong currency, low inflation and minimal levels of fiscal debt. To attract financial investors, Latvia adopted the lowest property tax rate of any industrial economy,

---

1. Two of the most prominent members of this group include Einars Repse, the Finance Minister responsible for Latvia's austerity budget, and Ilmārs Rimšēvičs, Governor of the Bank of Latvia (BoL). As we shall these members brought a fanatical, even fundamentalist, approach to Latvian economic policy.

while burdening its workers with one of the world's heaviest taxes on labour[2] (Hudson 2015: 54).

As Latvia transitioned to capitalist markets, it was also coming to grips with the challenge of representative democracy. As in many former communist states, Latvia's electoral pallet was both broad and colourful, with new parties coming and going in almost every election cycle. Between 1993 and 2008, the average government duration in Latvia was less than one year (more precisely, 325 days!). Most of the sixteen governments in place over this period (1993–2008) were coalitions, and most of these had only a slim majority, or no majority at all, with the cleavages separating them being largely ideological and ethnic in nature (Salines and Bērziņš 2012: 158–9; see also Conrad and Golder 2010). As can be seen in Table 6.1, this plethora of coalition governments continued throughout the first two decades of the 21st century, with the centre-right People's Party (*Tautas Partija*, TP) dominating before the crisis, and Valdis Dombrovski's Unity Party dominating afterwards.[3]

Even before the financial crisis, politics in Latvia was volatile, and dissatisfaction with the political elite (including complaints about perceived corruption) was clearly on the rise. Since 2006, the number of public protests in Latvia has been steadily rising (Kalačinska 2010: 45). Much of this protest activity was aimed at securing an amendment to the constitution, so that Latvians could dismiss their parliament (the *Saeima*) directly and call for extraordinary elections. Originating in the 2007 'umbrella revolution', and led by the trade unions, the constitutional reform movement aimed 'to give people more say in political matters and to increase the accountability of elected officials' (Ikstens 2009: 1017). But political elites – in both parliament and in government – resisted. After the government refused to address their concerns, the movement secured enough signatures to submit the proposal to the parliament – where it was again rejected! When put before the public in an August 2008 referendum, however, 97 per cent voted in favour of the amendments (ibid. 1018)!

In short, Latvia was saturated with a popular distrust of elected officials just one month before the collapse of Lehman Brothers. While the referendum failed to have a legislative effect (it fell beneath the 50 per cent turnout threshold required by the constitution), it signalled a deep level of popular distrust and dissatisfaction with Latvia's elected officials.

---

2. Latvian employers must pay a 25 per cent employment tax on wages, and a 24 per cent social service rate, in addition to the 11 per cent that wage earners are forced to pay. In effect these three tax rates constitute a remarkable 60 per cent flat tax on wages.

3. Many of these parties are tainted by a reputation for corruption – even the more successful of them. For example, Aigars Kalvītis' governing coalition retained power in the 2006 parliamentary election, to become the first government since 1991 to be re-elected. But just thirteen months later, Kalvītis was forced to step down in the face of widespread opposition to his dismissal of the head of the anti-corruption bureau, Aleksejs Loskutovs. Even as a lame duck, however, Kalvītis appears to have played an active role in forming the new (Godmanis) government, that was sworn in on 20 December (Ikstens 2008: 1042).

Table 6.1: Recent governments in Latvia

Government	Prime Minister	From	Until	Coalition Partners
Kalvītis I	Aigars Kalvītis	2 December 2004	7 November 2006	*TP*, ZZS, LPP, JL
Kalvītis II	Aigars Kalvītis	7 November 2006	20 December 2007	*TP*, ZZS, LPP/LC, TB/LNNK
Godmanis II	Ivars Godmanis	20 December 2007	12 March 2009	*LPP/LC*, TP, ZZS, TB/LNNK
Dombrovskis I	Valdis Dombrovskis	12 March 2009	3 November 2010	*JL*, TP, ZZS, TB/LNNK, PS
Dombrovskis II	Valdis Dombrovskis	3 November 2010	25 October 2011	*Unity*, ZZS
Dombrovskis III	Valdis Dombrovskis	25 October 2011	22 January 2014	*Unity*, RP, NA
Straujuma	Laimdota Straujuma	22 January 2014	5 November 2014	*Unity*, RP, NA, ZZS
Straujuma I	Laimdota Straujuma	5 November 2014	11 February 2016	*Unity*, NA, ZZS
Kučinskis	Maris Kučinskis	11 February 2016	Present	*Unity*, NA, ZZS

Note: In the right-hand column, the coalition party in italics is the Prime Minister's political party. Party acronyms are defined as follows:

TP	*Tautas partija*	People's Party (centre-right)
ZZS	*Zaļo un Zemnieku savienība*	Union of Greens and Farmers (centre-right)
LPP/LC	*Latvijas Pirmā partija/Latvijas Ceļš*	Latvia's First Party/Latvian Way (social conservative)
JL	*Jaunais laiks*	New Era Party (centre-right)
TB/LNNK	*Tēvzemei un Brīvībai/LNNK*	For Fatherland and Freedom/LNNK (right-wing)
RP	*Reformu partija*	Reform Party (centre-right)
NA	*Nacionālā apvienība 'Visu Latvijai!'*	National Alliance 'All For Latvia!' (radical right)
Unity	*Vienotība*	Unity (liberal-conservative)
PS	*Pilsoniskā savienība*	Civic Union (centre-right)

Banking on growth

With the start of the new millennium, it appeared as though Latvia's economy had turned the corner. Between 2000 and 2007, Latvia had the fastest growing economy in the EU, with double-digit real GDP growth rates in 2005–7. Following the Irish model, the country encouraged foreign capital inflows, and rapid credit growth with a business-friendly environment. To fuel its economic expansion, Latvia relied on three sources of foreign capital: 1) an aggressive 'carrying trade', run by foreign (especially Swedish) banks that borrowed in the US and Japan (at lower interest rates) and then lent out to Latvians (in foreign exchange); 2) a flood of hot (tax-avoiding) money from investors/depositors in the Commonwealth of Independent States (CIS); and 3) the EU's Structural Funds.

But Latvia's rising financial tide did not lift all boats, as is evident in the country's persistently high levels of unemployment and emigration (cf. Figures 3.7 and 3.12). Worse, Latvia's expanding financial bubble generated economic imbalances across several fronts: prices (property, wages and inflation generally) grew rapidly and imports outpaced exports year after year, creating a massive current account deficit (*see* below).

This inflationary pressure was being produced by a banking sector (and its regulatory keeper) that had learned little from two previous banking crises (in 1995 and 1998).[4] In the wake of these crises, the Latvian banking system had become much more concentrated in the hands of foreigners, as smaller Latvian banks began merging, and foreign (especially Swedish) banks snapped them up. As a consequence, the liabilities of foreign banks in Latvia rose from just six per cent of GDP in 2000 to 54 per cent in 2007 (Blanchard *et al.* 2013: 332)! By 2007, just four banks accounted for 75 per cent of Latvia's banking assets: three of which were Swedish (Swedbank, SEB, Nordea), and only one was domestically owned (Parex Bank).

It is important to note that most of Latvia's banks were subsidiaries (not branches) of foreign banks – so the regulatory responsibility for their activities lay with the host country (i.e., Latvia). This is almost the opposite problem from what we saw in Iceland: where a miniscule country's banks were establishing numerous branches abroad; here foreign banks from larger countries were establishing subsidiaries in miniscule Latvia. As most of these banks were subsidiaries of larger, more powerful, West European banks, Latvian regulators were too weak, timid and inexperienced to stand up to them. As states across the region were competing with one another to attract foreign banks, regulatory standards were set with an eye at attracting more capital, not protecting depositors or the surrounding economy. At the same time, financial regulators in the home countries (e.g., Sweden) did not seem particularly concerned about their banks' foreign activities abroad – at least not at first.

Although Latvian banks avoided high leverage, sub-prime mortgages and collateralised debt obligations, they were exposed to two other sources of financial instability. First, many of the foreign banks were heavily involved in a risky carrying trade, encouraging consumers (both households and firms) to take out loans in foreign currencies (at lower interest rates). We saw this sort of risky behaviour in

---

4. In 1995, Latvia's second largest bank at the time (*Banka Baltija*) became insolvent. Tellingly, the bank was encouraging foreign exchange speculation by offering high-return lat deposit accounts (offering interest rates approaching 90 per cent a year!). The BoL ended up closing down fifteen commercial banks (and revealed extensive fraud in the process), which accounted for 35–40 per cent of the banking assets and 53 per cent of household deposits (Åslund and Dombrovskis 2011: 11). In this first banking crisis, shareholders were forced to accept huge losses, while depositors received only partial compensation. Just three years later, in 1998, the Latvian economy was again hit by financial crisis, this time emanating from neighbouring Russia.

Iceland, and it reflects a lack of regulatory acumen or responsibility on the part of local banking officials (and a remarkable ignorance or naiveté on the part of the borrowers). In Latvia, this risky behaviour was especially prevalent: it is estimated that 87 per cent of all loans in the Latvian economy were made in a foreign currency – usually euros (Åslund and Dombrovskis 2011: 84)! In addition, much of the Latvian banking model depended upon hot-money deposits from Russia and other CIS countries. This was not a secret: the US had placed Latvia on a list of alleged tax havens in 2005. Because these are foreign deposits, not sunk investments, they are very mobile, highly sensitive to political risk, and always on the look-out for more lucrative destinations – i.e., they are potentially destabilising.

As foreign money poured into Latvia, it inflated the domestic economy. Between 2000 and 2010, corporate profit rates exploded, and stayed higher than the EU average – even at the height of Latvia's crisis (Di Comite *et al.* 2012a: 53). Even Latvia's meagre wages were on the rise before the crisis hit. But the clearest symbol of economic overheating in Latvia, as in Ireland, was the housing market: nominal housing prices rose by an astonishing 240 per cent between 2003 and 2007 (Bakker and Gulde 2010: 19)!

The easy availability of cheap credit, rising property values and years of strong economic growth generated optimistic expectations about future income, and encouraged households and business to increase their consumption, indebtedness and risk-taking. Lacking tools to dampen this economic fever, and with the lat bound to the euro, Latvian exporters found it difficult to compete on the European market, and the country came to rely upon cheap imports. Not surprisingly, the country's current account deficit ballooned, as shown in Figure 6.2 – to 23 per cent of GDP in the years immediately preceding the crisis (2006 and 2007).

Figure 6.2: Latvian exports and imports, 2000–2014

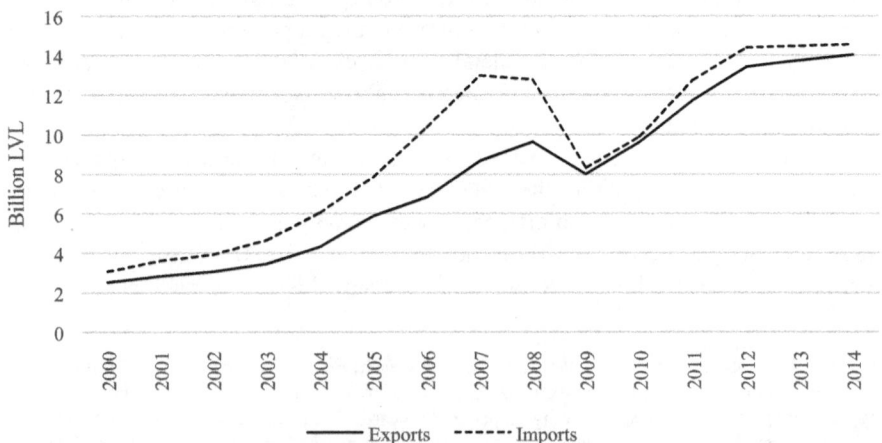

Note: Imports of goods and services at current prices (National accounts) (UMGS); Exports of goods and services at current prices (National accounts) (UXGS)
Source: Eurostat (AMECO: UMGS & UXGS)

This current account deficit was funded by those foreign capital flows noted above: by hot Russian money, by expanding foreign bank branches, and by EU Structural Funds. This is clearly evident when we break down the aggregate export indicator into its service and goods components, as is done in Figure 6.3. Here we can see that Latvia's merchandise trade balance had been deteriorating significantly since 1992, and remained negative throughout the entire period (1995–2011). Quite simply, Latvian goods were unable to compete in international and European markets. By contrast, Latvia's service trade balance has always remained in surplus (and relatively stable). While transport played an especially important part of this service surplus during the earlier transition period, financial services grew in importance as Latvia refashioned itself as low-cost banking centre.

Figure 6.3: Latvian net exports of goods and services, 1995–2011

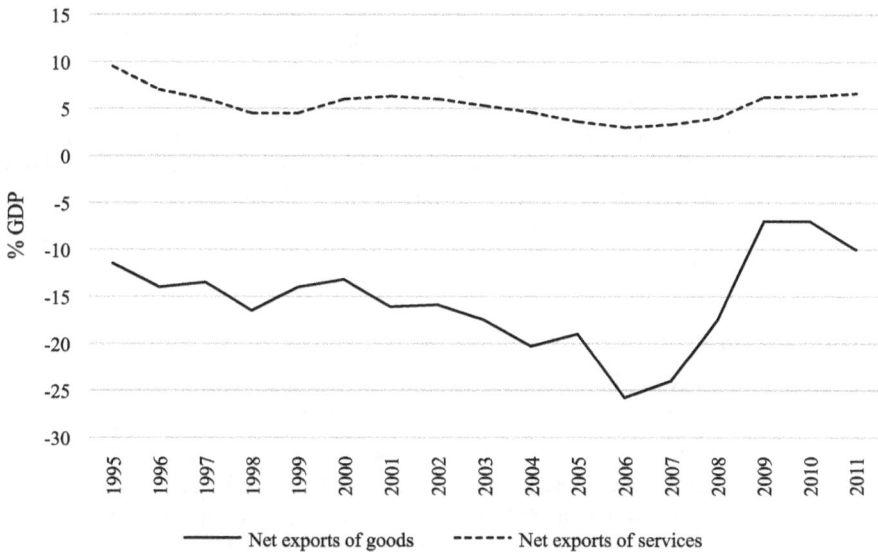

Source: di Comite et al. (2012a: 42)

Even before the collapse of Lehman Brothers, then, it was clear to most economic observers that the Latvian economy needed to be brought down to earth. The question debated was whether the landing could be soft or hard. In the words of a European Commission report,

'By 2007, the overheating reached its peak. Large current account deficits were compounded by new *types of vulnerability*. Galloping private credit, mostly in euro, was increasingly financing a housing bubble, heightening the bottlenecks and distortions on the supply side of the economy, including in terms of available skilled workforce and products. Financing to the private sector was increasingly dependent on a small group of common (foreign) lenders, dominantly Scandinavian banks, who themselves were increasingly dependent on market financing. At the same time, domestic banks (most notably Parex Bank in Latvia) at the zenith of the global financial crisis experienced major difficulties with rolling over their foreign loans in the face of extreme exposure to the housing sector' (Deroose *et al*. 2010: 5, emphasis in original).

Whiplash

As in Iceland, the impetus for the Latvian crisis was an over-extended domestic bank that had relied heavily on short-term financing from the international wholesale market. When that market dried up, Parex Bank shrivelled on the vine – and the Latvian government moved quickly to nationalise and recapitalise it. To do this, Latvia secured foreign financial support – calling on the IMF and the European Commission (and eventually neighbouring/Nordic countries) for assistance.

Unlike Iceland, the banking crisis in Latvia was challenging, but not overwhelming. 'According to the ECB's data on consolidated banking statistics, the loss incurred by foreign banks [in Latvia] was about 5.7 percent of GDP and the loss of domestic banks about 3.6 percent of GDP by 2010 – a large amount, but well below the banking sector losses in the two other case study countries [Iceland and Ireland]' (Darvas 2011: 8). More to the point, a significant share of Latvian banking activity lay in foreign hands, so Latvia could rely on the home country of these banks to assist during the crisis.

Distressed banks

As we have already noted, Latvia's banking sector was dominated by foreign, mostly Nordic, banks, including Swedbank, SEB, DnB, Danske Bank and Nordea (the latter two operate as branches, not subsidiaries). In 2008, Latvian subsidiaries of Nordic banks accounted for about 60 per cent of total bank assets. These banks were mostly (two-thirds) financed by their parent banks, with only one-third of their liabilities in the form of resident (Latvian) deposits.

When the international financial system froze up, these Nordic banks came to absorb many of the Latvian losses by recapitalising their subsidiaries and by staying put (not running for the exit, further exacerbating the situation). This was not just a matter of being good neighbours – Sweden's authorities were acutely aware that a run on Latvian banks could easily spread to the Swedish economy. Indeed, there was a lively debate in the Swedish government and its monetary authority about just how much responsibility Sweden needed to take for what was happening in the Baltics. Swedish banks were also aware of the need to limit any potential contagion – and these parent banks (and their home countries) worked together to protect their foreign subsidiaries in Latvia (and elsewhere in Eastern Europe), in the form of the so-called Vienna Initiative – also known as the European Bank Coordination Initiative (see Andersen 2009; Epstein 2014; de Haas *et al*. 2012; and EBRD/EIB/EU/IMF/World Bank 2014a).

This Vienna Initiative, involving seventeen parent banks, aimed to prevent foreign-owned banks from pulling out of emerging Europe, hence averting a systemic crisis.[5] These banks pledged a number of specific rollover and recapitalisation commitments in Latvia (and four other countries: Bosnia-Herzegovina, Hungary, Romania and Serbia). In Latvia, where Swedish banks dominated, those Swedish banks were expected to roll over at least 80 per cent of their lending – the majority of which was to their own subsidiaries (de Haas *et al*. 2012: 9). On 11 September 2009, the parent banks of the four largest foreign-owned banks operating in Latvia (DnB, Nordea, SEB and Swedbank), met in Stockholm to reaffirm their commitment to meet the liquidity and capital needs of their Latvian branches and subsidiaries, and to promote financial stability across the greater Baltic region (IMF 2009b; 2009c).

Although the biggest hole in the Latvian banking system was patched by this coordination initiative among European banks, there was still a serious problem at home. Indeed, the main source of Latvia's banking woes rested with its largest domestic bank (and the country's second largest bank), Parex Bank, which accounted for about 14 per cent of Latvia's total bank assets. Parex Bank was used as a honey trap for non-residential shell companies owned (mostly) by Russian and Ukrainian depositors.[6] The bank was one of the few big survivors from the first wave of Soviet private banks, and Anders Åslund (2010: 27) describes how the bank was known for wooing Russian depositors with 'extraordinary chutzpah'. For example, in 1992 Parex advertised that, 'We exchange all currencies and ask no questions'; and in 2005, the bank proudly boasted that Riga was closer to Moscow than was Switzerland, and that the staff at Parex was fluent in Russian. In short, Parex was a bank that was known for its shady dealings, and dirty money.[7]

Like the failed banks in Iceland and Ireland, Parex Bank enjoyed very strong political connections. The banks' founders, Valerijs Kargins and Viktors Krasovickis – who began their careers as Latvian Komsomol (Communist Youth League) functionaries – became especially powerful in Latvia, on both political and economic fronts. Kargins, in particular, was known as one of Latvia's most influential oligarchs. Among other luminaries, Parex's advisory council had previously included two former prime ministers, and a former prosecutor general sat on the board at the time of troubles (Raudseps 2008).

Parex's problems lay in the nature of its liabilities. Unlike the other banks in Latvia, Parex could not rely on a mother bank (either in a foreign country, or at

---

5. The first meeting of the Vienna Initiative occurred on 23 January 2009, and included central banks and ministries of finance from many Central and Eastern European countries, key advanced EU countries which are home authorities of cross-border banks, and IFIs (IMF, EBRD, EIB, World Bank, IFC). Only on 24 September of that year does the first Full-Forum meeting of the Initiative meet in Brussels (EBRD/EIB/EU/IMF/World Bank 2014b).

6. In addition, Parex also serviced national and local government institutions, including Riga city.

7. Although details are fuzzy, an earlier Parex employee, John Christmas, claims that he was fired for whistleblowing. He alleges that the EBRD in April 2009, made a €106 million investment in Parex, buying shares that the government had earlier bought for pennies on the dollar from the bank's founding oligarchs. When documents of the sale were leaked, they showed that the EBRD had a secret 'put option' to sell back the shares to the government in the future. In short, they didn't really buy them, they were just holding them. See Christmas (2012).

the central bank[8]) for support. In the summer of 2008, foreign depositors began to flee with their money, creating a cascading series of challenges that undermined faith in Parex and left it vulnerable to a massive risk of rollover. Worse, Parex was holding €775 million (roughly $1 billion, or 3.5 per cent of GDP) of syndicated loans that would mature in February and June of 2009; in addition to a €200 million Eurobond that was potentially callable – e.g. in the event of a default on the syndicated loans (Blanchard *et al.* 2013: 340).

As foreign depositors took flight, Latvia's central bank (the Bank of Latvia, or BoL) was forced to defend the fixed exchange rate peg. While this capital flight was occurring, I am not aware of any public deliberation over the utility of imposing capital controls, a devaluation, or any other administrative instruments to restrict the outflow. Rather, the central bank drained its reserves to protect the fixed exchange rate. In the final three months of 2008, the BoL sold €1.15 billion, or roughly one quarter, of its official reserves (Blanchard *et al.* 2013: 341; see also IMF 2009a: 8).

The Latvian government came to Parex's rescue. After a four-hour closed-door meeting of the cabinet – on Saturday, 8 November – Prime Minister Ivars Godmanis announced that his government would purchase 51 per cent of Parex's stock for the total price of two lats (roughly $3.65, or one lat for each oligarch). Later, we learn that Godmanis was instructed by the European Union, in the second half of 2008, to keep Parex (or any key domestic bank) afloat (Kolyako 2009).

Remarkably, the terms of the government buyout allowed the former owners to remain on the management board and retain significant influence over the bank's operations. It also gave them the right to buy back their shares in the following year (IMF 2009a: 8)! At the same time, the government introduced a partial deposit freeze (limiting withdrawal amounts from large non-commercial private deposits) to conserve Parex's liquidity, while the BoL secured a €500 million swap line with the Swedish Riksbank (Purfield and Rosenberg 2010: 27).

This initial effort proved insufficient, and the government was later (5 December) forced to take over 85 per cent of Parex's shares. Only then was a new professional management team brought in to run the bank (IMF, 2009a: 12). Finally, in May of 2010, the government divided Parex Bank into a good and bad bank, the latter of which assumed all the nonperforming loans (and was tasked with quickly selling the impaired assets before being closed down). The good bank, renamed Citadele, was to be sold.

External bailout

Recapitalising Parex required a significant injection of capital, the equivalent of 4.9 per cent of Latvia's GDP. Another 2.6 per cent of GDP would be needed in

---

8. Even though it is not supposed to happen under 'a strict currency board', the Latvian authorities did intervene to help Parex (but did so indirectly). In particular, the government placed Treasury bills and increased its Treasury deposits at Parex (to 1/3 of total deposits by the end of 2008). The bank could then use these bills to obtain financing from the BoL to fund deposit outflows. Then international donors replenished the reserves of the BoL: first with a swap line from Swedish and Danish central banks, later by the IMF/EU/Nordic program (Blanchard *et al.* 2013: 341)!

the form of additional guarantees (Åslund and Dombrovskis 2011: 35). All of this public money was marshalled to save a bank with a sullied reputation and a relatively limited impact on Latvia's productive capacity. To recapitalise Parex, and to keep it afloat, the government would need to divert a great deal of social and government spending; to prop up the country's fixed exchange rate, the BoL would need to draw from its foreign currency reserves (and borrow more, when these ran out). Given the rate Latvia was burning through its limited resources, the government quickly realised that it would need help to cover the bill.

Parex Bank was not the only economic institution in Latvia needing support. It was just the luckiest (or best connected). Throughout 2009, the Latvian economy was dragged through a severe recession, squeezed by the massive capital flight, a freeze on liquidity, and very weak external demand. Between 2007 and 2009, Latvia's GDP fell by 17.5 per cent, the largest in our sample, and second only to Estonia in Europe (*see* Figure 3.3). Worse – and as we saw in the other cases – Latvia's access to international financial markets dried up in the wake of Lehman's collapse.

Rather than consider the utility of letting this politically well-connected bank fail, the government turned first to the IMF for help (in October). Two months later it concluded a stand-by arrangement in which the IMF took responsibility for Latvia's stabilisation programme (IMF, 2009a). Realising that IMF support would be insufficient, Latvia turned to the European Union for help on 10 November. As Latvia was not yet a member of the Eurozone, it received no help from the ECB (Åslund 2010: 78), but the European Commission was willing to provide funding from its balance-of-payment facility – the European Stabilisation Fund (EC, 2012). The World Bank, the European Bank of Reconstruction and Development (EBRD) and the European Investment Bank (EIB) played more subsidiary roles, focusing on the need for bank restructuring (Åslund 2010: 32–33).

In total, the stabilisation package provided €7.5 billion (or $10.5 billion); roughly one-third of Latvia's GDP. The IMF ended up providing more than twelve times Latvia's quota, €1.7 billion ($2.37 billion), but less than a third of the total package. The European Commission contributed €3.1 billion ($4.3 billion), the Nordic countries another €1.8 billion ($2.5 billion), the World Bank €400 million, the Czech Republic €200 million, and the EBRD, Estonia and Poland each offered €100 million each (IMF 2008c).

Although the final deal provided €7.5 billion in assistance, Latvia only ended up using €4.5 billion (i.e. 60 per cent of what was made available).[9] To pay for this loan, the government agreed on a consolidation package that employed both revenue boosts and expenditure cuts. In particular, one third of the consolidation was to come from the revenue side – with an emphasis placed on increasing taxes on consumption and property, but also social security contributions (Dombrovskis 2012: 13). The remaining two-thirds was to come by way of expenditure cuts.

What is most remarkable about Latvia's bailout package was that it did not require a devaluation, or include any discussion about the utility of capital controls.

---

9. Latvia successfully returned to financial markets in June 2011 and again in February 2012, so it no longer needed additional disbursements – the last disbursement was made in October 2010 (Buti 2012: 10).

Indeed, at the height of the crisis (in 2009), Latvia did just the opposite: it introduced a law which made it even more attractive to foreign depositors: allowing anybody who invested 100,000 lats ($187,700) to get a residency permit (Tapinsh 2012).

The next section will consider why capital controls and devaluation were not on the table, but the government's willingness to defend the currency peg is especially noteworthy in light of the many international calls for a devaluation (both within the IMF, and beyond). Indeed, the social costs of shelving the devaluation option were made explicit in the text of the IMF stand-by arrangement:

> *The authorities' unequivocal commitment to the exchange rate peg has determined their choice of program strategy.* Though this commitment augurs well for program ownership, the authorities also recognize that their choice brings difficult consequences, including the need for fiscal tightening and the possibility that recession could be protracted, perhaps more so than if an alternative strategy had been adopted (IMF 2009a: 9, emphasis in original).

To pay down its loan, the government's budget was put in a fiscal vice. This is especially true during the first two years of crisis (2009 and 2010), as the general government deficit expanded, then shrunk, from 4.1 per cent of GDP in 2008, to 9.1 per cent (in 2009); to 8.5 per cent (in 2010); to 3.4 per cent (in 2011) and to 0.8 per cent in 2012 (Eurostat, [gov-10dd-edpt1]). Rather remarkably (in light of the promise to secure one-third of the consolidation from increased revenues), Latvia's total revenues, as a percentage of GDP, hardly changed between 2007 and 2011, and the tax burden even declined over the period – from 30.8 per cent of GDP to 27.9 per cent (di Comite *et al.* 2012b: 81, table 4.3). Indeed, by looking at the dashed revenues line in Figure 6.4, one can hardly see that Latvia was in the midst of a Great Recession.

Figure 6.4: General government finances, Latvia, 2000–2014

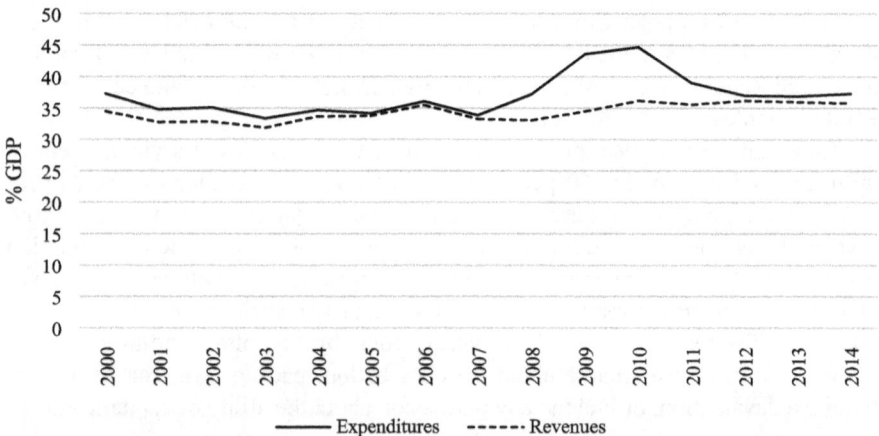

Note: Total general government revenues and expenditures as a percentage of GDP
Source: Eurostat [gov_10a_main]

Real change is only evident on the expenditures side, which increased sharply, albeit briefly, from 2007 to 2010 – as structural supports kicked in. After 2010, however, the state's expenditures fell rapidly. Most of these cuts came in the form of reduced government consumption, which dropped by almost a third (in nominal terms) between 2008 and 2010 (di Comite *et al.* 2012b: 81–82). In particular, public sector salaries came under the knife, resulting in a 25–30 per cent reduction in public sector wages, while 14,000 jobs (or 20 per cent of the total) were cut from the public payroll (Åslund 2010: 37–8). Among government services, health, education and defence-related expenditures suffered the deepest cuts.

The resulting economic collapse was jaw-dropping. From peak to nadir the nation's GDP fell by 25 percent (c.f. Figure 3.2). Among the 184 countries included in a 2011 IMF study, Latvia suffered the largest cumulative output loss from 2007 to 2010 (Darvas 2011: 10). And yet the resulting budget deficits contributed to a total government debt level that never exceeded 40 per cent of GDP. These fiscal steps are miniscule compared to what other states were willing (and able) to take. In short, fiscal discipline remained Latvia's top priority: it was unwilling or afraid to borrow in order to help its citizens survive the Great Recession.

Worse still, many of the imposed policies hurt the poor disproportionately hard, resulting in a sharp redistribution of income from the bottom to the top of the wealth scale (Sommers 2015: 27). In 2009, for example, the income tax rate for the self-employed was raised from 15 to 25 percent; the threshold for the non-taxable minimum for people with low incomes was reduced from €129 to €50; VAT or sales taxes increased from 18 to 21 per cent; and the new taxes significantly increased the cost of heat and hot water (Rizga 2012). The government's main tax increase (actually, a reduction in personal income tax allowances) was highly regressive – at the time, the IMF (2009d: 46) estimated that the effective tax rate for the poorest third in Latvia would go up by seven per cent (while it will only go up 1½ percentage points for those among the wealthiest ten per cent).

As we saw in Chapter Three, unemployment in Latvia skyrocketed to a point where almost every fifth worker was out of work in 2010 – the worst record in the European Union (Åslund and Dombrovskis 2011: 1–2). From 2007 to 2010, Latvia's unemployment level increased by a remarkable 13.4 per cent, the largest increase in our sample (Figure 3.8). These growing ranks of unemployed were filled in part by a rising number of public sector workers who had been laid off because of the austerity measures (Bauze 2012: 142). According to some calculations, the broader measure of unemployment – including those who involuntarily worked part-time, those who had given up looking for work, and those who had emigrated – approached nearly a third of Latvia's working population (Weisbrot and Ray 2011: 9; Salines and Bērziņš 2012: 164).

Sovereign will?

In order to bail out Parex Bank and to defend its fixed exchange rate peg, Latvia lined up a €7.5 billion loan (or 'stabilisation package') from the international community. This loan was the equivalent to one third of Latvia's GDP, and breaks down to about €3,750 for every man, woman and child in the country. This is a significant amount of debt per capita in a country where the average Latvian earned only €8,700 in 2009 (i.e., GDP/capita, from Eurostat, [nama_10_pc])! Worse, the conditions imposed on Latvia to repay that loan generated substantial hardship in the form of increased poverty, unemployment and emigration. It should not be controversial to suggest that the Latvian people paid a very high price for the failings of its financial system.

What is remarkable, and noteworthy, is the way this deal has been marketed as a political and economic success. As in Ireland, Latvia's political elites have taken pride in their people's capacity for suffering; they point to the lack of violent protest as evidence of support for the policies chosen. Indeed, Prime Minster Dombrovskis has been fêted for his ability to defy Juncker's Curse,[10] having demonstrated that it is possible to deliver austere economic policies, yet remain politically viable.

'Latvia's austerity was brutal, and many analysts around the world expressed surprise that it did not elicit mass protest. It was assumed that in a democracy any government imposing such measures, would be summarily removed at the ballot box. Thus, when not one, but two elections after austerity implementation kept the incumbent neoliberal administration in power, it was assumed voters approved the austerity measures imposed and accepted them without protest' (Sommers 2015: 18–19).

This section interrogates these claims and questions the democratic legitimacy of the decisions made. It begins by examining a number of broad-based indicators of public support for austerity, and then considers the electoral fall-out from the 2009 IMF stand-by arrangement, and its effect on emigration. At the centre of Latvia's political unease lies the contentious decision to maintain a fixed exchange rate (with an eye trained on eventual Eurozone membership). For this reason, the fourth section looks at the interests associated with the hard currency policy and its effect on Latvian monetary policy.

Voice

It is, quite simply, inaccurate to suggest that there was no public outcry over the austerity measures. This is a convenient political fiction, spun up by Latvian political elites (and an international financial press wanting to believe it), who recognised the necessity of manipulating public perceptions to maintain support for difficult policy choices.[11] I am not suggesting that Latvia's political elite were

---

10. As Luxembourg's former Prime Minister, Jean-Claude Juncker used to say 'We all know what we have to do, but then we don't know how to be re-elected once we have done it' (*The Economist* 2007).

11. ECOFIN's Director General, Marco Buti (2012: 10, emphasis added) makes this explicit: 'Such policies can be understood by the population—if they are *well explained*—and can eventually reward a government that has the courage to deal with these challenges. Valdis Dombrovskis, the Prime Minister of Latvia, is the prime example to show that if one is able to implement the programme and the adjustments successfully, if one does so with determination and also *manages*

disingenuous (at least, not any more than political elites elsewhere) – only that they believed firmly in the correctness of their decisions, were willing to do what was required to bring about that desired outcome, and influenced the nature of public debate accordingly. In the doing, they listened more to the needs of international creditors than their protesting and dissatisfied constituents.

Sommers (2015: 19ff) provides a detailed description of the Latvian health-workers, farmers, teachers and others who gathered frequently to protest the austerity measures. From the fall of 2008, and throughout 2009, Latvians came out in record numbers to protest the quality of their democratic institutions, the appearance of corruption, the distributional impact of government policies, and the nature of the austerity measures themselves. While these protests didn't result in sustained social unrest, and they began to fade after 2010, they offer a strong indication of the degree to which Latvians were upset about the decisions made by their political elites.

The largest of these protests occurred on 13 January 2009 at Dome public square, just blocks away from the parliament building in Riga. Estimates vary, but somewhere between 10,000 and 20,000 people participated (Åslund and Dombrovskis 2011: 66; Sommers 2015: 19). While the protest was mostly peaceful, a handful of hooligans started rioting, resulting in the injury and arrests of dozens of people.[12] This was the largest protest in Latvia since the pro-independence rallies against Soviet rule, and it was interpreted by some as a frustrated response to what had transpired in Latvia ever since (e.g. Sommers, 2009). For our purposes, this protest is important in at least two regards: it demonstrates significant public resistance to the government's austerity measures; and it triggers a change of government.

The 13 January gathering was organised by several opposition party politicians, civic organisations and trade unions to protest the irresponsiveness of elected officials in the Saeima. As noted earlier, Latvia's parliament had already rejected a popular grassroots-initiated referendum on the calling of extraordinary elections. Latvians were still fed up with unresponsive politicians, and they gathered in the streets of the capital to demand that their President call for new elections.

On the following day, President Zatler took up the matter and formulated an ultimatum to the Saeima, and its government. His list of demands, on behalf of the people, was impressive: give citizens a direct right to vote on the calling of extraordinary elections; limit the number of electoral districts in which a person can run for parliament; set up a council for supervising the use of the international rescue loan; immediately draft a plan for reorganising the system of public administration; recruit able ministers or broaden the coalition; and choose the

---

to explain it well, then one can definitely defy the so-called Juncker Curse…Obviously, policies can be understood by the population. This requires, as I indicated, *careful communication and a lot of pedagogy*. The Latvian example is something encouraging also from a political viewpoint: if governments are willing to take action with determination, being re-elected is indeed possible.'

12. In particular, twenty-five people were injured and 106 were arrested (Åslund and Dombrovskis 2011: 66).

new head of the Anti-Corruption Bureau. If the Saeima failed to comply with the President's request by 31 March, he promised to initiate the procedure for extraordinary elections (Ikstens 2010: 1055).

Latvia's President seemed – for a brief moment – to be taking a popular stand to defend democracy, in the face of corruption and the intrusion of market (as opposed to democratic) values. When the Saeima refused to comply to his ultimatum, however, President Zatlers balked: his office announced that he would *not* launch the dismissal procedure because the country needed strong government institutions in order to address the economic crisis (Ikstens 2010: 1055).[13]

For anyone willing to look, Latvia's public contempt for its political elites is evident across several indicators. The crisis package agreed to by Godmanis' government was one in a long line of decisions that benefited Latvia's political and economic elite, at the expense of the general public. A dwindling level of public support is clearly evident in a number of Eurobarometer polls, which show how Latvians' perception of the home economy bottoms-out during this period. In 2009, 97 per cent (!) of the Latvian respondents to a Eurobarometer survey described the national economic situation as 'bad'. Latvians' negative perceptions remain worse than the EU-average over the entire period under study. Latvian attitudes with regard to domestic political institutions are equally bleak: from 2004 to 2014, Latvians consistently trusted their political parties, their national parliament and their government less than the EU average (Eurobarometer).[14] On one political trust indicator after the other, we find strong evidence that Latvians are very dissatisfied with their political elite and political institutions.

Perhaps the best indicator for political dissatisfaction in Latvia can be found in their response to a question about how democracy works in their country. In these surveys, Latvians are remarkably disgruntled with the quality of their democracy (and much more so than the EU average). As shown in Figure 6.5, this level of dissatisfaction peaks in 2009, when only 21 per cent of the population is satisfied with the way democracy works in Latvia.[15]

There are two trends worth mentioning in Figure 6.5. First, Latvians are very unhappy with how democracy works in their country, and the height of this dissatisfaction occurs at the very time that the government's austerity programme is being adopted. While several countries in the EU had to tighten their fiscal belts, and experienced substantial economic hardship, the general level of discontent in the EU-average remains fairly stable, if growing slowly over time. In this respect, the Latvian response is especially strong and abrupt. Second, we see the level of democratic dissatisfaction in Latvia slowly declining over time (after 2009). It

---

13. This happened before the Icelandic President challenged the political status quo and called for a referendum on Iceland's foreign debt repayment plan. It is not clear whether President Grímsson was influenced in any way by the Latvian President's (failed) attempt to follow the public's lead.

14. Only in 2005 did the EU-average distrust their national governments more than the Latvians (but only slightly).

15. In particular, 21 per cent were satisfied; 76 per cent were not satisfied, and three per cent didn't know.

Figure 6.5: Dissatisfaction with democracy at home, Latvia and EU-average, 2004–2014

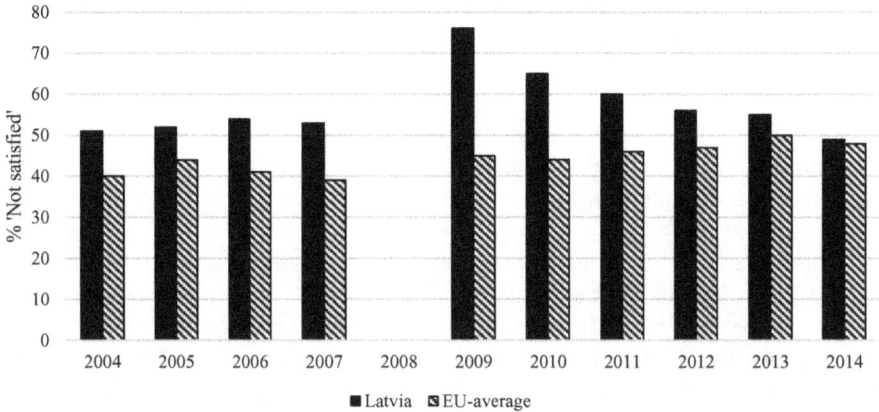

Note: Total share of those who responded 'Not satisfied' to the following question: 'On the whole, are you very satisfied, fairly satisfied, not very satisfied or not at all satisfied with the way democracy works in (OUR COUNTRY)?' The actual question number varies from year to year, but the question text remains the same in each survey. The question did not seem to appear in 2008. Contact author for more detailed information about the source.
Source: Eurobarometer [EB62-EB82]

would seem that the level of dissatisfaction is dissipating, as people slowly became accustomed to the crisis response. In other words, there is no abrupt change in the level of satisfaction with the arrival of a subsequent (new) government.

Finally, I would be remiss if I didn't note that it appears (to these foreign eyes) quite difficult for Latvians to voice critical dissent of their government's policies, or to find a venue where an open discussion of real policy alternatives can take place. BBC News (2008) reports of a university economist who was arrested and detained by Latvian security police for bravely questioning the government's commitment to the fixed peg. The domestic media are controlled by the oligarchs, so there is little critical voice to be heard there. Worse, the parliament has enacted a prohibition on any public comment that is likely to provoke 'financial instability' (Sommers 2015: 21)! For me, the clearest indicator of a lack of honest discussion about real alternatives in Latvia can be found in a comment by the BoL governor, Ilmārs Rimšēvičs. In a European Commission report on Latvia's response to the crisis, Rimšēvičs (2012: 16) notes, 'There were absolutely no benefits, not a single one, which would speak for a devaluation.'

This is ridiculous. Sincere and reasonable people can disagree about the costs and benefits of pursuing a devaluation. Indeed, I think it fair to say that most international economists believed that a devaluation was the most appropriate response for the Latvian authorities to take at the time. Likewise, there can be good and legitimate reasons for not devaluing Latvia's currency. But this sort of blind and dogmatic embrace of an exchange rate policy by the governor of the BoL smacks more of ideological fundamentalism than critical social science (or democratic deliberation). If this response is indicative of the nature of public debate concerning economic policy in Latvia, it is no wonder that people are dissatisfied with the way democracy works.

Vote

The most obvious casualty from Latvia's popular protests was the sitting (Godmanis) government, whose fate was linked to the unpopular IMF agreement it had signed.

Godmanis was no political amateur: he was an experienced politician, having been the first Prime Minister of Latvia when the country regained its independence. As Prime Minister, he had led Latvia through turbulent economic times (following the fall of the USSR), but his party was dogged by corruption scandals and Godmanis himself was seen to be part of an old, untrustworthy political establishment. Consequently, many people thought that the bailout smacked of old-school favouritism when they learned that some of Godmanis' party members held jobs in Parex Bank.[16]

The Prime Minister's resignation, in February, was clearly triggered by the violent riots in the month preceding. Godmanis' government fell because of the economic crisis, and its attempt to impose radical austerity measures (Salines and Bērziņš 2012: 173). Thus, when voters went to the polls in early 2009, they were voting out a corrupt government that had rescued a favoured bank and accepted onerous conditions imposed by international creditors. Indeed, the nature of the bailout confirmed the public's suspicions that this was simply business as usual. As the opposition politician (and former Economics Minster) Aigars Štokenbergs noted, the elite were shielded from the government's crisis program: 'Godmanis found tens of reasons not to end tax holidays for dividends, not to introduce capital gains tax and not to tax magnificent villas…where those "spoilt by the fat years" built their castles. This government defends only the rich, who need endless tax holidays' (Štokenbergs (2008), quoted in Åslund and Dombrovskis 2011: 41).

On 12 March 2009, a new government rallied behind Valdis Dombrovskis and his 'New Era' Party.[17] Dombrovskis enjoyed a reputation for being honest, educated and (perhaps most importantly) not corrupt. But to secure a majority, Dombrovskis had to work together with three parties from the previous government,

---

16. There are also widespread rumours of misconduct associated with the takeover of Parex Bank, and the special arrangements made for the bank's owners and their family members (see US Embassy in Riga 2008). In October 2009, a public prosecutor was assigned to investigate whether state officials had acted criminally, after state auditors had noted irregularities in the Parex Bank takeover. But as most of this (auditor) report was made classified by the government, cynical Latvians were not surprised to learn that the prosecutor dropped the criminal case after nearly one year (Greenhalgh 2010).

17. In 2011, the New Era Party merged with 'Civic Union' and the 'Society for Other Politics' to form the Unity Party.

including the People's Party (TP).[18] What is most noteworthy, however, is the lack of ideological light (with regard to economic policy) that separates the Godmanis II and Dombrovskis I governments – a point emphasised by most analysts, even Dombrovskis himself.[19]

As in Ireland (but unlike Iceland), the change in government did *not* result in a new policy course or response to the public protests. Instead, the people got a more efficient provider of austerity measures. There was no change of leadership at the central bank, no larger discussion about the appropriate balance between economic and political authority, no serious discussion about the exchange rate regime, or the need to punish those that were responsible for the financial mess. Indeed, the new government depended upon the TP, perhaps the one party most associated with Latvian corruption and economic mismanagement.[20] The Saeima subsequently certified that the international loan was being used in accordance with the government's objective (Saeima 2010), and the new government continued the previous government's austerity program with full vigour – indeed, it now set Latvia's course firmly in the direction of euro membership.

While it is convenient and common to see the election as a referendum on the IMF-bailout (and the austerity measures associated with it), it is not certain that Latvians supported the new (Dombrovskis) government because it embraced austerity. Jeffrey Sommers, for one, argues that the 2010 and 2011 elections in Latvia were 'fought entirely on different grounds than economic policy' (Sommers 2015: 21). At the time, a growing Russian nationalist movement was building steam under the Harmony Centre (HC) Party. Sommers argues that ethnic Latvians rallied behind the Unity Party because it was the strongest non-Russian party untainted by corruption – not because it embraced austerity (Sommers 2015: 21–22).[21] Indeed, several other foreign commentators have explicitly noted the role of geopolitical pressure in explaining government policy (and voter attitudes).[22]

In fact, Dombrovskis' first government was itself divided over how to respond to the crisis. Hoping to distance itself from its previous economic record (and the New Era Party, with which it shared government), the TP began to argue for a devaluation, and the need to avoid raising taxes.[23] The difference separating

---

18. The TP had led the ruling coalition during years of rapid economic growth after Latvia joined the EU, and had proven victorious in the 2006 election (*see* Table 6.1), but its popularity had fallen dramatically; its reputation sullied by rumours of corruption and its perceived responsibility for the country's current economic woes.

19. See, e.g., Salines and Bērziņš (2012: 165). Åslund and Dombrovskis (2011: 65) note that Dombrovskis' incoming government is only a 'slightly different center-right coalition.'

20. See, e.g., Ikstens (2010: 1052). In the first election after the crisis (2 October 2010), the TP was decimated at the polls: its 'For a Good Latvia' (*Par Labu Latviju!*) coalition lost twenty-five seats.

21. In an earlier piece, Hudson and Sommers (2011) introduced this argument and buttressed it with reference to the lack of a strong labour movement, and massive emigration.

22. See, e.g., Buti (2012: 11) and Salines and Bērziņš (2012: 158).

23. This position became especially evident when the party's long-time leader, Andris Šķēle, officially returned to politics (Salines and Bērziņš 2012: 172).

the parties in government became obvious during the annual budget negotiations (in October 2009, and again later in January 2010), when the TP opposed the government's mandate to conclude talks with the IMF (the vote was eventually carried with support from opposition parties). In March 2010, the TP left the government, leaving Dombrovskis with a minority government (*see* Table 6.1).

The TP's changing position seems to reflect an awareness that public opinion is opposed to the government's policies. By early 2010, the TP sensed the public's growing disillusionment with the IMF programme of fiscal adjustment and austerity.[24] After they left the government in March, the TP promised to oppose the IMF-backed programme, and devalue the lat. Curiously, however, the TP never managed to develop an alternative economic policy of any substance (Ikstens 2011: 1039–40).

As we saw in Table 6.1, this new government coalition was unable to hold on to power, as it also suffered from a corruption scandal that hit several leading parties and politicians (in 2011). President Zatlers ended up calling for the dissolution of parliament (prompting the first extraordinary Saeima elections in the history of Latvia) and starting his own party, Zatlers' Reform Party, or ZRP (Ikstens 2012: 179).[25] Zatlers' condemnation of parliament received strong support from voters: in a national referendum, 94.3 per cent voted in favour of throwing out the sitting Saeima, and new elections were called for 17 September. This time Dombrovskis' Unity Party failed to win the election outright (even though Dombrovskis was never implicated in any of the scandals), and Unity formed a coalition government with the ZRP (in an effort, once again, to exclude the Russian-leaning HC). Indeed, the HC attracted the largest number of votes in the election, followed by the ZRP, while Dombrovskis' Unity Party came in third place.

Throughout this period, as pro-austerity parties enjoyed a certain degree of electoral success, the Latvian parliament suffered from dismal approval ratings – only 5–15 per cent during much of the austerity period (Sommers 2015: 23).

---

24. A similar realisation can be found in the HC's Jānis Urbanovičs, who tried to establish an alternative platform by criticising Dombrovskis cabinet and calling on 'an end to the country's shameful dependence on international lenders'. But, the implied solution for the Russophilic HC was to secure a rescue loan from 'some unspecified sources in the East' – but this was not politically tenable for most Latvians (Ikstens 2011: 1040–41).

25. Zatlers is a bit of a slippery fish. When backstage negotiations to secure his re-election for President failed, he initiated a procedure for dismissing the Saeima and called for new (extraordinary) elections. In a live televised address to the nation on 28 May 2011, Zatlers cited a 'serious conflict' between the legislative and judicial branches and the danger of 'privatisation of democracy' as prime reasons for calling a referendum on extraordinary elections (Ikstens 2012: 180). Earlier, President Zatlers had used his constitutional powers to convene and preside over extraordinary meetings of the Cabinet, including an 11 June 2009 meeting in which he helped to strike a budget deal, where the disbursement of the EU/IMF loan was linked to onerous conditions. In the run-up to the parliamentary elections of 2010, he also made it clear that the key criterion for nominating the next Prime Minister was the successful continuation of the EU/IMF programme (Salines and Bērziņš 2012: 161).

These dismal approval ratings are also evident in the monthly polls that track the government's popularity, as shown in Figure 6.6.

Figure 6.6: Popular support for Latvian governments, 2008–2011

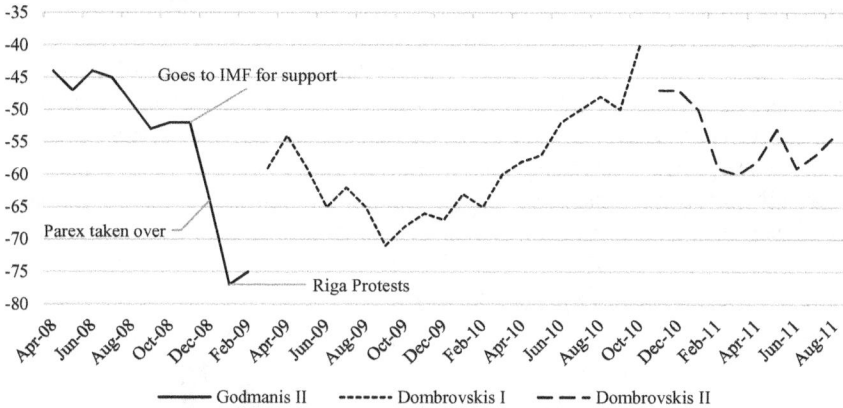

Note: The chart represents the evolution of the weighted difference between the total of positive and negative opinions on the Latvian government. Hence, the farther down on the graph, the less popular the government.
Source: Nord LB (2011), as used in Salines and Bērziņš (2012: 174, figure 7.3).

Here we can see how the popularity of Godmanis' government suffered greatly when the crisis hit, and as it turned to the IMF for support. At the time of the actual decisions (to bail out Parex, secure international support, and impose austerity measures), it seems clear that the government did not enjoy popular support – it seems to be pursuing another (less democratic, more economic) objective. Recall that the streets of Riga were filled with protestors at this time, and that just about everybody agrees there was little significant difference in policy (with regard to austerity) between the outgoing and incoming governments. In effect, Latvia's elites were in agreement about what to do, but they don't seem to have the Latvian people behind them. Neither does the Dombrovskis I government enjoy much popular support: for most of 2009, its popularity plummeted. Things begin to change around October 2009, and the government's popularity slowly begins to rise – up until the 2010 election, when it loses the support of the TP. Popular support for the Dombrovskis II government is mostly lower than what the Godmanis' government enjoyed prior to the crash.

Exit

Facing an economy in freefall, and a government that is corrupt – or at best, nonresponsive – tens of thousands of Latvians gave up hope altogether and left their country in search of jobs elsewhere. As we already saw in Chapter Three,

Latvia has long suffered from a serious emigration problem – but this problem worsened significantly with the crisis.

Figure 6.7 depicts a gut-wrenching rise in the number of registered emigrants from Latvia (these are not net-migration figures, as in Figure 3.12, but actual emigration tallies, as a share of population). Between 2007 and 2011, over 150,000 people left Latvia in search of better livelihoods elsewhere (Eurostat, [migr-emi2]). This exodus occurred in a country that has fewer than two million people, and whose population is shrinking each year. While 150,000 emigrants may not seem exorbitant to a Brit or a German, Latvia's annual emigration rates (per mil) are extremely high – anything above ten emigrants per thousand residents is historically noteworthy and large enough to generate significant political pressures (see Moses 2011).

Figure 6.7: Latvian emigration, 2000–2013

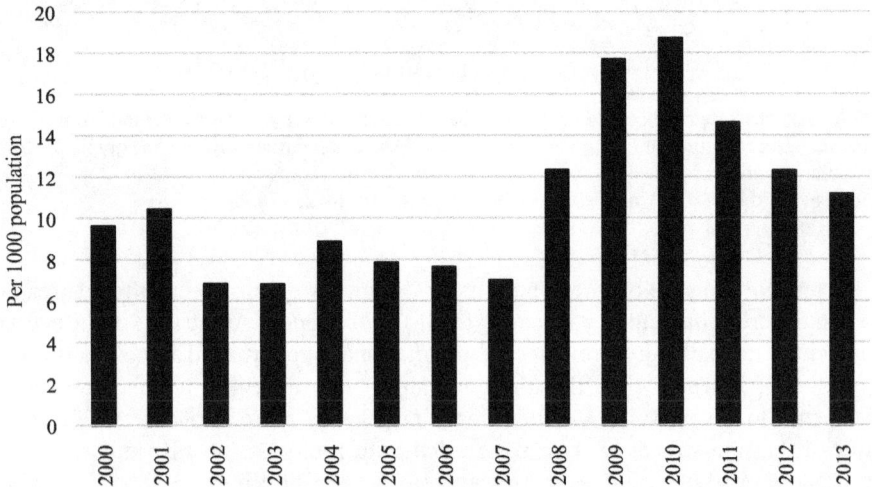

Note: Emigration, per 1,000 of population (per mil)
Source: Eurostat [migr_emi2] and [demo_pjan]

We all recognise that there are enormous costs, both personal and social, from having to leave one's family, friends and home to search for jobs elsewhere. Workers tend to choose this option only after other, less costly, measures have been tried. What we are seeing is a generation of Latvians voting with their feet: a flood of young Latvians who would rather leave their home than hope that their elected officials will (or can) improve local economic conditions.

Devalued priorities

Despite the significant cost of bailout, the Latvian authorities never wavered in their intent to maintain the lat's fixed exchange rate to the euro. Instead of following Iceland's lead (by imposing capital controls, or leveraging a devaluation to improve its international competitiveness), Latvia's plan for economic recovery was to force domestic prices and wages downward. This section considers why Latvia chose the Irish, as opposed to the Icelandic, path forward.

Latvian officials have provided us with two (related) types of arguments for their choices in policy: 1) Latvians supported their government in its policies; and 2) Latvia enjoyed no real alternative. I have used the previous section to raise doubts about the first of these arguments. We have been told that the government's policies (defending the exchange rate peg, bailing out Parex, taking on a massive international loan, and the austerity measures needed to pay it down) were difficult, but necessary – and embraced by the public. Implicitly, Latvian elites (and their supporters) would have us believe that their economic policy reflects a democratic consensus, borne of broad-based deliberation. For example, Anders Åslund (2010: 35) notes, that: '[a]s late as August 2009, an opinion poll reported that almost two-thirds of Latvians wanted the lat peg to the euro to remain unchanged.[26] They were prepared to do what it took, including large wage cuts, to keep the euro peg and adopt the euro early…'

I find this argument very difficult to swallow in a country that: 1) has so little trust in its politicians and political institutions; 2) is so dissatisfied with the way its democracy works; and 3) has used its voice to recall not only the government, but the entire parliament, for their misdeeds and policies. More telling yet is the fact that young Latvians, having witnessed the inadequacies of more traditional democratic channels of influence, are voting with their feet and fleeing *en masse*.

The authorities' second argument is more credible, but only if we ignore the Icelandic case. This argument holds that Latvia really had no choice. In particular, Latvian officials were afraid of the inflationary consequences of a possible devaluation, they were concerned about the large number of Latvian loans being held in foreign currencies (which a devaluation would make even more burdensome), and they didn't want to delay membership in the Eurozone.[27] But the currency of this second argument was greatly devalued in the wake of Iceland's actions.

Latvia could have devalued its currency, introduced capital controls, let Russian hot-money depositors bear the costs of Parex's failures, and examined allegations of corruption and mismanagement. Indeed, Iceland paved the way forward, by demonstrating the viability of these policy choices. But Latvia chose to listen to the needs of its international creditors more than the needs of its people – and

---

26. Åslund makes reference to this poll in several different pieces, but I have not been able to track it down. His reference is always brief: 'IMF External Relations Department, *Morning Press*, August 4, 2009.'

27. There is another argument, which I find more credible, but which was not explicitly used to justify the policy choice: that Latvians are afraid of their Russian neighbours and are willing to accept a costly economic arrangement if it means greater (formal) integration into the (western) European sphere. If this sort of geopolitical argument had been made to justify the country's fixed exchange rate policy, then it might have been buttressed by economic sweeteners for those Latvians hardest hurt by the policy.

those creditors feared a devaluation and/or a reduced banking sector; and they discouraged the use of state finances to stimulate jobs and domestic demand. As in Ireland, the government chose to pursue an undemocratic path, by prioritising the interests of international creditors (over those of domestic workers and borrowers), and by legitimising that decision with reference to economic necessity.

In choosing an internal devaluation strategy, the Latvian authorities leveraged the crisis to secure *unpopular* economic reforms. In particular, the government initiated deep cuts 'aimed at streamlining the public sector, which had been so far strongly resisted and thus postponed by previous governments for fear of unpopularity' (Salines and Bērziņš 2012: 164). Even if there were strong economic arguments for reforming Latvia's health and education sectors (and I believe there were), the authorities were callous in implementing these reforms at the height of the Great Recession, and they were dishonest to suggest that Latvia didn't have an alternative.

Indeed, when the Prime Minister met resistance in the Saeima, and it seemed as though his government's 2010 austerity budget would not pass muster, the European Commission and foreign governments (especially Sweden) applied enormous pressure on party leaders to secure support for the budget. In the face of such foreign pressure, a prominent TP politician (Vents Armands Krauklis) declared that: 'Nothing else is left other than to fulfil the unreasonable demands of the international lenders' (Willis 2009).

Worse yet, the internal devaluation did not end up fixing the underlying shortcomings of the Latvian economy – the ones that had produced the serious imbalances preceding the crisis. Although Latvia's GDP has returned to its pre-crisis level, the country's unemployment and emigration levels remain extremely high. More to the point, GDP growth has not secured a current account surplus (*see* Figure 6.2): Latvia still imports more than it exports, and the financial gap is still being filled by foreign capital/deposits (*see* below). Rather than using a devaluation to recalibrate Latvian prices, vis-à-vis its main trading partners, Latvian workers have been squeezed without any noticeable gains to their international competitiveness.[28]

The Icelandic example also provides a lesson as to how Latvia might have dealt with a cascade of failed foreign-currency denominated loans (in the wake of a devaluation). Indeed, the Hungarian authorities chose a similar solution, as we shall see in the next chapter. As it was originally the bank and regulatory officials that had encouraged such risky behaviour, they might be expected to bear the cost of fixing the problem. In order to protect consumers from the costs of the devaluation, the Latvian authorities had access to tried-and-true options. As in Iceland, Latvia could have used its sovereign court

---

28. To the extent that the internal devaluation was effective at generating economic growth it was because of productivity increases, rather than nominal wages cuts. But increased productivity generated greater profit margins, rather than a decrease in prices (Blanchard *et al.* 2013: 325). There are, however, differences in opinion as to why Latvia's productivity levels increased. Paul Krugman suggests it was due to productivity catch-up (Krugman, response to Blanchard *et al.*); while Oliver Blanchard and colleagues think it may be associated with labour-shedding, i.e., decreased employment (Blanchard *et al.* 2013: 351).

system to help desperate debtors/borrowers, under crisis conditions. Indeed, the court system is one of the few public institutions in Latvia that still enjoys the people's trust, and Latvians relied on it to protect their pensions from the government's austerity cuts.[29] At the same time, a devaluation would have hit wealthy Latvians disproportionately hard, as only the wealthiest Latvians held mortgages (whether in euros or in lats).

Unlike Ireland, Latvia still had a choice. Latvia maintained its own central bank, issuing its own sovereign currency. Indeed, Latvia enjoyed an even stronger position than Ireland, in that it faced an international consensus that was divided over what it should do. On the one hand, the IMF (initially), and many foreign experts (e.g., Paul Krugman, Nouriel Roubini, among others), argued that Latvia should employ a devaluation in response to the crisis. Market consensus at the time even held that Latvia would devalue (Krukowska 2009). On the other hand, Latvia's international creditors (especially the European Commissioners and the Swedish government) remained concerned about the potential for contagion. Sweden was especially concerned about the effect a Latvian devaluation would have on its own banks (as Swedish citizens – rather than Latvians – would then have to bail out the risky behaviour of their banks). But the European Commission was also forceful in reminding Latvians to pay the piper: '[t]he necessity of cuts was underlined by a special visit by Joaquin Almunia, European Commissioner for Economic and Monetary Affairs, who came not to cheer up the public, but to remind Latvia's political elite of its international obligations' (Ikstens 2010: 1056).

It should not surprise anybody that international creditors, who were lending Latvia money, should be advocating reforms that could ensure Latvia's loan is repaid quickly. After all, it is not their job to defend the interests of Latvians. But when nobody seems to be defending the interests of workers, or those who depend upon public support,[30] then the objectives of policy can easily become one sided, to the benefit of the creditors.

We can catch a glimpse of this inherent imbalance when we study the European Commission's (EC 2012) report on the 'foundations of success' behind the EU's Latvian bailout. Among the opening remarks to this study (totalling nineteen

---

29. While only about 19 per cent of Latvians trust their parliament, some 70 per cent trust their Constitutional Court. More to the point, it is relatively easy to launch a case with the Constitutional Court. As the Latvian constitution guarantees several fundamental social rights, including the right to social security, the Court has played an important role during the crisis. Latvians have used the courts to contest those austerity measures that have undermined their fundamental rights, e.g., cuts to the pension system (see, e.g., Salines and Bērziņš 2012: 162).

30. Buti (2012: 11) complains that negotiations with the Latvian government were tough, as the government didn't seem to care about its constituents (!): 'It has to be said that the discussion with Latvian authorities was not always easy. We had at a certain point to insist that the composition of the adjustment would not be done in a way which could undermine the social fabric of the country. Unlike in other countries, where we have to insist on having an adjustment which is essentially expenditure-based, in the case of Latvia we took the view that, whilst cuts in expenditure were absolutely essential, reforms on the revenue-side were also important in order to guarantee the social balance and social acceptability of the programme.'

pages of comments from a number of Latvian and EU dignitaries and analysts), we find no mention of poverty, migration, workers or emigration, and only limited mention to the problem of unemployment (twice, when explicitly linked to Latvian conditions). On the other hand, as we can see in Table 6.2, these officials made frequent reference to banks (18 references) prices (15), GDP (13), economic growth (12), deficit (9) and even 'confidence' (7).

Table 6.2: Concept analysis of EC (2012)

Total words (minus names and titles)	9,962
Of which:	
Bank	18
Price	15
GDP	13
Economic growth	12
Deficit	9
Confidence	7
Unemployment	5
Budget deficit	5
Inflation	3
Employment	2
Unemployment, with reference to Latvian conditions	2
Contagion	1
Migration, including emigration	0
Poverty	0
Worker(s)	0

Note: Number of times that a given concept was included in the combined 'introduction' and 'opening remarks'. Comments include remarks from the following analysts and dignitaries: Marco Buti (Director General, DG ECOFIN, European Commission); Valdis Dombrovskis (Prime Minister, Latvia); Gatis Eglitis (DG ECOFIN, European Commission, Latvia Desk); Elena Flores (Director, DG ECOFIN, European Commission); Gabriele Giudice (Head of unit, Economies of the Member States: United Kingdom, Estonia, Latvia, Sweden, DG ECOFIN, European Commission); Ilmārs Rimšēvičs (Governor, Bank of Latvia); and Christian Weise (Deputy Head of unit, Economies of the Member States: United Kingdom, Estonia, Latvia, Sweden, DG ECOFIN, European Commission)
Source: EC (2012: 3–17)

The Latvian response to the crisis is frequently touted as a success, and EU and IMF officials believe the Latvian example should be emulated by other members of the Eurozone, in order that European monetary policy can function more efficiently. All this, I suppose, depends upon one's definition of success. As Jeffery Sommers (2015: 24) would have it, 'Latvia's "success" has meant, first and foremost, that banks get paid.'

Recent developments

Latvia's economic turn-around has been remarkable, even if the fruits of its economic rebound are not broadly shared. While the rest of the Eurozone continued to suffer from recession, Latvia was able to generate substantial economic growth (around five per cent) after 2011 (*see* Figure 3.3) – the strongest among our cases. As a result of this growth, Latvia was able to prepay the outstanding amount of its IMF loan in December of 2012 – three years earlier than originally agreed (IMF 2012b). This is clearly impressive, but needs to be put in a larger context. When we lift our gaze above the headline statistics, and consider Latvia's broader experience relative to the other cases in this study, we see less of an economic miracle and more of a five-year struggle to return Latvia's GDP to where it was prior to the crisis (*see* Figure 6.1, above).[31]

Worse, this recovery was secured with great suffering: unemployment and income inequality levels remain high (cf. Figures 3.7 and 3.11), and the current level of poverty in Latvia is shocking. In 2015, over 30 per cent of Latvia's population was at risk of poverty and social exclusion. As seen in Figure 6.8, this is significantly above the EA-18 average, the worst among our cases, and the fourth worst among all European countries.

Figure 6.8: People at risk of poverty and social exclusion, European states, 2015

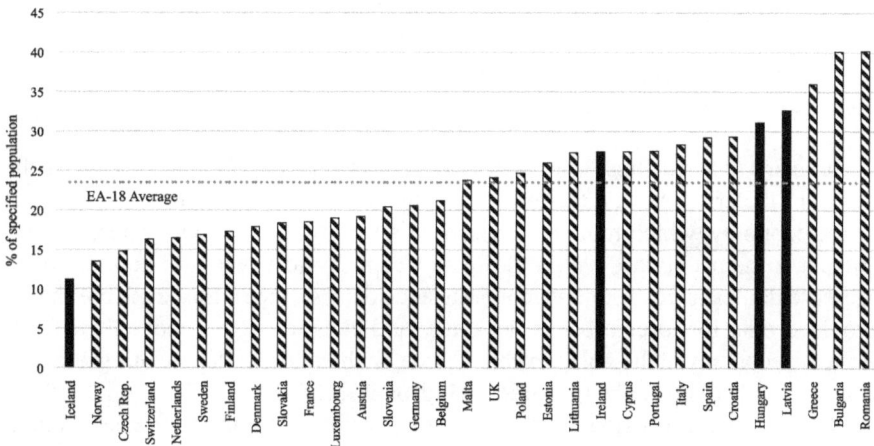

Source: Eurostat (2015)

In short, the headline economic statistics are woefully inadequate and conceal more than they reveal. Many Latvians are not benefiting from Latvia's impressive economic recovery. The reason for this is evident when we look at where this

---

31. Although some observers have referred to this as a 'dead cat bounce', more recent evidence suggests that what we see is a genuine recovery (in the sense of a return to pre-crisis levels). But references to a dead cat bounce are understandable in the sense that the scope of the rebound is only impressive if one ignores the scope of the decline that proceeded it.

recent economic activity is being generated. In 2015, the largest share (39 per cent) of the country's Foreign Direct Investment is being drawn into financial and real-estate activity, rather than in the form of investments that can secure jobs and productive activity (*see* Figure 6.9).

Figure 6.9: Foreign direct investment in Latvia, 2014–2015

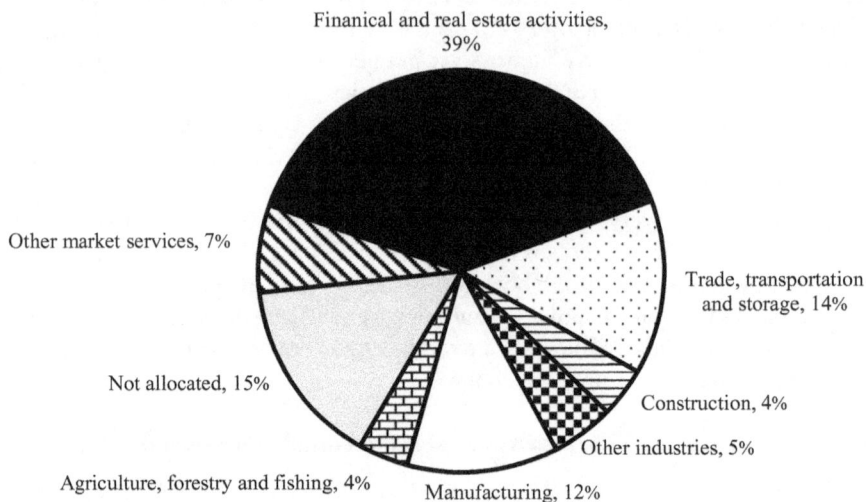

Note: Foreign direct investment in Latvia. The 2015 figures end in the third quarter.
Source: Bank of Latvia, as quoted in EC (2016: 8)

It seems that all those 'necessary' structural reforms, forced through at the height of the crisis, have done little to change the underlying nature (or structure) of the economy, which remains focused on attracting hot money. 'There was no attempt to help Latvia develop the export capacity to cover its imports, nor to preserve domestic government economic and social services. Eurozone credit was provided only for foreign banks, investors and kleptocrats to remove their funds from the economy at the going exchange rate, without the lat depreciating and thus leaving less hard currency to extract' (Hudson 2015: 56).

The government remained steadfast in its desire to join the Eurozone, even in the face of strong and persistent public opposition. Already on 31 January 2013, the Saeima passed a law (52 to 40) allowing the country to apply for adoption of the euro, despite strong public resistance.[32] Worse, when the opposition party, HC, tried to secure a referendum on adopting the euro, Prime Minster Dombrovskis

32. The unpopularity of this move has been well documented in the polls: a May 2013 poll commissioned by the Finance Ministry, found that 62 per cent of respondents did not favour the currency switch, compared to 36 per cent who said they do. Indeed, opinion surveys have consistently shown very few Latvians support the change (Baltic Course 2012). In an April survey by TSN, twenty-four percent said they were 'very negative' about the switch, compared to just seven per cent who were 'very positive' (BBJ 2013), and anti-euro parties won more than half the

made it clear that public opinion was less important than securing entry into the inner sanctum of the European Union: 'It's quite clear from the signals we are getting from Brussels that we will not receive an invitation to join the euro zone with a referendum pending' (Seeder 2012).

Despite strong opposition from the public, Latvia's currency was decommissioned in 2014, and the country is now a full member of the Eurozone. As the former Prime Minister (and now European Parliament member), Ivars Godmanis, noted in a 2013 interview:

'After Latvia joins the eurozone, the Bank of Latvia will not even have a theoretical opportunity to pursue an independent monetary policy. However, the lat has been pegged to the euro for seven years already, therefore the Bank of Latvia's policies cannot be considered fully independent' (Baltic Course 2013).

Conclusion

The Latvian response to the crisis is both unique and impressive. But it is also cruel and short-sighted. Latvia's remarkable economic collapse (and rebirth) is astonishing – but it becomes even more so when placed in a comparative context. Compared to the other countries in this study, the size of Latvia's bank crash was relatively small, and the country enjoyed significant international support provided by neighbouring states/banks. Throughout the crisis, the government's deficit and debt levels remained remarkably modest. If the government wanted to wait with the structural reforms, it could have. Instead, the government was myopically focussed on paying down its debts, balancing its budget quickly and entering the Eurozone. In the doing, it made the crisis more difficult for everyday Latvians. In the end, full Eurozone membership may provide reward for all the suffering required of working Latvians – but it will take time (and much luck).

For these reasons, the Latvian story is a contested one, in that many people seem desperate to show that the country's embrace of austerity offers a moral lesson for the rest of Europe. Latvia's economic rebound was remarkably (and thankfully) rapid: the country was able to escape from the recession, and return to economic growth, relatively quickly. For many policy makers in Europe, the Latvian example demonstrates that a monetary union in Europe can work, if only people are willing to sacrifice sufficiently.

In this chapter I have endeavoured to show that it stretches credibility to claim, as so many international observers have, that Latvians realised the necessity of austerity, and embraced it with a strong dose of sombre realism. Latvians have protested at every step along the way, but it has done them little good.

---

vote in local (June 2013) elections in the capital, Riga (McHugh 2013). See also Ikstens (2014: 202–3).

But this is not the main lesson of this chapter. The main lesson is that Latvia still had a choice in 2008 and 2009, and it could have chosen otherwise. When the crisis hit, Latvia found itself in a unique, middle-ground, position: it could decide whether it should devalue its currency (following the Icelandic strategy), or maintain investor confidence in its ability to ride out the economic storm. It chose the latter strategy, but at great cost to its people.

'In the end, the IMF accepted that Latvia not devalue. Christoph Rosenberg, who led the December 2008 IMF mission to Latvia, laid out the arguments against devaluation. The key reason was that *this was the Latvian choice*. The IMF was also persuaded by the substantial financing of the European Union and the Nordic countries, which supported the Latvian choice' (Åslund 2010: 36, emphasis added).

Latvian officials, if not the Latvian people, still enjoyed some freedom to manoeuvre when deciding to keep the lat pegged to the euro. After all, the choice to *not* devalue is still an example of policy autonomy, and the Latvian authorities had one more option than did the Irish: they could have chosen an easier path to recovery, but they chose not to. Indeed, it was the Latvian authorities' strong and explicit preference to maintain the peg that eventually convinced the IMF to support the decision not to devalue (Rosenberg, 2009).

So far, we have compared the policy responses of three very different states, and this variance appears to correspond to the sundry relationships that each state had to its exchange rate regime (and corresponding monetary policy). Iceland enjoyed the most monetary policy autonomy; Ireland the least; and Latvia – when given an opportunity to choose between the two paths – followed the Irish route out of the crisis. But what about states that are not neck-deep in crisis – can they also find recourse in an autonomous monetary policy? The next chapter examines the Hungarian case, with this question in mind.

Chapter Seven

Hungary

In Hungary, the crisis was different. Whereas the other three countries in this study were forced to deal with a banking crisis that threatened to sink their (broader) economies, Hungary suffered from a cash-flow problem. The international financial crisis ignited a political crisis in Hungary by making it more difficult for the country to pay back the bonds used to cover its growing debt. In short, in the midst of a global financial crisis, Hungary's elected officials were hoping to secure a little more breathing space.

To accomplish this, Hungary was one of the first European countries to turn to the international community in search of assistance. In exchange for economic support, Hungary's political elites pledged economic austerity and agreed to a number of political conditions, imposed by the IMF and the EU. As the crisis unfolded, however, Hungarians became increasingly disgruntled with the options they faced. In 2010, responding to growing signs of political and economic incompetence, a landslide election cleaned Hungary's political house. Unlike in Ireland and Latvia, however, this landslide actually affected the political landscape: the new government that emerged changed the country's political direction and set Hungary down its own *sonderweg*, or 'special path'. The election mattered in Hungary, and it mattered because Hungary still enjoyed the policy instruments needed to blaze an autonomous path.

This is why I have included Hungary as a case in this study, even if its case characteristics don't lend themselves to Mill's comparative design. Hungary, is a case *unlike* the others. But Hungary's *sonderweg* still offers evidence of the political breathing space that is afforded states that keep their own currency. In Hungary, this breathing space is partly the result of its underlying economic position – it didn't suffer a crippling financial crisis in the same way as in the other cases, and (hence) was less reliant on the international community (and its political conditions) to survive. But Hungary's *sonderweg* is also the result of an explicit and political decision to prioritise domestic needs over the demands of the international market. Because Hungary could sever the conditions imposed on it by international lenders; because it did not feel obliged to defend the interests of foreign banks; and because the Hungarian central bank was not forced to defend a fixed rate of exchange to the euro, Hungary's elected officials enjoyed more freedom to set their own political course.

Hungary's political path leads in a very different direction: where Iceland turned left, Hungary turned right. Although the Hungarian path may be more difficult for many (liberal-leaning) Europeans to follow – as the deluge of international criticism of Hungarian policy attests – the country's willingness to do something different clearly demonstrates the scope of political autonomy that is afforded to states that retain their own currency.

A different start

Before 2007, Hungary was seen as a model for post-communist transitions to capitalism; Hungary was the darling of the international community.[1] The country joined the European Union in 2004, and quickly adopted a series of liberal reforms that were designed to attract foreign capital and jobs to the Hungarian economy. Like Latvia, it seems that Hungary chose Ireland as its model for economic transformation. Even before Hungary joined the EU, its central bank – the National Bank of Hungary (*Magyar Nemzeti Bank*, or MNB) – adopted an inflation-targeting regime (in 2001) in hopes of securing early membership in the Eurozone.[2] Indeed, Hungary's central bankers lead the country's charge for greater economic liberalism: they quickly adopted EU norms and pressured Hungarian politicians into accepting more and more liberal economic solutions:

> 'The central bankers wanted to adopt the euro quickly in order to tie the hands of their own increasingly unsupportive governments, forcing the governments to first cut their fiscal deficits enough to meet the Maastricht criteria, and then to cede control over monetary policy to the more powerful ECB' (Johnson 2006: 363–4).

At first, this embrace of liberalism seemed to deliver economic reward: the country attracted a large influx of foreign direct investment, which fuelled a slow but steady economic growth trajectory. Although the country had built up a sizeable level of debt in the early years of transition,[3] its debt burden was slowly receding at the end of the 1900s. In the 2000s, however, Hungary's debt level started to grow slowly again, on a string of government deficits that exceeded six per cent of the country's GDP (between 2002 and 2007). Consequently, Hungary's gross government debt level punctured (slightly) the 60 per cent ceiling set by the EU's Stability and Growth Pact (SGP). Although Hungary was clearly finding it difficult to live within its means, its debt-level remained at, or below, the Euro-area average throughout most of this period (*see* Figure 3.4).

The two most important challenges facing the Hungarian economy, prior to the international financial crisis, were inflation and unemployment. Given the oddly perverse incentives of Europe's Economic and Monetary Union, the former

---

1. For a concise overview of this economic transition, see Djankov (2015).

2. The then governor of the MNB, Zsigmond Járai, hoped that Hungary might join the Eurozone in January 2006, and subsequent, well-publicised research by MNB analysts (Csajbók and Csermely 2002) argued that Hungary and the Eurozone would function as an optimum currency area, bringing a cornucopia of economic fruits to the country (Johnson 2006: 370–71).

3. Much of this debt was left-over from the Communist era, as Hungary (unlike Poland) did not receive partial debt forgiveness at the time of transition.

requires swift and immediate action, the latter does not. While the level of inflation in Hungary had been reduced to single-digit levels in the new millennium, it still tended to fluctuate between 3–8 per cent, as we saw in Figure 3.6. Not surprisingly, the level of unemployment remained high (above 10 per cent before 2013: c.f. Figure 3.7), but has been fallen significantly in the past couple of years.

In this context, Hungary's level of debt was mostly an irritant, not an existential threat. While Hungary was having difficulty meeting the fiscal criteria of Maastricht and the SGP, its economic record was not significantly worse than the Eurozone average, as we saw in Chapter Three. The problem lay in what the debt represented. Hungary's debt was not seen as an investment for improving the future lives of Hungarians, or the result of some master plan to redirect and/ or reinvigorate the Hungarian economy. Rather, Hungary's debt was mostly a reminder of the incompetence of its political elites, and a threat to future membership in the Eurozone. This impression only grew after the April 2002 elections, when a Socialist-led (MSZP) coalition, headed by Prime Minister Péter Medgyessy, came to power and increased public spending (*see* Table 7.1). In the doing, the government raised the spectre of even greater inflation and increased government debt in the future.

Table 7.1: Recent governments in Hungary

Government	Prime Minister	From	Until	Coalition Partners
Orbán I	Orbán, Viktor	8 July 1998	27 May 2002	*Fidesz*, FKGP, MDF
Medgyessy I	Medgyessy, Péter	27 May 2002	29 Sept 2004	*MSZP*, SZDSZ
Gyurcsány I	Gyurcsány, Ferenc	29 Sept 2004	9 June 2006	*MSZP*, SZDSZ
Gyurcsány II	Gyurcsány, Ferenc	9 June 2006	14 April 2009	*MSZP*, SZDSZ
Bajnai I	Bajnai, Gordon	14 April 2009	29 May 2010	*MSZP*
Orbán II	Orbán, Viktor	29 May 2010	6 June 2014	*Fidesz*, KDNP
Orbán III	Orbán, Viktor	9 June 2014	Current	*Fidesz*, KDNP

Note: In the right-hand column, the coalition party in italics is the Prime Minister's political party. Party acronyms are defined as follows:

MSZP	*Magyar Szocialista Párt*	Hungarian Socialist Party (socialists)
SZDSZ	*Szabad Demokraták Szövetsége*	Alliance of Free Democrats (liberals)
Fidesz	*Magyar Polgári Szövetség*	Hungarian Civic Union (conservatives)
KDNP	*Kereszténv Demokrata Párt*	Christian Democratic People's Party

By the end of September 2004, Medgyessy was forced to resign due to a growing realisation that he was unable to mobilise the political support necessary to shrink the budget deficit down to a size required by the EU's SGP. The three governments that followed (Gyurcsány I & II, and Bajnai I) were equally doomed:

each refused to take serious action for fear of the electoral consequences. In the case of Ferenc Gyurcsány, the public reaction was most venomous: his popularity was torpedoed when a recording of his infamous 'lie' speech to MSZP members of the National Assembly (in Balatonőszöd) was leaked in September 2006, revealing a vulgar, deceitful and duplicitous prime minister (BBC News 2006). Political frustration with the government's apparent ineptitude began to pour out as public demonstrations in the streets.

Despite Gyurscány's dwindling popularity, he responded to these public demonstrations with promises of increased fiscal austerity. It was almost as if he was trying to align all the country's political and economic forces in a perfect storm of political retribution. In 2006, the Hungarian budget deficit fell to its lowest level (the structural deficit reached almost 12 per cent of GDP), and the European Commission and the European Council were prescribing very strong medicine in an effort to restore Hungary's economic health (EC 2006). By the fall of 2006, Gyurcsány's government announced a number of austerity measures to satiate the Council's demand (and in response to the Excessive Deficit Procedure) and to try and reel in the government's budget deficit. In the summer of 2007, the Ministry of Finance introduced draft legislation that would require strict fiscal rules and an independent parliamentary office. As elsewhere, the EU was using the economic crisis as an excuse to limit the policy scope of elected officials.

All the while, the government found itself under attack, from both within and beyond. Internally, the government coalition was divided: Socialists and Liberals couldn't agree on a number of pressing issues, borne of the drive for austerity (including whether to privatise the health insurance system, reduce taxes and/ or introduce women's quotas). Outside of government, the opposition began to challenge the government's policies by exposing them to public referendums. The National Election Commission was asked to handle several hundred referendum initiatives in 2007 (Ilonszki and Kurtán 2008: 999). In the doing, the governing Socialist Party's (MSZP) popularity took a pounding: falling from roughly 40 per cent in January to about 26 per cent in December (among those who were certain to vote), and to just 15 per cent in the general population (Ilonszki and Kurtán 2008: 1002).

The fate of the government was sealed when the 9 March 2008 referendums clearly revealed the level of voter dissatisfaction with government policies. When asked to support the government's proposals to raise fees for government services (e.g. in-patient care; family-care dentistry; and higher education), Hungarians turned up in droves to reject (by over 80 per cent) the government's program. Although neither of the main opposition parties (Fidesz or the KDNP) demanded a vote of confidence in parliament,[4] the referendum outcomes constituted, in effect, a landslide victory for the opposition.

The government was left to implode on its own: the Liberals left the government in May, leaving the Socialists to run a minority (caretaker) government headed

---

4. A smaller party, the MDF (Hungarian Democratic Forum) did initiate a vote of confidence in September, but it failed 204/171 (Ilonszki and Kurtán 2009: 976).

by the former Economy Minister, Gordon Bajnai (*see* Table 7.1, above). Bajnai didn't have a chance: not only did he lack a popular mandate, but his economic options were severely limited by the conditionality requirement of the EU/IMF/ World Bank stand-by arrangement that Gyurcsány had signed while still in office (see below).

On the eve of the international financial crisis, in the early fall of 2008, Hungary's elected officials had already destroyed what little good will they might have had at their disposal. The MSZP/SZDSZ coalition government had twiddled its thumbs as the economic situation deteriorated, then tried to address the problem by accepting onerous austerity conditions on behalf of its constituents.

Austere beginnings

As the international financial storm was brewing in the fall of 2008, a dark cloud of economic and political crises was already hanging over Hungary. On 6 November 2008, about one month after the fall of Lehman Brothers, Gyurcsány's government was forced to secure financial support from abroad (IMF 2008d). As the previous section suggested, the reason had less to do with an overheated financial market (or the need to bail out corrupt bankers), and everything to do with good, old-fashioned, economic mismanagement. Hungary needed money to pay for its growing debt burden.

It is important to note that the Hungarian government was not insolvent. Like Latvia, Hungary's economic challenges were manageable, not crushing. After all, the Hungarian central bank could continue to buy more debt – but doing so would require printing more money, and risking a further fall in the value of the forint (HUF). In short, Hungary was being caught in a credit squeeze, driven largely by fear in foreign markets. Since the second half of 2007 – and as we've seen in the preceding chapters – the world's financial system experienced a sharp decline in interbank liquidity, and banks in Europe had begun to deleverage both at home and abroad (even if they weren't directly exposed to US sub-prime markets). After the collapse of Lehman Brothers, this activity accelerated, creating some concern in Hungary (and elsewhere) that multinational banks would withdraw from the Hungarian market and starve Hungarian borrowers (and their local subsidiaries) of needed capital.

At the same time, and as a result of the political and economic turmoil described above, the value of the forint had been falling, and the government's paper was being dumped by non-residents – leaving the country with a number of failed auctions and a growing financing gap (Mabbett and Schelkle 2015: 515). As much of Hungary's debt, both private and public, was held by foreigners, the economy was being squeezed by its dwindling access to foreign capital. Hungary's international lending costs were rising quickly, making it expensive to borrow more money. The Hungarian authorities needed to calm market fears, so that foreign banks would not pull up stakes and return home. If some foreign banks began to flee, they could trigger a stampede, with significant consequences for Europe's financial system (and the banks that remained in Hungary).

The Gyurcsány (II) government found itself in a fiscal vice. To loosen that vice, the government approached the international financial community for help. In response, the IMF and the EU offered a €20 billion loan to the MNB (€12.5 billion from the IMF, the rest from the EU): the 6 November 2008 agreement, mentioned above.[5] The loan was to help the central bank finance the government's deficit, refinance the public debt (that was falling due) and to help service the private sector's liquidity needs. Borrowing abroad was seen to be necessary, as increased money creation would depreciate the currency all the more, creating severe hardships on domestic borrowers, many of whom had undertaken foreign loans (see below). In its Letter of Intent to the IMF, the government noted its willingness to pursue austerity measures to correct the fiscal imbalances, and to introduce to parliament an amended fiscal responsibility law and a law to strengthen the emergency powers of the Hungarian Financial Supervision Authority (GoH, 2008: 40). What is remarkable about this document is the lack of any reference to the need for Hungary to maintain a fixed exchange rate, or a clear signal about the need for Hungary to stay on track for joining the Eurozone.[6]

This growing international crisis had revealed how reliant Hungary (and other East European countries) had become on foreign banks. As in Latvia, foreign banks had pursued a subsidiary strategy in Hungary (unlike the banks in Iceland, which had expanded using a branch strategy). Consequently, banks in Hungary were able to turn to their home banks (and their authorities) to secure additional funding and support. As we saw in the preceding chapter, the Vienna Initiative aimed to do just that by securing a series of agreements among parent (multinational) banks, host and home country regulators, central bankers and politicians, and representatives from the international financial institutions.

In Latvia, Swedish banks (and their home authorities) played an important role in calming the financial waters. In Hungary, this role was played by Austria and its banks. Austrian banks were especially active in much of central Europe (and in Hungary, in particular) – and (not surprisingly) the Austrian government cooperated with a number of multinational banks to try to overcome collective action problems (among banks) and to secure greater macroeconomic stability in Hungary. Formally, this process began on 27 November 2008, when six bank groups[7] wrote a letter to

---

5. This 2008 Stand-By Arrangement was never completely tapped. Five program reviews were completed on schedule and only about €14.2 billion was dispersed (€8.7 billion from the IMF, €5.5 billion from the EU), before a new Orbán (II) government decided in mid-2010 to let the programme lapse (IMF 2011: 9, box 1).

6. There is only a vague reference, from the IMF on the need to '…continue focusing on medium term structural development and growth goals, including accession to the euro' (IMF 2008d: §36, p. 20). The Hungarian Government's Letter of Intent shows no-such concern, but notes that the country now enjoys a floating exchange rate, so it is not exposed to one-way bets against the forint, and can focus its attention on domestic price developments (GoH 2008: 45).

7. The six major bank groups that signed the communique were: Raiffeisen, Erste, Intesa SP, Société Générale, KBC and Unicredit. These banks came from Germany, Belgium and Italy as well as three from Austria.

the European Commission about their concerns over financial stability in Central and East Europe.

While there are differences of opinion about the initial motivation for this Initiative,[8] it resulted in a rescue package of €24.5 billion to support large cross-border banks and a number of initiatives aimed at averting a banking crisis in the region (de Haas *et al*. 2012: 8).[9] To convince parent banks to stay and maintain a certain level of exposure (e.g. rollover or maintain exposures to the extent possible; recapitalise subsidiaries following stress tests; provide support packages from home country national banks to support their subsidiaries), Hungary promised to comply with IMF conditionality while pursuing prudent macroeconomic policies, supporting deposit insurance schemes, and supplying local currency liquidity, irrespective of bank ownership. As in each of the other cases in this study, the need to secure external financing was being used to leverage Hungary into accepting liberal (free-market) policy conditions/reforms.

In short, at the very start of the financial crisis, and before it became vogue in the rest of Europe, Hungary's political elites signalled their willingness to pursue austerity in exchange for international financial support. While Hungary's economic situation was less dire than in the other cases in this study, its political elites – at least, initially – found it necessary to protect and support the financial sector, at the expense of the common voter. In the doing, they were being forced to circumscribe their authority and agree to a number of conditions that would limit their political and fiscal autonomy.

Freedom fight

In 2008, Hungary stood at a crossroads with regard to its future euro-membership. Although its financial sector was in much better shape, and its economic challenges were nothing like those facing the other cases in this study (c.f. Table 1.1), Hungary still needed to develop a response to the forthcoming financial crisis. Formally, as a member of the European Union, it was obliged by treaty to join the Eurozone. As part of that obligation, Hungary had promised to pursue an economic policy that would fulfil the criteria for adopting the euro, including exchange rate stability. As we saw in the Latvian and Irish cases, fulfilling these criteria would bring significant economic hardship to the Hungarian people. The alternative, still available to Hungary, was to leverage the autonomy provided by its independent currency to secure more popular outcomes.

---

8.   While some authors point to the Vienna Initiative as an example of international organisations stepping in to fend off the retreat of foreign banks from the region, Rachel Epstein (2014) argues that the Initiative was a bank-driven process: an attempt to maintain their dominant exposure in Central and Eastern Europe.

9.   For example: in Hungary, banks promised to ensure a 'prudent capitalization of their subsidiaries' and to maintain at least 95 per cent of their September 2008 exposure in that country. See de Haas *et al*. (2012: 9).

As we saw in the previous section, Hungary's initial response to the financial crisis was to embrace austerity and to pursue business as usual. By 2010, however, Hungarian voters opted to change direction and lunged to the right – in a desperate attempt to maintain some degree of democratic control and/or accountability. In a series of national, local and European elections, Hungarians made it abundantly clear that business would *not* continue as usual. Voters punished the incumbent parties, embraced a new, more conservative coalition (Fidesz/KDNP), and introduced two new parties to parliament (Jobbik and the Green LMP[10]).

Winning two-thirds of the country's parliamentary seats,[11] a new government was well-positioned to introduce radical change, and it worked quickly to distance itself from the perceived corruption and inefficiency of the old government (and its embrace of austerity). In his June 2010 speech to the Hungarian Parliament (the *Országgyűlés*), the incoming Prime Minister, Viktor Orbán, announced a 'new social contract', which would create some breathing space between the austerity demands of international organisations and Orbán's explicit desire to secure 'debt reduction through economic growth' (Bod 2013: 22). While most of Europe's political elites came to embrace austerity, the Orbán (II) government promised its voters a bold new plan, where the government would regain influence over important economic policy instruments, and where the economy would be allowed to outgrow its debts.

The resulting policy shift has received a great deal of international attention. Most of the critical focus has been trained on the illiberal and nationalist nature of the policy response: on how 'Hungary's government, though elected democratically, is misusing its legislative majority to methodically dismantle democracy's checks and balances, to remove constitutional constraints, and to subordinate to the will of the ruling party all branches of power, independent institutions, and the media' (The Budapest Appeal 2011).[12] The Orbán II government introduced a wide-ranging series of reforms, including a new constitution, and a radical new media law, on the tails of its impressive electoral victories – and many of these reforms run counter to the more liberal (market) trend in Europe.

For the purposes of this study, it matters not whether policy autonomy is used to secure policies of the left or the right. The question before us is whether the new government was able to: 1) take advantage of the fact that Hungary was not yet bound to the euro; and 2) maintain a degree of policy autonomy (as a result). The answer to both these questions is clear: the government leveraged its policy autonomy to secure outcomes that were popular (at home, if not abroad), if not always (economically) successful. The new government's policy was three pronged: a depreciating exchange rate, increased monetary policy autonomy, and a series of unorthodox fiscal policy measures.

---

10. *See* the notes to Table 7.1 for a list of party acronyms. Jobbik is a populist right party, whose English translation is 'For the Right Hungary'; LMP stands for *Lehet Más a Politika* (or 'Politics Can be Different').

11. Fidesz gained just 53 per cent of the total vote, but used the country's disproportional electoral system to leverage these votes into a two-thirds majority in the parliament.

12. See, e.g., Kirchick (2012).

The forint floats

The first step in Hungary's return to autonomy was to put its euro-ambitions on ice. While the government would work hard (using very unconventional means!) to bring its budget deficit and debt-levels under control, it was not interested in defending a fixed exchange rate with the euro. Instead, the government allowed the forint to float, resulting in a significant depreciation in the forint's value over time. This depreciation has allowed Hungarian firms to improve their price competitiveness vis-à-vis foreign firms, such that exports have consistently out-performed imports since the crisis began (*see* Figure 7.2, below).

To be clear, the abandonment of a fixed exchange rate precedes the Orbán II government and reflects a broader political consensus (among elected officials, if not within the central bank) on the need to maintain policy autonomy. After a long period with an adjustable peg regime, Hungary adopted a crawling band regime in March of 1994 (with a relatively narrow, +/- 2.25 per cent, band). Over time, the market rate evolved into something more like a crawling peg system (as it was almost always hovering at the strong edge of the band) – and the band was expanded substantially (+/- 15 per cent) in May of 2001, when inflation targeting was introduced. For most of the subsequent period, until 2008, the forint/euro exchange rate stabilised around 250–260 forints per euro, as seen in Figure 7.1.

Figure 7.1: Forint/€ exchange rate, daily, 2000–2016

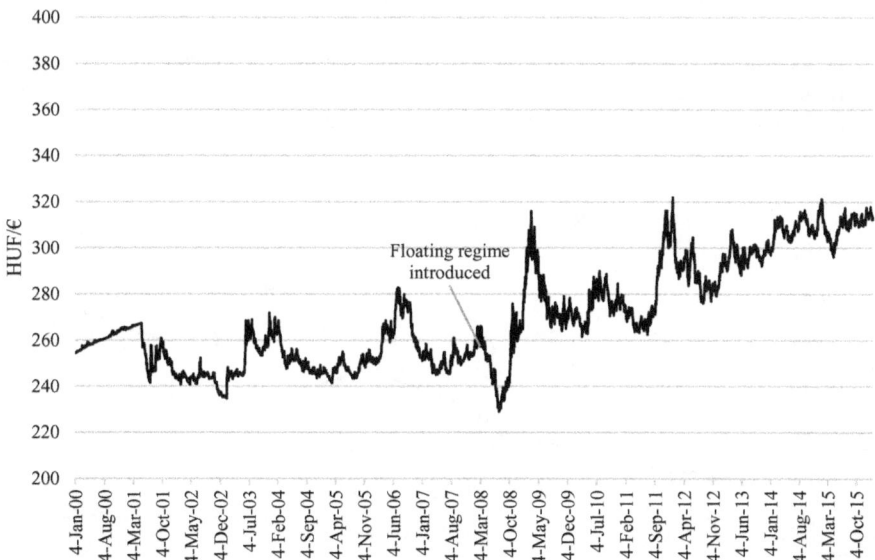

Note: Nominal official daily exchange rate vis-à-vis euro.
Source: MNB (2016b)

On 26 February 2008, the Gyurcsány (II) government, together with the MNB (and pursuant to Act LVIII of 2001), dissolved the currency band and allowed the forint to float freely vis-à-vis the euro (Darvas 2012: 5). Since that time, the forint has fluctuated in value, but gradually depreciated vis-à-vis the euro – driven less by any underlying economic fundamentals and more by market psychology (e.g. negotiations with the IMF, EU responses to the crisis in Greece, Spain, etc.). From the day that the floating regime was introduced (26 February 2008) until the last day of the time series in Figure 7.1 (29 January 2016), the nominal value of the forint has fallen by over 20 per cent (from about 260 to about 312). In the meantime, Hungary's entry into the Eurozone has been put on indefinite hold. This adjustment fuelled a quick economic turn-around – and helped the economy grow its way out of debt – as promised by the new government. Compared to Latvia, where the adjustments took place in the form of an internal devaluation – driven by an unemployment-induced fall in wages and increased productivity (*see* Chapter Six) – the Hungarian economy went through a much shallower economic recession, and came out of the slump much more quickly. As we saw in the preceding chapter, the Latvian economy nosedived in response to the crisis: from a booming (11.6 per cent) growth rate in 2006, to a frightening -14 per cent, three years later (2009). Hungary's economic trajectory during this same period tracked the euro-average: a substantial (but short) drop into negative territory in 2008 (-5 per cent), and another brief and minor return to negative growth in 2012.

The reason that Hungary was able to buoy its national economy is complex, but a significant part of the story is the ability to maintain competitiveness by means of the depreciating currency, as seen in Figure 7.1. This effect is clearly evident when we compare the level of Hungarian imports and exports over time, as is done in Figure 7.2. Here we see how the value of Hungarian exports begin to surpass imports in 2008 (the year the floating regime was introduced), and how it increased in each subsequent year. This is the engine of Hungary's economic growth, and it is fuelled by the depreciation depicted in Figure 7.1.

Figure 7.2: Exports and imports, Hungary, 2000–2013

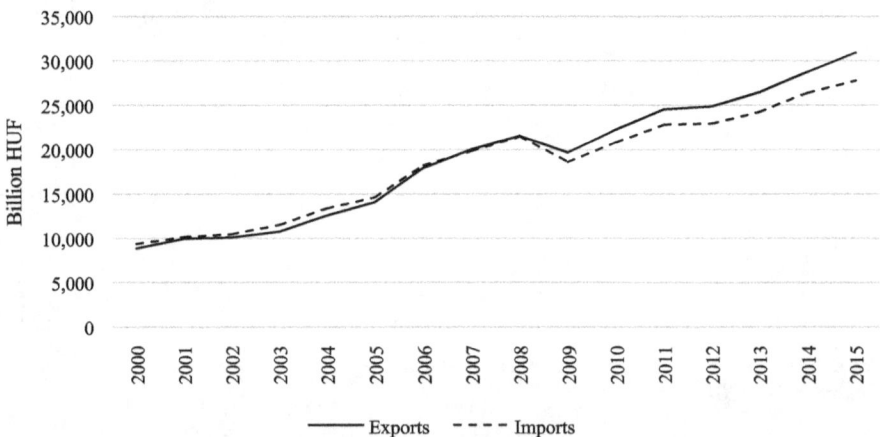

Note: Imports and exports of goods and services at current prices (National accounts; UMGS).
Source: Eurostat/AMECO

Of course, there are economic casualties to letting the forint float, and these were significant in Hungary. This is because foreign banks and previous governments had been irresponsibly encouraging Hungarians to take up loans (for homes and cars, mostly) in foreign currencies (especially Swiss francs, or CHF). As we saw in Iceland, these loans began to balloon, due to the forint's fall in value. Like Iceland, the Hungarian government worked quickly to relieve this burden and ensure that demand in Hungary would not sink along with the foreign loans. The Hungarian parliament passed a law (on 19 September 2011) to help borrowers pay back their (foreign) mortgage loans in a lump sum at a preferential exchange rate that was about 20 to 25 per cent (eventually 30 per cent) lower than market rates (Bod 2011: 10–11).[13]

This policy was designed to pit the interests of domestic constituents (borrowers) against foreign bankers (lenders), as the economic relief for borrowers would be paid for by losses in the banks' balance sheets. This expense was not trivial: banks did not have a CHF deposit base in Hungary, so they had to borrow funds abroad (typically short term), and then lend out again over the long-term.[14]

Hungary allowed its currency to depreciate in a way that provided the country with economic opportunities that most other states in Europe – being bound to the euro – didn't enjoy. Rather than force economic austerity on its workers (in the form of an internal devaluation), it grew the economy by tapping into international demand, fuelled by a cheaper forint, and protected those Hungarians who were overly exposed to the costs of a depreciating forint.

Monetary policy autonomy

Although the new government did not instigate the floating forint regime, it exploited the policy space that opened up in its wake. Almost immediately after his re-election into government in 2010, Orbán introduced his plans for a 'freedom fight'. This freedom fight would be secured in two, related, ways: by gaining greater political control over other instruments of monetary policy, and by using this political autonomy to improve Hungary's financial position with a handful of very unconventional budgetary measures.

In order to secure greater political control over the country's monetary policy (and its institutions) – and to fuel a broader-based, demand-driven, economic recovery – the new government realised it needed to disentangle itself from

---

13. By requiring the entire loan be paid back in a lump sum, it was difficult for some families to take advantage of this scheme: analysts estimate the take-up rate to be about 10 to 35 per cent. The plan clearly helps some households to escape their foreign exchange liabilities; but these households are probably the most well-off. More troubled borrowers, who lacked the funds or capacities to secure a new loan, were not able to participate in this scheme. For them, another government initiative provided temporary relief: a previous Act allowed the temporary fixing of forint instalments on foreign exchange mortgage loans, with rescheduling of the remaining debts (Bod 2011: 11).

14. For example: if borrowers repay their debt at 180 HUF/CHF, banks still had to buy foreign currency at the going rate (in the fall of 2011 this was 240 or more).

the political conditions imposed upon it by its international creditors: the IMF and the European Union.[15] In announcing their radical change in policy, Orbán was explicit: 'We want to regain Hungary's lost economic sovereignty' (quoted in Fairclough and Gulyas 2010). This change in policy direction began almost immediately, in the summer of 2010, when the new government suspended talks with the IMF over future loans (while announcing the series of unorthodox fiscal policies that would constitute his freedom fight).[16]

The government then tried to secure greater influence over the country's central bank, the MNB. At first, the government tried to oust the sitting governor, but it met strong opposition from the ECB (as doing so would have contravened the Maastricht Treaty, which Hungary had signed).[17] Later, in March 2013, the government found a path around that political roadblock: Orbán appointed his own Minister of Economy, György Matolcsy, as the new central bank governor. (It is important to point out that this decision was entirely within the government's legal authority, as the sitting governor was due to retire after his six-year stint in office.) Matolcsy was not just any old Minister of Economy: he was previously the main architect behind the government's unorthodox budgetary policies (see below).

As governor of the MNB, Matolcsy pledged to cooperate closely with the government; indeed, one of his first tasks as governor was to create a position, within the central bank, of director in charge of 'fiscal cooperation' (Kopits 2013). Even more revealing, I think, is Matolcsy's willingness to think about monetary policy *autonomy* in a very different light, as revealed in a November 2013 interview with CNBC (2013). In that interview, Matolcsy underscored the importance of central bank independence – but broadened its scope: the MNB needed to (and would) be independent from political influence, but it also needed to be independent from the financial industry. In the world of central banking, this is a horse of a different colour!

As the Hungarian banking sector had already been backstopped by the Vienna Initiative, Hungarian officials were less desperate than those in other countries experiencing severe banking crises. Unlike their counterparts in Ireland, Portugal,

---

15. As noted above, the 2008 IMF agreement required the Hungarian parliament to pass a fiscal responsibility law, which established a technocratic monitoring group (the Fiscal Council). The new government first ignored the Fiscal Council, then (with the 2011 budget) cut its funding, promising to narrow its remit (see, e.g., Kopits and Romhányi 2013: 226). The government also tried to merge the MNB with the Hungary Financial Supervisory Authority, but eventually agreed not to do so, when the plan appeared to stand in the way of subsequent negotiations between Hungary and the IMF (Várnagy 2013: 96).

16. Once freed from the political constraints that were originally imposed on it, the Hungarian government was willing and able to turn the tables on the IMF. In 2011, the Orbán government returned to the IMF, in what appears as a clever means at appeasing markets (Csaba 2013: 162–3). In the end, Hungary did not need to secure external financing, it simply wanted to reduce its financing costs, and it did so by playing nice with the IMF. When the negotiations with the IMF finally broke down, in mid-December 2011, Hungarian bonds were selling for less than their Italian and Spanish counterparts.

17. See Feher (2014a and 2014b) for more on the ECB's resistance to the politicisation of the MNB.

Spain, Italy, Greece, Estonia and Cyprus, Hungarian banks hadn't been forced to accept public financing solutions. Consequently, Hungarian authorities had little need or interest in transferring any of their regulatory authority or financial sovereignty over to a European banking union. As in Iceland, Hungary's ability to stay just beyond the reach of EU and IMF-imposed financial obligations (and subsequent designs for European banking union), allowed it to sustain a higher degree of popular authority and financial sovereignty.[18]

The new government was adamant about making foreign banks pay for their excesses in the run-up to the financial crisis (see below), and intended to weaken the country's reliance on foreign banks. Indeed, the government had an explicit goal to secure domestic ownership over 'at least' half of the Hungarian bank sector (Feher 2014c). To reach that goal, the state has re-established itself as a significant actor in the banking sector. Through a series of acquisitions, between 2013 and 2015, the government's ownership share of bank assets has increased significantly, to something like 20 per cent (Djankov 2015: 6).[19]

Finally, the government used the MNB to open up a new line of credit to help small and medium sized enterprises access forint-denominated loans. This was necessary to compensate for the excessive risk aversion of banks and the tight credit conditions that resulted. To meet these needs, the Funding for Growth Scheme was introduced in April 2013. During the first phase of the program (in 2013), about $2.8 billion (750 billion HUF) of credit was allocated to Hungarian firms. In 2014, the program was expanded by another $8 billion (*circa* eight per cent of GDP!), and broadened to include more types of borrowers, with increased lending limits. This innovative funding scheme is estimated to have contributed to an increase in the 2014 GDP on the order of 3.6 per cent (Djankov 2015: 7; MNB 2016a; MNB n.d.).

Unorthodox fiscal policies

The third prong of Hungary's novel response to the crisis was a series of unorthodox budget policies. Here the objective was to try and reduce indebtedness (in part, to secure greater political autonomy, as in the second prong) by making the wealthy pay for their (fair) share of the crisis and by adopting popular measures that could stimulate economic demand.

As we saw in Ireland, Hungary's debt problem was reframed from an economic to a political phenomenon – and became part of a drive to defend political sovereignty. In his (February 2011) State of the State address, Orbán declared

---

18. The eventual cost of bank recapitalisation in Hungary was so small that it doesn't show up as a separate item in the IMF's analysis. Emergency lending from the government to the banks in 2008 was repaid. 'It was Hungary's good fortune that other sovereigns bailed out the foreign-owned banks' (Mabbett and Schelkle 2015: 518).

19. In particular, the government secured control over two small banks (Széchenyi Bank and Gránit Bank) in 2013, Hungary's fifth largest bank, MKB, in 2014, and its eighth largest bank, Budapest Bank, in 2015. It has also developed an extensive bank branch network through the Hungarian Post, and opened new branches of the Hungarian Development Bank Group (a state-owned bank).

a '...war against government debt...We must and will defeat government debt, which is the source of most of our problems and difficulties today. If we do not overcome it, then it will overcome us once and for all' (Lambert n.d.). Later in that same year (21 June), Orbán noted that the battle against debt was a battle for political autonomy: he compared foreign debt to foreign domination, with reference to the Cold War:

> 'For us Hungarians this is important also because it has been around twenty years since the last soldier of the occupying Soviet army left Hungary and at that time many of us thought . . . that Hungary had thus regained its freedom and independence.' Over the past twenty years, Orbán noted, 'We had to bitterly experience the validity and truth of the old wisdom' that a nation can be subjugated in two ways – with the sword or with debt. Today in Hungary, seven of every ten forints in tax revenue must be used to pay off the government debt and "this cannot be called freedom even with the greatest amount of goodwill"' (Lambert n.d.).

The government's plan to pay down the debt was a radical one, and rested on three pillars: 1) drawing on those that had benefited most in the run-up to the crisis; 2) transferring significant wealth from private pension plans to a public pension plan; and 3) helping borrowers who were burdened with foreign loans (that had been growing due to a depreciation in the forint's value). We have already considered the third pillar – so let's take a closer look at the first two.

To help get its finances back on track, the government decided to milk the wealthy, rather than squeeze its workers: i.e., it chose just rewards over austerity. In particular, the government introduced a series of controversial taxes[20] on those sectors that were seen as most responsible for the crisis. These included the introduction of:

- a flat-rate personal income tax (set at 16 per cent);[21]
- a special 'bank tax' on corporations working in the financial, energy and telecommunication sectors;
- one of the biggest bank levies in Europe – at 0.6 per cent of the banks' total assets – in 2011 (Djankov 2015: 6); and
- a 98 per cent tax on severance pay packages (when they exceeded 3.5 million forints for ordinary employees; two million forints for state and local (public) officials).[22]

---

20. In addition, the marginal rate of the value added tax was raised to 27 per cent, the highest level in the EU (Djankov 2015: 5).

21. At the same time, the corporate income tax level was reduced.

22. The Constitutional Court ruled against this bill, and there was a subsequent debate about the tether of the court. In November 2010, the government initiated a constitutional amendment that curbed the constitutional court's powers over fiscal matters, and reinstated the legislation that the court had rejected (Várnagy 2011: 995).

While each part of this plan was controversial, the one that attracted the most critical attention was the one that did most to shrink the government's debt burden: the abolishment of mandatory private pension funds. The controversy resulted from the government's willingness to sacrifice one of the EU's sacred cows: paying down the debt was done by moving money from private to public hands.[23] Members of private funds were allowed to choose between moving their savings to the government-run programme, or opting for private funds (which meant that they would lose the right to a state pension after retirement). The assets managed by these private pension funds were then moved into the state budget, to reduce the level of public debt. As a result of this policy, $14 billion in assets (3,000 billion HUF), or roughly ten per cent of GDP, were transferred to the government, allowing it to significantly reduce its debt-level (Csaba 2013: 161).

'The Hungarian version of the private pension fund system did indeed exhibit many of the problems which persistently afflict us: it was expensively run, client protection was weak, and its regulation kept changing constantly. But there was a choice between two options: one was a reasonable re-regulation and the other was abolition. The government opted for the latter, and the restoration of the pay-as-you-go system: the whole amount of the social security contribution of the active workforce goes to the public fund, from which pensions are paid. Those who have paid their tax-like contributions receive in exchange a promise – which is legally difficult to interpret – that decades later the Parliament at the time will enact budget laws which ensure fair pensions for the retired, and impose taxes on the then active workforce. In any case, the government integrated the accumulated pension fund wealth into the 2011 national budget, and partly spent it in 2011' (Bod 2013: 23).

Hungarian officials responded to the crisis by choosing a radically different path: they hoped to grow their way out of the crisis (rather than embrace austerity), and transfer the burden of adjustment over to those who were best able to bear it: foreign banks and capital. Elected officials enjoyed this freedom of manoeuvre because they had not yet committed their forint to the Eurozone, and (consequently) were able to negotiate more scope for political autonomy.

As we shall see in the next section, this action attracted much critical attention from foreign bankers (and their home countries) and the European Commission – but it proved to be largely popular with Hungarians.

Relevant constituents

The Hungarian *sonderweg* attracted much critical attention from foreigners who are concerned about Hungary heading down a nationalist, illiberal, path. On

---

23. There is an enormous irony here, in that much of the sovereign debt crisis in Europe is the result of a similar sort of transfer (but of debt, not assets). As we saw in Latvia and in Ireland, governments have taken on significant levels of debt in order to bail out their financial sectors – in order to keep the European financial market afloat.

several different occasions, the financial sector (both domestic and foreign), the European Commission, and the home countries of those foreign banks that are active in Hungary have opposed the Hungarian government's attempt to pursue an autonomous policy.

I have already quoted from the 2011 Budapest Appeal, where a number of those that had fought against Communist regimes in Central and Eastern Europe came together and voiced concern about the direction of Hungary's political choices. While most of these criticisms have been aimed at the nature of constitutional reforms, a major reform of the media law, and the way that Hungary treats minorities and immigrants, there have also been significant criticisms of Hungary's economic policy.

For example, the Hungarian Banking Association asked the Hungarian Constitutional Court to declare the government's scheme to help foreign-mortgage borrowers to be unconstitutional, and an unjustified intervention into contracts between private parties. As foreign banks were hardest hit by this measure, Hungarian officials have been under significant pressure from their host governments (especially Austria, Italy and Germany).

The European Commission has also voiced opposition to the government's plan to punish the foreign banks (by helping borrowers unload their foreign loans), and it has opposed Hungary's special tax on telecommunications. In January 2012, the Commission launched three accelerated infringement proceedings against Hungary over: 1) its judiciary; 2) its data protection authorities; and 3) the independence of the MNB (Várnagy 2013: 96). At roughly the same time, on 18 January, the European Parliament dedicated a session to debate Hungarian affairs, where a number of concerns were voiced about Orbán's government and the functioning of Hungarian democracy.

Most interesting of all was the reaction to Hungary's effort to reduce its debt and deficit levels. As a result of the Orbán government's unorthodox policies, Hungary's deficit and debt positions have shown remarkable improvement: in 2011, the Hungarian budget recorded a surplus of 4.3 per cent, and in 2012 a small deficit (of just 1.9 per cent of GDP).[24] In short, the Hungarian economy is now preforming as expected, with a deficit well below the three per cent ceiling. But the European Commission didn't care for the way in which Hungary balanced its budget (especially the public takeover of private pension funds), and proposed (on 22 February 2012) that Hungary be punished by suspending some of the country's access to the EU's Cohesion Fund.[25] This marked the first time that the European

---

24. The European Commission and ECOFIN refused to recognise the 2011 budget surplus. On 11 January 2012, the European Commission proposed that the Excessive Deficit Procedure be maintained against Hungary; and on 24 January 2012, the ECOFIN approved the Commission proposal.

25. The EU Cohesion Funding is allocated to member states whose GDP is less than 90 per cent of the EU average in order to finance investments to improve infrastructure and protect the environment. In particular, the Commission proposed to suspend 29 per cent of the 2013 Fund, worth €1.7 billion. On 13 March 2012, the ECOFIN approved the Commission's proposal to suspend Hungary's 2013 Cohesion Fund support.

Commission had *ever* initiated a suspension of the Cohesion Funds subsidies for an EU member state. Eventually, the European Commission reversed its decision: on 30 May 2012 it withdrew its recommendation that the Cohesion Fund subsidies be withdrawn, and lifted the Excessive Deficit Procedure that had been in place against Hungary since 2004.

While the international community's condemnation of Hungarian policies is disconcerting, that community is not really the appropriate constituency for evaluating the success of Hungarian policy. More relevant are the attitudes of those living in Hungary, those who Hungary's elected official are supposed to represent. Is it possible to gauge the degree to which Hungarians, themselves, are satisfied with the government's unique political path?

Before the crisis, in 2007, Hungarians were among the most pessimistic citizens in Europe: about half of the Hungarian respondents to the 2007 Eurobarometer did not expect any improvement in their life situation in the coming year, and a significant proportion expected things to get worse. At the time, Hungarians were pessimistic about the future of their country: only ten per cent expected an improvement over the following twelve months, whether it was in the country's economic or employment situation, or in their own job or household financial situation. In 2007, a higher proportion of Hungarians trusted the EU, while a smaller share trusted in their own national government, relative to the EU-average (Eurobarometer 2007: 2–3).

While the level of pessimism remains high in Hungary, it has decreased in recent years and is approaching the European average. This can be seen in Figure 7.3, which compares the share of those Hungarian (and EU-average) respondents who think that their current economic situation is bad. While it is not possible to see a noticeable impact of a new (2010) Orbán government on the Hungarian indicator, the level of economic optimism begins to increase (the share of 'bad' responses decreased) in 2012, and continues to fall to this day. Still over 70 per cent of the Hungarian respondents (and over 60 per cent of the EU-average respondents) perceive their 2014 economic situation to be bad. This is not very encouraging – even if it is a slight improvement over pre-crisis perceptions.

The impact of Orbán's *sonderweg* may be more evident when we look at the level of faith that Hungarians have in their domestic political institutions, which has been increasing since 2009. Each of the Eurobarometer's domestic trust indicators (trust in political parties, trust in national parliament, trust in national government), shows a strong rise in trust among Hungarians in 2010 – although there is a serious correction in 2011–12 and the effect dissipates somewhat since. In 2010,[26] it would seem, Hungarians were excited (and supportive) of

---

26. Note that the Hungarian election was set on 11 and 25 April, and the Orbán II government came to power on 29 May 2010. This is precisely the time when the Eurobarometer (EB73) questions were being fielded: in May 2010. Hence, when the 2010 score appears as an outlier (as it does here), we should be aware that it is probably affected by the ongoing election campaign. In November, when EB75 was conducted, the trust in political institutions questions were not asked.

Figure 7.3: Belief that current economic situation is bad, Hungary and EU-average, 2005–2014

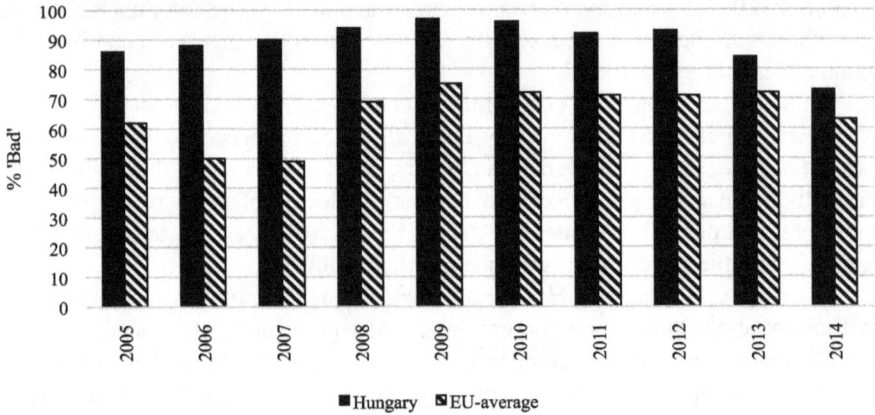

■Hungary ▨EU-average

Note: This is the response of those who answer 'Bad' to the question: 'How would you judge the current situation of the (NATIONAL) economy?' EU-average varies over time: 2003 = EU-15; 2004–6 = EU-25; 2007–2013 = EU-27; 2014 = EU-28.
Source: Eurobarometer, various years.

Figure 7.4: Trust in national government, Hungary and EU-average, 2004–2014

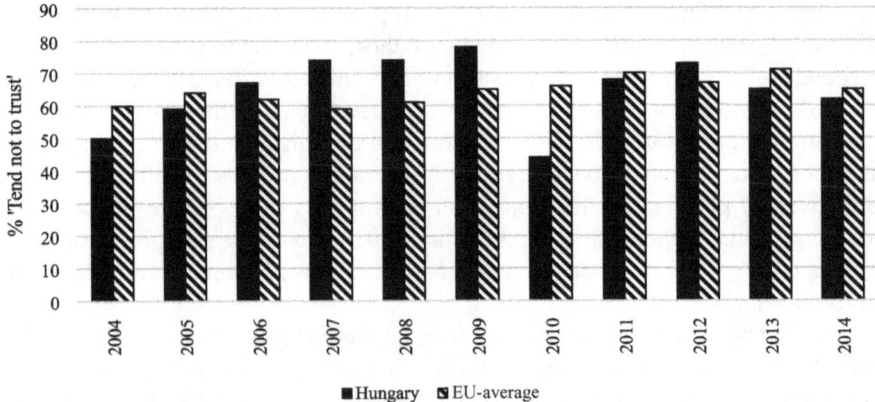

■Hungary ▨EU-average

Note: Tracks those who respond 'Tend not to trust' to the following question: 'I would like to ask you a question about how much trust you have in certain institutions....Please tell me if you tend to trust or tend not to trust the (NATIONALITY) GOVERNMENT.' EU-average varies over time: 2003 = EU-15; 2004–6 = EU-25; 2007–2013 = EU-27; 2014 = EU-28.
Source: Eurobarometer, various years.

the new government's plans for a radical change in direction. This may simply signal a critical judgement of the earlier government (rather than support for the *sonderweg*) – but at least we are seeing some progress in the trust indicators.

Figure 7.4 compares Hungarian and EU-average scores on trust in national governments.[27] As the level of trust is low, below 50 per cent most of the time, Figure 7.4 compares the share of respondents who 'tend not to trust' their home government. In the figure, we see the EU-average level of distrust (i.e., those who 'tend not to trust') in their national governments to be rising slowly but steadily. The Hungarian distrust figures, by contrast, are much more volatile, but the level of Hungarian trust in government (and parliament) has actually grown, relative to the pre-crisis period. In other words, whereas Hungarians were less trustful than the average European before the 2010 election, they have since become more so – with the exception of 2012 (but even in 2012, the lack of trust is lower than it was in the 2007–2009 period).

While Hungarians have begun to trust their political institutions more, their attitude towards the euro has grown much more sceptical. Since joining the EU in 2004, Hungarians have always been less sceptical to the euro than the average European. But that scepticism grew significantly after 2010 (and much faster than it was growing in Europe, on average). For example, when we look at the share of the respondents that oppose the adoption of a single currency (euro), as is done in Figure 7.5, we see a remarkable rise in opposition after 2010. In 2011, the level of Hungarian opposition to the euro approaches the European average, and this opposition stays at the higher level for the remainder of the recorded period.

Figure 7.5: Opposition to euro, Hungary and EU-average, 2004–2014

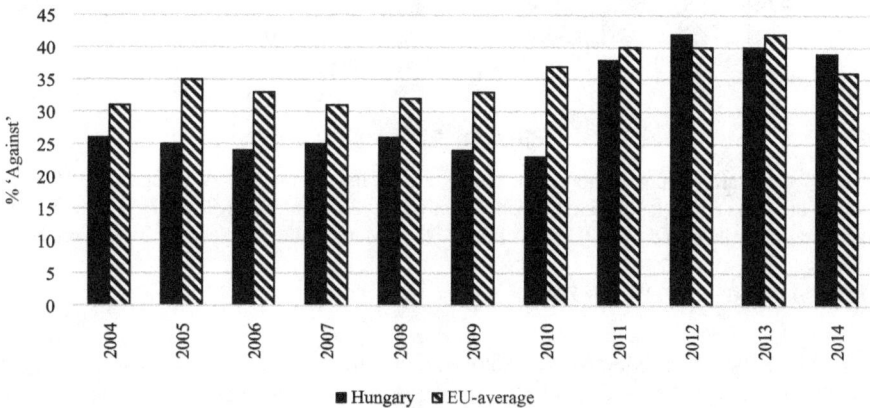

■ Hungary ◩ EU-average

Note: Share who responded 'Against' to the following question: 'Please tell me whether you are for or against a European Monetary Union with one single currency, the euro?' EU-average varies over time: 2003 = EU-15; 2004–6 = EU-25; 2007–2013 = EU-27; 2014 = EU-28.
Source: Eurobarometer, various years.

---

27. Hungarian levels of distrust in political parties and the national parliament are closer to the European average, but reveal a similar pattern: higher in 2007–2009, but lower and more similar since.

It is important not to read too much into these opinion changes, as a more pessimistic account can be found in responses to another Eurobarometer question: one that gauges whether Hungarians are dissatisfied with the way in which democracy works at home (Figure 7.6). Given the government's willingness to pursue a more populist response to the financial crisis, we might expect this indicator to show a market improvement after 2010, compared to the EU average. But the highest point of democratic satisfaction in Hungary seems to be in 2006 (before the Orbán government!), when roughly half of the respondents were satisfied/dissatisfied with the way democracy works. Instead, Hungarians tend to be much more sceptical than the average European about how democracy works at home, and these levels have stayed relatively constant since the turn of the millennium.

Figure 7.6: Dissatisfaction with democracy at home, Hungary and EU-average, 2004 – 2014

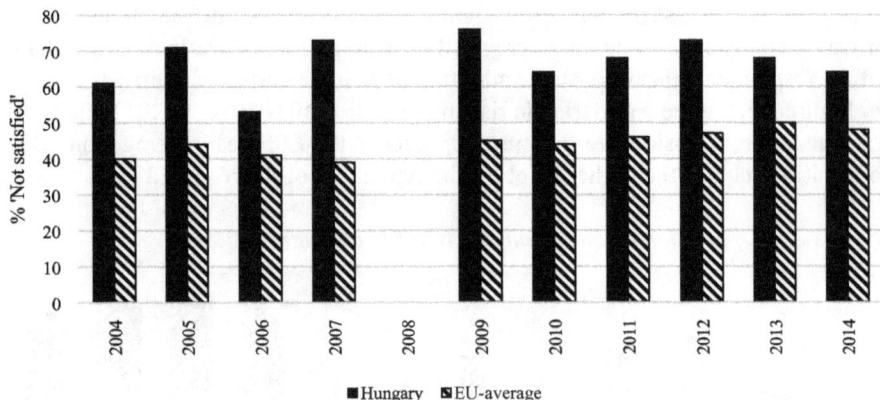

Note: Total share of those who responded 'Not satisfied' to the following question: 'On the whole, are you very satisfied, fairly satisfied, not very satisfied or not at all satisfied with the way democracy works in (OUR COUNTRY)?' NB: the question does not seem to have been asked in 2008.
Source: Eurobarometer, various years

This lack of satisfaction is also evident in another set of responses to a question that is directed squarely at the home government's response to the financial crisis. In 2012, Eurobarometer asked whether respondents felt that their national government had acted effectively in response to the crisis. A comparison of European and Hungarian responses, as shown in Figure 7.7, shows that Hungarians were less forgiving than the average European respondent: the share of those that thought the government responded effectively was actually lower than the European average. Hungarians don't seem to think that their *sonderweg* has been very effective at dealing with the crisis – compared to the average European response. More worrisome, perhaps, is the size of the 'Not effective' response – for both Europeans and Hungarians: 76 per cent of Hungarians respondents felt that the government response was 'Not effective'.

Figure 7.7 Attitudes about government response to the crisis, Hungary and EU-average, 2012

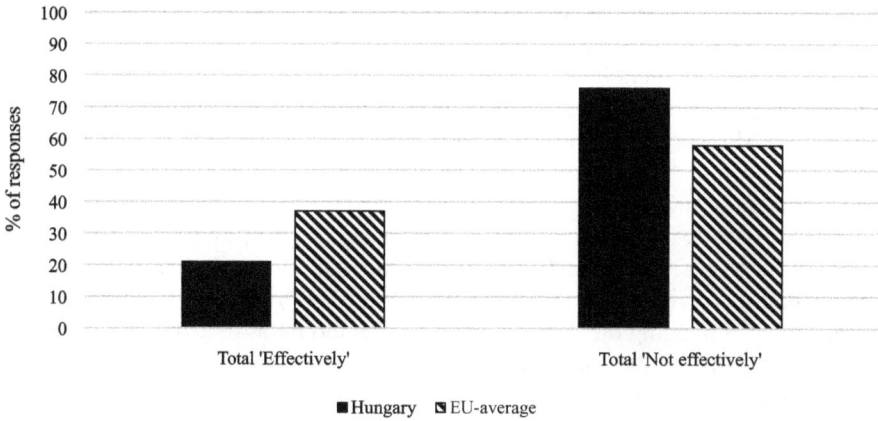

Note: Aggregate responses of those that answer 'Effectively' and 'Not effectively' to question QC82: 'Since the beginning of the crisis, would you say that the (NATIONALITY) GOVERNMENT has acted effectively or not to combat the crisis up to now?' Questions asked in May, 2012.
Source: Eurobarometer (2012: QC82)

While it is difficult to find strong support for the *sonderweg* in the Eurobarometer data, there are no signs that Hungarians are terribly dissatisfied with the direction their country is headed – if anything, one can see feint signs of support, in that trust figures have increased, along with opposition to the euro. Unlike in the other cases, we do not see massive demonstrations against the government. Quite the contrary: in January 2011, more than 100,000 demonstrators came out in support of government policies. The counter-demonstration on 15 March, was only able to mobilise 15,000 citizens (Várnagy 2012: 130). Perhaps the best indicator of the support that Hungarians are willing to give to the government's unorthodox policies is in returning the government to power in the 2014 election, with another substantial majority.

Recent developments

As Hungary didn't have to bail out a failed banking system, the state of its economy was neither as precarious or as dire as it was in the other cases. Contrary to the expectations of many who have criticised the reforms, the Hungarian economy has not been adversely hit by the decision to stake out a more autonomous economic path. Economic growth has returned to Hungary, without any noticeable sign of inflation; the government has pursued a very conservative fiscal policy, producing small budget deficits (and reducing the national debt slowly over time); and Hungary enjoys a healthy current account surplus. While income inequality has grown since 2010 (*see* Figure 3.11), it remains lower than both the EA-average and three of the other cases (the exception is Iceland). Neither is Hungary haemorrhaging its workforce, as are Ireland and Latvia. Conditions remain good enough to keep Hungarians looking for work and economic opportunity at home.

The darkest shadow in the Hungarian economy is cast by the country's stubborn unemployment level, which remains high (7.8 per cent in 2014) – but is improving. In the most recent Eurostat data at the time of this writing (February 2016 data), Hungary's unemployment level was down to 5.8 per cent – below both Ireland (8.8 per cent) and Latvia (10.1 per cent), but above that in Iceland (3.2 per cent) (Eurostat, [une_rt_m]).

On the political front, Hungary continues to draw critical attention for its willingness to blaze an autonomous path, and this has provoked a number of commentators to voice concern about the country's retreat from liberalism, even democracy.[28] Engaging this literature will take us too far away from our objective, which is to consider whether Hungary was able to use an autonomous monetary policy to secure a more popular, democratically-accountable, outcome. On this account, the answer is clear: Hungary's capacity to be different is, in large part, due to the autonomy provided by the country's willingness to maintain its own currency and monetary policy.

Conclusion

Hungary is one of the most politically unique and independent states in Europe. As a result, Hungary has gained a reputation as a political maverick: Hungarian authorities have prioritised national (and nationalist) solutions, at the expense of international commercial and financial interests. More recently, Poland seems to have joined Hungary in wishing to break out of what is perceived to be a European policy straightjacket: it too has embraced more nationalistic positions, and shown a willingness to impose greater political constraints on its constitution and media. It seems that the political constraints being imposed by liberal economic doctrine (and Europe's one-size-fits-all economic policies) are creating conditions that feed the flames of nationalism in Europe.[29]

Most of Hungary's headline-grabbing activities are focused in the areas of migration, media control and constitutional reform. This chapter had endeavoured to show that this spirit of policy autonomy is also evident in Hungary's approach to economic policy, especially monetary policy.

As Abby Innes has noted, since 2010 Hungary has steered away from the liberal, market-oriented stance that the EU and IMF have been selling, to embrace a new type of economic nationalism:

'...the Orbán government has nationalized Hungary's largely foreign-controlled private pension funds; levied windfall taxes on banking, telecommunications,

---

28. For a sampling of this recent literature, see Ágh (2015); Bayer (2013); Berend and Bugaric (2015); Hanley and Dawson (2016) and Innes (2015).

29. For a discussion of the Polish cases along these lines, see, e.g., Karolewski and Benedikter (2016).

energy, and retail companies (sectors with a high proportion of foreign companies); made mandatory cuts in utility prices and bought out the companies exiting in response; restricted international corporate takeovers; nationalized and in short order reprivatized Hungary's largest banking cooperative; and passed a law that enabled a significant redistribution of lucrative—and EU-subsidized—agricultural land...' (Innes 2015: 95).

Much of this economic nationalism could have occurred in the absence of an autonomous monetary policy – but having an independent central bank, a national currency, and a financial system that was still under domestic regulatory authority surely helped. Obviously, the advantage of currency depreciation and major central bank reforms are not available to states that have jettisoned their currencies to join the Eurozone. But many of Hungary's other policy choices (e.g. special taxes on finance; forcing the banks to clean up their mess; increasing the state's role in securing financing...) are still available to other states in the Eurozone. In making those choices, however, states risk alienating the international market and the international political community which supports it (read the EU).

Hungary was willing to take those risks. Indeed, those risks were smaller in Hungary, because it still enjoyed an autonomous monetary policy and an independent central bank. In taking on those risks, however, Hungary needed to secure a degree of economic self-sufficiency from international banks, the IMF and the EU. The government used its political influence over the central bank, and the parliament, to put its economic house in order. This, in turn, allowed it greater freedom of manoeuvre in dealing with both its internal and external constituents.

It is not necessary to embrace Hungary's policy choices to recognise that they are both unique and a reflection of domestic preferences. If states are free to pursue autonomous policies, we should expect to see more variation across national policies—as this variation will reflect the (varied) will of their domestic constituents. By maintaining a degree of monetary policy autonomy, governments can pursue policies of the left, or the right, depending on the pressures emanating from within.

Chapter Eight

Conclusion

Roughly eight years have passed since a global financial crisis rocked Iceland, Ireland, Latvia and Hungary. Eight years should be long enough to evaluate their varying national responses to that crisis and to establish whether small states were able to exert autonomous and effective monetary policies. In this concluding chapter, I pull together the case study evidence from Chapters Four–Seven, along with the descriptive statistics in Chapter Three, to tally the political and economic costs and benefits of weathering a major financial crisis as a member of Europe's monetary union.

This post-crisis tally reveals clear costs – both political and economic – to membership in the monetary union. Contrary to popular perception, small states still wield effective monetary policies, to the benefits of their constituents. Hence, when entering a monetary union, states jettison an effective set of policy tools, and this has important economic and political consequences. In economic terms, this study reveals that states outside the Eurozone experienced a briefer and shallower economic crisis, compared to those who were bound to the euro. Politically, citizens of states with their own currency enjoyed greater influence over policy outcomes; while the voice of citizens in Eurozone countries – by contrast – fell mostly on deaf ears. Consequently, Eurozone citizens were more often forced to vote with their feet.

Economic benefits of monetary policy autonomy

This study was designed to test the effectiveness of two competing strategies for economic recovery: an external and an internal (devaluation) strategy. States in a monetary union lose the possibility of pursuing an external devaluation strategy. These states must improve their international competitiveness by lowering wages (and prices, more generally). This is done by succumbing to the market: unemployment is allowed to rise such that workers will accept lower wages (for fear of being underbid by a growing army of unemployed), or move to another country (where there are jobs to be had). This period of transition can be painful and slow, as it takes time for market incentives to work their way through the economy.[1] The political benefit of this strategy is that the resulting pain can be blamed on a faceless market (not elected officials). The economic benefit of this strategy is that it promises to deliver stronger, more resilient, long-term growth.

---

1. After all, how long would you wait, and how high would unemployment rates need to rise, before *you* would accept a reduction in your salary/wage rate?

On the other hand, states that control their own monetary policy can use capital controls, depreciations/devaluations, and a more responsive central bank (and regulatory institutions) to respond to constituent needs. In allowing their currency to depreciate in value, national authorities shift domestic demand away from foreign goods and services, while their exported goods and services become more price competitive, internationally. On both domestic and foreign fronts, the resulting increase in demand can propel an economy out of recession. While a depreciation provides an immediate adjustment in prices and demand, detractors of this strategy note that it can produce unwanted inflation (as domestic wages and prices fill the resulting price gap, produced by the depreciation) and increased lending costs (due to decreased market confidence).

In this study, variants of these two strategies were employed by four very different states. Among them, Ireland enjoyed the fewest options: having jettisoned its currency, the Irish people were obliged to follow an internal devaluation strategy (as the cost of re-instituting an autonomous monetary policy – e.g., a return of the punt, the imposition of capital controls – would be too costly). Iceland, by contrast, enjoyed the greatest scope for policy autonomy: being less entwined in the demands of Eurozone membership, it could devalue and regroup around its sovereign institutions. Hungary and Latvia found themselves somewhere in between: they had to commit to one strategy or the other in responding to the crisis. For reasons that were elaborated upon in the preceding country chapters, Latvia chose the Irish path; Hungary the Icelandic.

This section assesses the economic costs and benefits of these two very different recovery strategies. While Chapter Three provided very rough indicators of the scope of the crisis in our four cases, these indicators are not very useful for evaluating the policy responses to the crisis. For this, I propose to compare, across time and cases, the depth and the length of the economic crisis – measured in terms of both GDP and unemployment.

Figure 8.1 compares GDP developments over time. At the heart of this figure lie seasonally and calendar-adjusted GDP data, by quarter, in the national currency for each case (Latvia was denominated in euros). This data is used to establish a proxy date for when the crisis started in each country: the first quarter of negative growth. I then created an index for each GDP time series, anchored to that particular point in time (the start of the crisis). For example, in Iceland, the first quarter of negative growth came in the fourth quarter of 2009 (2009Q4). For the Icelandic data, then, the GDP was re-calibrated at this date (t = 100), and the time series was indexed accordingly. Hence, for Iceland, t = 2009Q4; t+1 = 2010Q1; t+2 = 2010Q2, etc. The same procedure was conducted on the other three cases. This sort of re-calibration allows us to compare both the depth and the length of the crisis in each case, where time 't' represents the (varying) start of the crisis. The resulting Figure (8.1) clearly depicts two very different recovery trajectories: a high road and a low road. States that maintained their national currencies (and corresponding monetary policies) were able to ascend the high road through the crisis; those linked to the euro were bound to the low road.

Figure 8.1: GDP trends

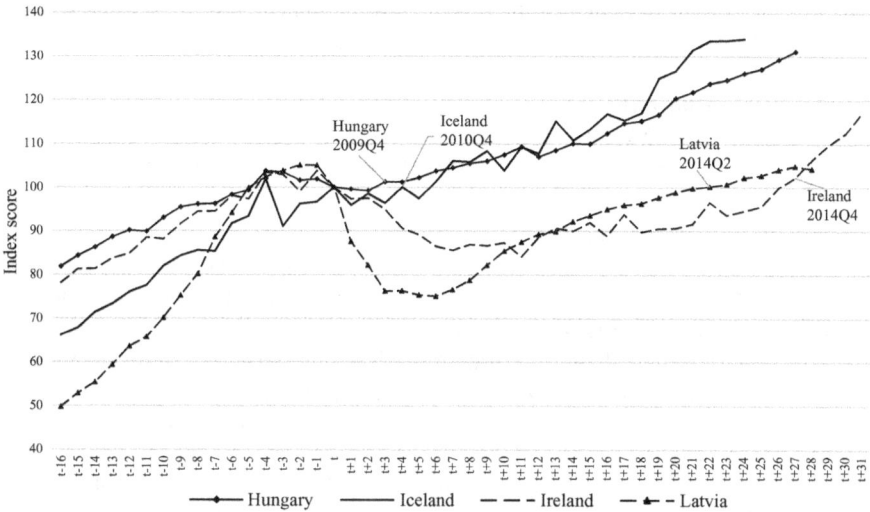

Note: Each GDP indicator uses seasonally- and calendar-adjusted data in the national currency (Latvia was in euros). I then set the index year (t) for the first quarter that GDP actually fell (negative growth). Thus, for Hungary, 100 = 2009Q1; Iceland, 100 = 2009Q4; Ireland, 100 = 2008Q1; and Latvia, 100 = 2008Q4. I then compared quarterly developments, both before (t-16) and after (t+31) the start of the recession. Hence, for Hungary, t = 2009Q1, t+1 = 2009Q2, t+3 = 2009Q3, etc. The figure also notes the date at which GDP in each country returned to its pre-crisis level. By comparing this initial point with the point at which the same level of GDP was restored, we find that the crisis lasted for only three quarters in Hungary; four quarters for Iceland, 27 quarters for Ireland, and 22 quarters for Latvia.
Source: Eurostat (2016)

Consider first, the high-growth path taken by Hungary and Iceland. We know that the nature of the crisis in Hungary was different – so we should ignore this case for now, and focus on Iceland's recovery. In Iceland, despite a huge financial crisis (where 13 per cent of the country's GDP was used to bail out the banking sector, cf. Table 1.1), the economy recovered very rapidly. As just described, Iceland first experienced negative growth in 2009Q4, but just one year later (2010Q4), its GDP had returned to the same level as before the crisis, and it has continued to grow ever since. Iceland's recession was remarkably shallow and short-lived: it took just one year (four quarters) for the economy to return to its pre-crisis GDP level. It should go without saying (but I'll say it anyway): a longer and deeper recession would have increased the suffering of Iceland's most vulnerable residents.

Along the low-growth path we find Ireland and Latvia enduring much deeper and longer-lasting crises. In Latvia it took 22 quarters (over five years!) before the country's GDP was able to rebound. While Latvia's celebrated economic recovery is evident in the figure (from t+7 onward), it appears far less impressive when placed in this sort of comparative and temporal context. Although the Irish crisis was less deep than in Latvia, it took longer for Ireland's economy to recover. It was not before 2014Q4, or *28 quarters later*, that the Irish economy was back to where it had been before the crisis had started.

If you were an unemployed worker in one of these three countries, where would you rather be? Would you prefer to live in a country where the crisis was limited in depth and length, or one where it took years to recover? In responding to questions like these, Irish and Latvian workers left their country in droves, in hopes of finding better employment opportunities elsewhere.

When evaluating a country's response to the crisis, it is useful to consider its relative debt burden. Figure 3.5 compared increases of government debt in response to the financial crisis (measured as a percentage of GDP, over the years 2007–2013), to suggest that the overall cost of the recession was largest in Ireland, followed by Iceland, Latvia and Hungary. In light of these varying debt burdens, it is easier to see why the Irish recovery (illustrated in Figure 8.1) was so lengthy, while the Hungarian recovery was so short.

In making this comparison, however, we implicitly assume that each country shares similar priorities with respect to how a government should respond to the crisis, and its willingness to go into debt. As we have seen, this is clearly not the case. While some states used debt and deficits to shield their workers from the crisis, others preferred to appease international investors and creditors by quickly balancing government budgets and minimising their debt load. Latvia is a prime example of the latter: its level of government debt is remarkably low (never exceeding 40 per cent of GDP), given the depth of its economic crisis (and the misery it caused for so many Latvians).

By comparing both debt and GDP-growth levels, we can better see how quickly Iceland managed to recover (given its larger debt burden), relative to Latvia. In light of its relatively light debt-burden, Latvia should have experienced a shorter (and shallower) recession. Iceland's success, by this measure, is a function of its ability to wield an autonomous monetary policy.

The same two-track pattern – between states that were bound to the euro, and those that were not – is also evident in their unemployment trends. Figure 8.2 offers a temporal comparison of unemployment levels across the four cases, using the same sort of comparative framework as in Figure 8.1. In this figure, however, the unemployment figures are not indexed, so that they retain their intuitive value.[2] Like Figure 8.1, the time series in Figure 8.2 is re-calibrated, such that time 't' is set for the first quarter of negative economic growth in each case.

---

2.   In other words, the numbers are already comparable (per cent of labour force that is unemployed), and we understand what 20 per cent unemployed means (whereas reading a '94' on the index scale has less intuitive value).

Figure 8.2: Unemployment trends

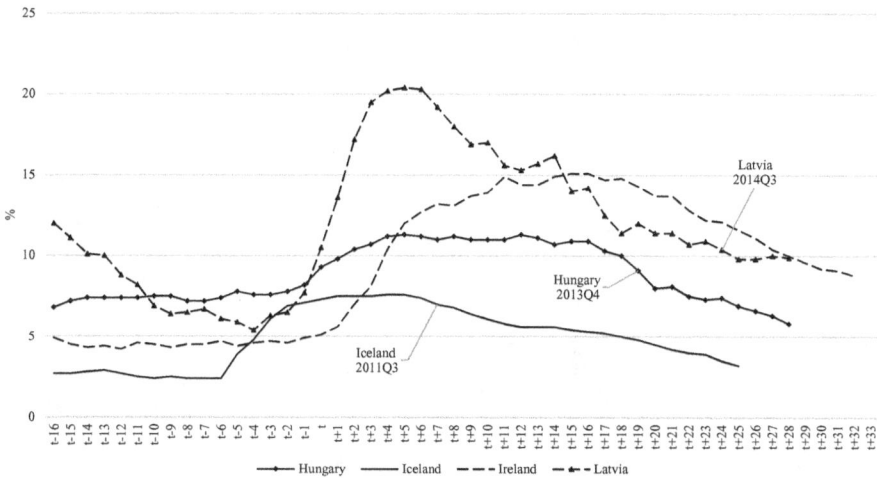

Note: The unemployment rate is based on the quarterly average, per cent, seasonally adjusted. The index years are set for the same time as in Figure 8.1 (i.e., for Hungary, t = 2009Q1; Iceland, t = 2009Q4; Ireland, t = 2008Q1; and Latvia, t = 2008Q4). I then compared quarterly developments in each country's unemployment rate, both before (t-16) and after (t+32) the start of the recession. Hence, for Hungary, t = 2009Q1, t+1 = 2009Q2, t+3 = 2009Q3, etc.
Source: Eurostat [une_rt_q]

In Figure 8.2 we can see how states that maintained monetary policy autonomy suffered less unemployment over a shorter period of time than those that were bound to the euro. In Iceland, unemployment returned to its pre-crisis level after seven quarters (2011Q3); whereas it took Latvia 24 quarters (2014Q) to manage the same task (albeit at a higher level of unemployment)! At the end of the quarterly unemployment data (2016Q1), Ireland has still not managed to return to its pre-crisis unemployment level. Not only did it take longer for euro-bound states to return to their pre-crisis unemployment levels, but the overall level of unemployment in both Latvia and Ireland is significantly higher than what we see in Iceland (especially) and Hungary.[3]

The EU's most recent (monthly) unemployment data, set in real time, show how all four countries have experienced a gentle reduction in their unemployment levels (*see* Figure 8.3). In January 2016, Iceland's unemployment rate has shrunk to just three per cent. The unemployment levels in Latvia and Ireland, by contrast, are three (!) times higher: 8.9 per cent in Ireland and 10.6 per cent in Latvia. In Hungary, the unemployment level in January 2016 is about twice that in Iceland: 6.1 per cent.

---

3. The Hungarian unemployment figures are relatively flat, revealing – once again – that the Hungarian situation was not as dire as in the other states.

Figure 8.3: Recent unemployment rates, monthly

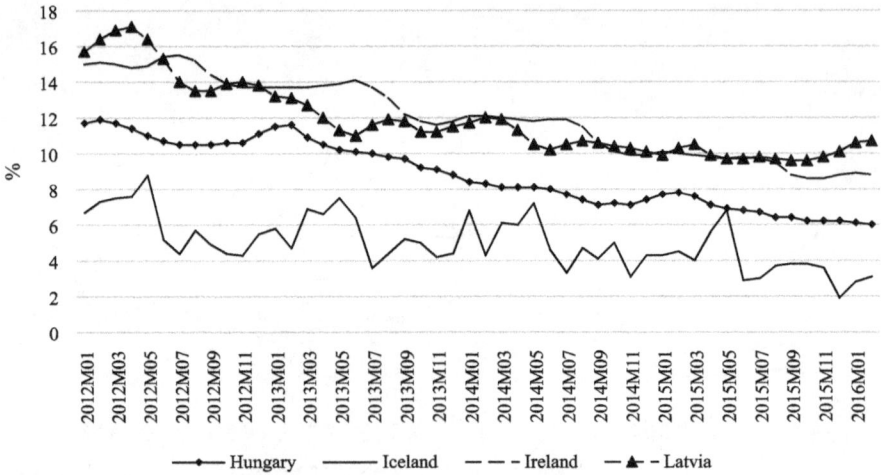

Note: Unadjusted unemployment rate, monthly average, per cent
Source: Eurostat [une_rt_m]

From these figures we can clearly see two very different policy paths available to small states in Europe. Those states that did not jettison their monetary policies have been able to secure better economic outcomes (in terms of both GDP performance and unemployment levels). As we found in the case study evidence, these countries used capital controls, currency depreciations and domestic legislation to prioritise the interests of domestic constituents over those of international markets and creditor institutions. But what about the potential downsides of these decisions? After all, detractors of this approach warn of an increased threat of inflation (undermining the very gains secured by the depreciation) and lending costs (as a signal of market's dissatisfaction). Have these costs come to bear?

Chapter Two has already noted the distributional consequences of pursuing a low inflationary path. Still, nobody benefits from a very high (or worse, volatile) rate of inflation. Hence, if Iceland and Hungary suffered run-a-way inflation as a result of their (monetary) policy autonomy, there would be good grounds for concern.[4] But we already know this did not happen: all four cases reveal relatively low levels of inflation after 2010, with little notable difference separating Latvia and Ireland from Iceland and Hungary (*see* Figure 3.6). Indeed, the two states that suffered the highest levels of inflation (in 2008–2009), were Iceland and Latvia – with Latvia experiencing the worst cases (both in 2008, but again in 2012). While Iceland's inflation rate is slightly higher than the other cases in 2013, and this inflation is probably the result of the króna's depreciation, a four per cent inflation level is a relatively small price to pay for a shorter and shallower economic crisis.

---

4. This is not to suggest that a moderate level of inflation is necessarily detrimental for a country. A moderate level of inflation can be used to pay down debts and smooth the transition to recovery.

Market sentiment seems to concur about the benefits of an external devaluation strategy. Figure 8.4 shows the rates offered on long-term (10-year) government bond yields, and this figure can be used as a surrogate for market confidence in a government's policy. If the market believes a country is not pursuing sound economic policies, it will punish it by demanding a higher yield on that state's bonds.

Figure 8.4: Harmonised long-term interest rates

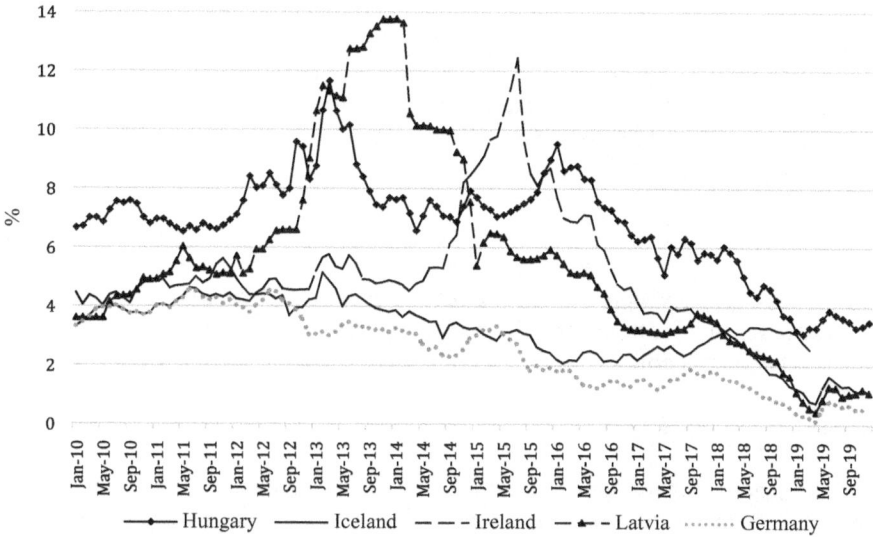

Note: ECB data is the monthly, long-term interest rate for convergence purposes. Debt-security issued, 10-yr maturity. The FRED data is long-term government bond yields, 10-year main (including benchmarks), monthly, not seasonally adjusted. For Germany, Hungary, and Ireland, the ECB and FRED data are exact duplicates, but the Icelandic figures were limited to FRED (2016).
Sources: ECB (2016) and FRED (2016)

When interpreted in this light, Figure 8.4 reveals significant market scepticism about the internal devaluation strategy. In the heat of the crisis – when the financing needs of the state are most precarious – both Latvia and Ireland faced cripplingly-high bond yields (above 12 per cent). The Icelandic rates, by contrast, remained remarkably low (always below six per cent). Indeed, the Icelandic yields seem to track Germany's for most of the period (until January 2014, when they began to increase, moderately). After 2011, the interest rates on Irish and Latvian long-term government bonds decreased significantly, so that by 2015 these countries are able to borrow at roughly the German rate. Today it is possible for all four states to sell government bonds with relatively reasonable yields, with Hungary having to pay the highest price, followed by Iceland, then Ireland and Latvia.

With regard to both inflation and lending costs, then, it would seem there are small, long-term costs to maintaining an autonomous monetary policy, relative to those economies that were bound to the euro. But the economic gains derived from that autonomy – in the form of quicker economic recovery and lower rates of unemployment – clearly trump those relatively minor costs.

The political costs of monetary union

The four cases also sort themselves with regard to political costs and benefits. Here too, it is possible to detect two very different routes to recovery. One group of countries is more able (or willing) to respond to domestic pressures and immediate needs. The other group of countries is betting on the long game: they have directed policy to satisfy international constituents (whether investor confidence or the demands of institutional creditors, such as the EU and the IMF) and the hope of long-term growth – at the expense of more immediate constituent needs.

The first group of countries chose the Embedded strategy depicted in Figure 2.1: they prioritised the needs of the demos over that of markets. The second group of countries chose a Faustian strategy: in exchange for immediate democratic accountability, they opted for what they hoped would be a greater economic reward (over time). These very different political choices were largely determined by whether a state could control its own monetary policy.

Embedded responses

Iceland and Hungary employed their own constellation of monetary policy instruments to create more sovereign space in a global economy under crisis. Among these instruments were different regulatory and legislative orders, capital controls, explicit constraints on the central bank (and its governors) and – of course – currency depreciations. As a consequence, political agitation in these countries – whether in the form of protests or elections – delivered real policy changes. This popular pressure resulted not just in elections, and changes in government, but in different (and better) economic results, for the benefit of the entire population (including the most vulnerable). By allowing the value of their currencies to fluctuate, political leaders were able to secure some sovereign breathing space, and an opportunity to do the right thing.

> 'Indeed, the right of devaluation is nothing other than an institutional expression of respect for nations (represented by their states) as special communities involving a shared life and destiny. It serves as a brake on the pressure for capitalist expansion and rationalization spreading outward from core to periphery. And to the interests and identities confronted with that pressure, which in the free trade world of the Great Single Market would otherwise be driven toward populism and nationalism, it offers a realistic collective alternative to the obedient self-commodification demanded of them by the market. Countries able to devalue can decide for themselves whether, and at what speed, they wish to discard their pre-capitalist or anti-capitalist heritage,

and in which direction they want to transform it. For this reason, more than anything else, the option of devaluation is a thorn in the flesh of single-market totalitarianism' (Streeck 2014: 181–82).

Having an independent currency (and central bank) provides countries with real policy latitude. This latitude allowed Iceland more options than those states that had committed to defending the Eurozone. Only in Iceland did a newly-elected prime minister (Johanna Sigurdardottir) demand the resignation of the country's central bank governors. No other country held its politicians accountable to the same degree; no other country conducted such a transparent review of the wrongdoings; no other country held a referendum to decide whether foreign bank interests should be bailed out; no other country responded with such a widespread reform of both its economic and political institutions. Even the *Financial Times* (2011) noted with approval that Iceland had put its citizens before its banks. Iceland's success in overcoming the crisis is evidenced by the fact that it scored third in the *World Happiness Report 2016*, after Denmark and Switzerland (Helliwell *et al.* 2016).

This sort of policy latitude was also evident in Hungary, where a newly-elected government turned the tables on international creditors who wished to impose austerity on the country. In an effort to stimulate economic growth, pay down its debt, and protect its constituents, the Orbán government introduced a number of radical (and protective) measures, while letting the forint depreciate vis-à-vis the euro. Although the economic situation in Hungary was less dire than in Latvia, both countries had previously been committed to Eurozone membership, and both countries enjoyed the option of loosening their ties to the euro. Unlike Latvia, Hungary chose to attend to constituent needs rather than defend its commitment to the Eurozone.

In both Iceland and Hungary, political elites were willing to consider and pursue unconventional (even radical) approaches to monetary policy – whether it was redefining the scope of autonomy at the central bank (à la Hungary), or re-thinking the fractional reserve system of money creation (in Iceland). In both countries, political authorities were willing to protect the scope of sovereign authority and impose real costs on those who had been responsible for the financial crisis. In both country responses, politics was allowed to trump markets.

Faustian responses

None of these options were available in Latvia or Ireland: euro membership (or the lure of such) kept them off the table. Elected officials in Ireland and Latvia were committed to defend the Eurozone system, and the interests of their own (domestic) economic elites. In doing so, they prioritised the needs of creditors (both national and international; individual and institutional) over the explicit demands of their constituents. This is especially evident in the Irish case, where the futility of national elections, in the face of signed international agreements, was evident for all to see.

Ireland could neither devalue nor let its banks fail, as the ECB insisted that Ireland hold the line (for fear of contagion to the rest of the Eurozone). Irish authorities, early on, decided to play the confidence game, and it has cost the people of Ireland dearly. Even after a tumultuous election, with much talk about radical reforms, the new government was unable to deliver any sort of significant improvement on its bailout terms. In Ireland, voters asked for change, but the hands of policy makers were tied by their commitment to the larger (European) community and their willingness to protect the interests of financial elites over those of the Irish electorate. When given a choice between 'Labour's way' or 'Frankfurt's way', the Irish electorate chose Labour's way, but ended up with Frankfurt.

Latvia enjoyed more options, but the country's political elites chose to signal their commitment to the Eurozone. Latvia's workers (and those who relied on public services) ended up paying the cost. Latvia began the crisis with the smallest bank sector (relative to the other two, as a percentage of GDP), but it ended up paying the highest price for rescuing that sector (in terms of unemployment), because it was unwilling to increase its debt exposure, and/or devalue its currency. As a consequence, Latvia's electorate (as in Ireland) was hammered by unemployment, emigration, reduced public spending and growing levels of poverty.

In the end, of course, Ireland and Latvia may yet secure the promised economic reward of monetary union. These rewards will need to be substantial if they are to cover the years of suffering and sacrifice. Not only has a significant share of the workforce in these countries emigrated, or are otherwise alienated from the domestic labour force, but the national labour markets of Ireland and Latvia are only now climbing out of the crisis. While these economic costs are staggering, the political costs may be even more substantial, as elected governments have proven unwilling or unable to respond to constituent pressure and/or generate effective policy responses.

In comparing these different paths to recovery, this study has revealed two important lessons. The first lesson is that small states still benefit from monetary policy autonomy, and this benefit is clearly revealed in the two paths described above (and in the case narratives in the preceding chapters).

Of course, this option may not suit voters across all of Europe – many of whom continue to believe in the need for monetary union in Europe (for whatever reason). For those voters and states, other tools are available to protect European citizens from the full force of market fluctuations. It is only when we recognise the true costs of this union that we can begin to devise an appropriate institutional response. This study draws our attention to the size of those costs. It is possible to create a currency union that allows member states more freedom to secure democratically-accountable outcomes. Doing so will require a much larger economic and political commitment.

The second, and perhaps most important, lesson is a recognition of the continued need for national (or regional) tools of economic management. The financial crisis has clearly revealed the absence of any Great Moderation – i.e., that the efficiency of modern markets has somehow made them immune to boom/bust cycles, or the need for political management, regulation and intervention. In the wake of this financial crisis, we have become more aware of the political extremism that is generated by the injustice and suffering produced by unfettered markets. To avoid political extremism, democratic states need to maintain economic stability and wellbeing. This means providing our policy makers with the tools they need to manage our economies effectively.

Caveats

This study has revealed a clear pattern, consistent with expectations, that demonstrates the continued utility of monetary policy for small states in Europe. It has leveraged a comparative approach to show how this pattern is related to the degree of policy autonomy derived from keeping one's currency. The advantage of such a comparative approach is that it lets us climb into the case material and get a better feel for the political processes; we can move beyond simple measures of GDP, inflation and debt to consider why and how particular policy decisions were made, and who benefited most (or least) by them.

But there are a number of limitations to a study like this, and I would be remiss for not mentioning them. Even though the cases were chosen with great analytical care, a sample of four states is clearly too small. Also, there could be any number of additional variables that might explain the successes and failures uncovered in the preceding chapters. There is much more separating Iceland from Latvia than the latter's willingness to defend an exchange rate peg. Iceland's history, culture, traditions and institutions are all radically different from Latvia's, and are undoubtedly an important part of Iceland's unique path out of the recession. National idiosyncrasies like these are found in every country – and they need to be taken seriously. Indeed, this is a major point underlying my argument: that national differences require different approaches and solutions. Elected officials need to be able to manoeuvre their own ships of states through uncharted economic waters, and be held responsible by those who have selected them for the task.

It is also not clear that the lessons derived from a study of small states can, or should, be extended to larger states. As most states in the EU are relatively small, however, it is important we consider the policy options available to such states. In contrast to small states, larger states may need to consider the systemic consequences of their policy decisions.[5] The design of this research project does not shine any light on the question of whether the international system (or the Eurozone itself) could handle a larger state (e.g. Spanish or Italian) default and/ or devaluation/exit from the Eurozone). But as small states are policy takers, not hegemons – and they reap none of the larger rewards of the hegemon – it would be rather odd to expect them to pay the eventual costs for maintaining the system.

Size also played an important role in this comparison, but not in the way we might expect. In all four of these countries, we find very strong links between

---

5. For example, in terms familiar to Hegemonic Stability Theorists. See Kindleberger (1986); Gowa (1989); Snidal (1985) and Webb and Krasner (1989).

political and financial elites. It would appear that these relationships facilitated favourable bailout arrangements to protect vested interests. It is possible that small states have a tendency towards corruption and group think,[6] but I remain sceptical. This sort of elite network is just as evident in the US Treasury and Federal Reserve as it is in Latvia's corresponding institutions. In Iceland this sort of cosy arrangement eventually proved impossible, as the size of the necessary bailout was too large for the government to cover. I fear that the people of Iceland would have been saddled with even more debt (and more ominous repayment terms) had the ECB been obliged to play the role of lender of last resort to Icelandic banks (as it did in Ireland).

Other concerns might be flagged about the important role that devaluations play in the Embedded Strategy. Many believe that devaluations/depreciations can encourage a tit-for-tat, beggar-thy-neighbour, type of response among competing countries (as was seen during the interwar period). If this were to happen, it could have devastating consequences for subsequent trade flows and international relations. While this is a real concern, it is not limited to an external devaluation strategy – it is a function of competitive markets, not policy choices, per se. The same sort of tit-for-tat cycle can happen among states that employ an internal devaluation strategy, as states are forced to squeeze wages and prices in a competitive race-to-the-bottom. Indeed, this is exactly what we are witnessing within the Eurozone, where states lack alternative means to buoy demand for their goods and services.

Finally, it is important to note that autonomy doesn't mean success. The fact that Iceland enjoyed a significant degree of policy autonomy before the crisis didn't protect it from making a number of stupid decisions that exacerbated the crisis. Freedom also means the freedom to fail – and countries are no different than people in this regard. Likewise, there are those who are unhappy about the way in which Hungary wields its political autonomy. In giving states more latitude to follow their constituent demands and needs, we should expect states to pursue very different policies (and consequently, experience very different outcomes). The size of the distance that separates the Icelandic and Hungarian responses to the crisis is proof to that effect.

Conclusion

In comparing the outcomes of these four different states, I have revealed the scope of alternatives still available to small states in a global economy. In the doing, I have demonstrated the existence of policy options (and cross-national variance) that many had thought to be lost. Monetary union in Europe was premised on the belief that monetary policy autonomy was no longer useful, effective, or desirable. The global financial crisis shows this to be nonsense: an independent monetary policy proved effective for both Iceland and Hungary, and might have

---

6. See, e.g., Carolan (2016).

been fruitfully employed by others – given the requisite political will. Using capital controls and devaluations to insulate and build the domestic economy on a more competitive export-based footing, Iceland and Hungary managed to recover quickly, with a relatively small hit to their employment levels. Although many mistakes were made along the way, the examples provided by these two very different states demonstrate the continued utility of monetary policy autonomy.

In the end, the legitimacy of democratic states requires that elected officials have tools that allow them to secure popular outcomes. As countries will continue to have different economic objectives, different factor endowments, and varying political balances of power, any monetary union needs to provide its member states with enough latitude and tools to secure outcomes that are democratically sustainable over the long run.

As skippers on very different ships of state, elected officials need to be able to respond quickly and effectively to the sort of unforeseen challenges that continually arise, while listening carefully to the needs of the crew and passengers they serve. As we have seen in response to the financial crisis, the global economy is more like a tempestuous ocean than an object at rest in equilibrium. For this particular passenger, the last thing I want is for my skipper to be tied to the mast, while our economic ship of state flounders.

References

Ágh, A. (2015) 'De-Europeanization and de-democratization trends in ECE: from the Potemkin democracy to the elected autocracy in Hungary', *Journal of Comparative Politics*, 8(2): 4–26.

Alþingi (2009a) 'Comparing Act No. 26/2009 and the acceptance and amendment agreements', 21 October, http://www.althingi.is/pdf/icesave/ Icesave_2009_comparing_EN.pdf (accessed 11 June 2016).

Alþingi (2009b) 'Bill amending Act No. 96/2009, draft translation', 21 October, http://www.althingi.is/pdf/icesave/138_0076_Icesave_2009_%20 frumvarp_med_grg_EN.pdf (accessed 11 June 2016).

AMECO (2015) 'Economic and financial affairs dataset', http://ec.europa. eu/economy_finance/ameco/user/serie/ResultSerie.cfm (accessed 29 January 2016).

Andersen, C. (2009) 'Agreement with banks limits crisis in emerging Europe', *IMF Survey Magazine: Interview*, 28 October.

Åslund, A. (2010) *The Last Shall Be the First. The East European financial crisis*, Washington DC: Peterson Institute for International Economics.

Åslund, A. and Dombrovskis, V. (2011) *How Latvia came through the financial crisis*, Washington DC: Peterson Institute for International Economics.

Bakker, B. B. and Gulde, A. M. (2010) 'The credit boom in the EU new member states: bad luck or bad policies?' *IMF Working Papers*, WP/10/130.

Baldursson, F. M. (2011) 'A sovereign insolvency mechanism? Lessons from Icesave and the Icelandic banking crisis', paper prepared for the UNCTAD/IPD Seminar on resolution of debt crises, 11 February.

Baltic Course (2013) 'Godmanis listed the reasons why Latvia should join Eurozone', *The Baltic Course*, 5 July.

Baltic Course (2012) 'Euro introduction mostly opposed by uneducated persons in Latvia', *The Baltic Course*, 20 December.

Bauchard, P. (1986) *La guerre des deux roses: Du rêve à la réalité, 1981–1985*, Paris: Bernard Grasset.

Bauze, K. (2012) 'Labour market flexibility and fiscal consolidation', in EC [European Commission], EU balance-of-payments assistance for Latvia: foundations of success. *European Economy*, Occasional papers 120 pp. 141–144.

Bayer, J. (2013) 'Emerging anti-pluralism in new democracies – the case of Hungary', *Österreichische Zeitschrift für Politikwissenschaft*, 1: 95–100.

Bayoumi, T. and Eichengreen, B. (1993) 'Shocking aspects of European monetary unification', in F. Torres and F. Giavazzi (eds.) *Growth and Adjustment in the European Monetary Union*, Cambridge: Cambridge University Press, pp. 193–229.

BBC News (2012) 'Iceland ex-PM Haarde "partly" guilty over 2008 crisis', 23 April, http://www.bbc.com/news/business-17820739 (accessed 7 April 2016).

BBC News (2008) 'Latvia defends economist's arrest', 7 December, http://news.bbc.co.uk/2/hi/business/7768696.stm (accessed 17 May 2016).

BBC News (2006) 'We lied to win, says Hungary PM', 18 September, http://news.bbc.co.uk/go/pr/fr/-/2/hi/europe/5354972.stm (accessed 19 February 2016).

BBJ (2013) 'Most Latvians oppose joining euro zone, poll', *Budapest Business Journal*, 14 May.

Bearce, D. H. and Hallerberg, M. (2011) 'Democracy and de facto exchange rate regimes', *Economics and Politics*, 23(2): 373–410.

Benediktsdottir, S., Danielson, J. and Zoega, G. (2011) 'Lessons from a collapse of a financial system', *Economic Policy*, (April): 183–231.

Berend, I. T. and Bugaric, B. (2015) 'Unfinished Europe: transition from communism to democracy in Central and Eastern Europe', *Journal of Contemporary History*, 50(4): 768–785.

Bergström, H. (1991) 'Devalveringens politiska tillkomst och logik', in L. Jonung (ed.) *Devalveringen 1982—rivstart eller snedtändning?* Stockholm: SNS, pp. 280–311.

Besley, T. and Hennessy, P. (2009) 'British Academy letter to Her Majesty The Queen', 22 July, http://www.feed-charity.org/user/image/besley-hennessy2009a.pdf (accessed 24 August 2016).

Blanchard, O.J., Griffiths, M. and Gruss, B. (2013) 'Boom, bust, recovery: forensics of the Latvia crisis', *Brooking Papers on Economic Activity* (Fall): 325–388.

Block, F. (2001) 'Introduction', in Karl Polanyi, *The Great Transformation*, Boston: Beacon Press, pp. xviii-xxxviii.

Bloomberg View (2012) 'Fighting Recession the Icelandic Way', *Bloomberg View*, 26 September, http://www.bloombergview.com/articles/2012-09-26/is-remedy-for-next-crisis-buried-in-iceland-view-correct- (accessed 8 April 2016).

Blyth, M. (2013) *Austerity. The History of a Dangerous Idea*, NY: Oxford University Press.

Bod, P. A. (2013) 'Crisis after crisis – any lessons learnt?' *Hungarian Review* 2: 18–28.

Bod, P. A. (2011) 'A not too original sin: Hungarian indebtedness in foreign currency', *Hungarian Review* 6: 5–13.

Boyes, R. (2009) *Meltdown Iceland: Lessons on the world financial crisis from a small bankrupt island*, New York: Bloomsbury.

Brennan, D. (2010) 'The difference between Iceland and Ireland: one letter and the ability to default', *Politico*, 7 December, http://politico.ie/archive/difference-between-iceland-and-ireland-one-letter-and-ability-default (accessed 21 April 2016).

Brogger, T. and Einarsdottir, H. K. (2008) 'Iceland reaches deposit accord with UK, Netherlands', Bloomberg, 11 October.

Budapest Appeal, The (2011) 'Appeal to the European institutions', 7 January, http://www.iprotest.hu/budapest-appeal.html (accessed 11 June 2016).

Buti, M. (2012) in EC [European Commission], 'EU balance-of-payments assistance for Latvia: foundations of success', *European Economy*, Occasional papers 120, pp. 10–12.

Caporaso, J. and Rhodes, M. (eds.) (2016) *The Political and Economic Dynamics of the Eurozone Crisis*, New York: Oxford University Press.

Carolan, E. (2016) 'Are small states susceptible to groupthink? Lessons for institutional design', *EPS* doi:10.1057/s41304-016-0003-9.

Carswell, S. (2008) 'Irish bailout cheapest in world, says Lenihan', *Irish Times*, 24 October.

CBI [Central Bank of Iceland] (2016) 'Exchange rate time series', http://cb.is/exch.-rates/time-series/ (accessed 25 March 2016).

CBI [Central Bank of Iceland] (2008a) 'New foreign exchange regulation', http://www.cb.is/publications/news/news/2008/11/28/New-foreign-exchange-regulation-/ (accessed 19 March 2016).

CBI [Central Bank of Iceland] (2008b) 'Rules on foreign exchange No. 1082', http://www.cb.is/lisalib/getfile.aspx?itemid=6631 (accessed 11 June 2016).

CBI [Central Bank of Iceland] (2007) *Monetary Bulletin*, 30/July (30), Reykjavik: CBI.

CBOI [Central Bank of Ireland] (2014) *Central Bank Quarterly Bulletin Q4*, 14 October, Dublin: CBOI.

Christmas, J. (2012) 'Latvian financial crisis – the multi-billion-euro Parex/EBRD/ Ernst & Young fraud', 26 June, https://www.youtube.com/watch?v=IBiYCPfIWFA (accessed 15 May 2016).

Claeys, G., Darvas, Z., and Leandro, Á. (2016) 'A proposal to revive the European fiscal framework', Bruegel Policy Contribution Issue 2016/07 (March).

Claeys, G., Darvas, Z., Leandro, Á. and Walsh, T. (2015) 'The effects of ultra-loose monetary policies on inequality', Bruegel Policy Contribution Issue 2015/09 (June).

Clark, T. E. and van Wincoop, E. (2001) 'Borders and Business Cycles', *Journal of International Economics*, 55(1): 59–85.

CNBC (2013) 'Hungary's central bank is "independent": Governor', video interview recorded 20 November 2013, http://video.cnbc.com/gallery/?video=3000220023 (accessed 26 February 2016).

Coakley, C. (2015) 'Ireland shares lessons after its recovery from the sovereign-bank loop', *IMF Survey*, 6 February.

Cohen, B. J. (1996) 'Phoenix risen: the resurrection of global finance', *World Politics*, 48 (January): 268–296.

Conrad, C. R. and Golder, S. N. (2010) 'Measuring government duration and stability in Central Eastern European democracies', *European Journal of Political Research*, 49(1): 119–150.

Cowen, B. (2012) 'The euro: from crisis to resolution? Some reflections from Ireland on the road thus far', Georgetown University, 21 March, http://cdn.thejournal. ie/media/2012/03/20120327cowenspeech.pdf (accessed 21 April 2016).

Csaba, L. (2013) 'Growth, crisis management and the EU: the Hungarian trilemma', *Südosteuropa Mitteilungen*, 03–04: 155–169.

Csajbók, A. and Csermely, Á. (2002) 'Adopting the euro in Hungary: expected costs, benefits, and timing', NBH Occasional Papers 24.

CSO [Central Statistics Office, Ireland] (2016a) 'QIHQ1: Table 3: number of employees by sex, industry sector and quarter', http://www.cso.ie/en/ databases/ (accessed 14 April 2016).

CSO [Central Statistics Office, Ireland] (2016b) 'HSQ06: average price of houses by area, statistical indicator, and quarter', Environment, community and local government, http://www.cso.ie/en/databases/ (accessed 12 April 2016).

CSO [Central Statistics Office, Ireland] (2016c) 'Monthly unemployment. March 2016', 5 April, http://www.cso.ie/en/releasesandpublications/er/mue/ monthlyunemploymentmarch2016/ (accessed 23 April 2016).

CSO [Central Statistics Office, Ireland] (2015) 'Population and migration estimates. April 2015', 26 August, http://www.cso.ie/en/releasesandpublications/ er/pme/populationandmigrationestimatesapril2015/ (accessed 23 April 2016).

Dahl, R. (1971) *Polyarchy: Participation and opposition*, New Haven: Yale University Press.

Danielsson, J. and Krisjánsdóttir, Á. (2015) 'Why Iceland can now remove capital controls', VOX, http://www.voxeu.org/article/why-iceland-can-now- remove-capital-controls (accessed 28 March 2016).

Darvas, Z. (2012) 'Monetary transmission in three Central European economies: evidence from time-varying coefficient vector autoregressions', Bruegel Working Paper 2012/08, May.

Darvas, Z. (2011) 'A tale of three countries: recovery after banking crisis', *Bruegel Policy Contribution*, 2011/9, December.

de Grauwe, P. (2014) *Economics of Monetary Union*, 10th Edition, Oxford: Oxford University Press.

de Grauwe, P. (2011) 'The governance of a fragile euro zone', https://www.ceps. eu/publications/governance-fragile-eurozone# (accessed 11 June 2016).

de Haas, R., Korniyenko, Y., Loukoianova, E. and Pivovarksy, A. (2012) 'Foreign banks and the Vienna initiative: turning sinners into saints', EBRD Working Paper No. 143, London.

Dellepiane, S. and Hardiman, N. (2012) 'The new politics of austerity: fiscal responses to the economic crisis in Ireland and Spain', UCD Geary Institute Discussion Paper Series, February.

Deroose, S., Flores, E., Giudice, G. and Turrini, A. (2010) 'The tale of the Baltics: experiences, challenges ahead and main lessons', ECFIN Economic Brief, no. 10, European Commission, July, http://ec.europa.eu/economy_ finance/publications/economic_briefs/2010/pdf/eb10_en.pdf (accessed on 8 May 2016).

di Comite, F., Giudice, G., Krastev, R. and Monteiro, D. (2012a) 'The evolution of the Latvian external sector: imbalances, competitiveness and adjustment', in EC [European Commission], EU balance-of-payments assistance for Latvia: foundations of success, *European Economy*, Occasional papers 120, pp. 40–59.

di Comite, F., Giudice, G., Lendvai, J. and Toming, I. (2012b) 'Fiscal consolidation in the midst of crisis', in EC [European Commission], EU balance-of-payments assistance for Latvia: foundations of success, *European Economy*, Occasional papers 120, pp. 77–99.

DIGF [Icelandic Depositors' and Investors' Guarantee Fund] (2007) 'Financial statements 2007', http://www.tryggingarsjodur.is/pdf/arsreikningur%20 2007_enska.pdf (accessed 8 April 2016).

di Muzio, T. and Robbins, R.H. (2016) *Debt as Power*, Manchester: Manchester University Press.

Dinan, Desmond (1999) *Ever Closer Union: An introduction to European integration*, London: Boulder.

Dineen, M. (2012) 'Government fights to keep NAMA debt off its books', 12 April, *Irish Independent*.

Djankov, S. (2015) 'Hungary under Orbán: can central planning revive its economy?' Peterson Institute for International Economics, July, Policy Brief Number PB15–11.

Dombrovskis, V. (2012) in EC [European Commission], EU balance-of-payments assistance for Latvia: foundations of success, *European Economy*, Occasional papers 120, pp. 13–15.

Donovan, D. and Murphy, A.E. (2014) *The Fall of the Celtic Tiger: Ireland & the euro debt crisis*, Oxford: Oxford University Press.

EBRD/EIB/EU/IMF/World Bank (2014a) 'Overview: Vienna Initiative I', http:// vienna-initiative.com/about/ (accessed 22 May 2016).

EBRD/EIB/EU/IMF/World Bank (2014b) 'Timeline: Vienna Initiative I', http:// vienna-initiative.com/vienna-initiative-part-1/timeline-4/ (accessed 23 May 2016).

EC [European Commission] (2016) 'Commission staff working document. Country report Latvia 2016', SWD(2016) 82 final, 26 February, Brussels.

EC [European Commission] (2012) 'EU balance-of-payments assistance for Latvia: foundations of success', *European Economy*, Occasional papers 120.

EC [European Commission] (2011) 'The economic adjustment programme for Ireland', *European Economy*, Occasional Papers 76.

EC [European Commission] (2010) 'Cross-country study: economic policy challenges in the Baltics', *European Economy*, Occasional Paper No. 58.

EC [European Commission] (2009) 'Economic crisis in Europe: causes, consequences and responses', *European Economy* 7/2009.

EC [European Commission] (2006) 'Communication from the commission to the council on the public finance situation in Hungary', Brussels, 26 September, SEC(2006) 1196 final, http://ec.europa.eu/economy_finance/

economic_governance/sgp/deficit/countries/hungary_en.htm (accessed 29 January 2016).

EC [European Commission] (1990) 'One market, one money. An evaluation of the potential benefits and costs of forming an economic and monetary union', *European Economy* 44.

ECB [European Central Bank] (2016) 'IRS: long term interest rate statistics', ECB Statistical Warehouse, http://sdw.ecb.europa.eu/browseSelection. do?dataset=0&ref_area=262&ref_area=179&ref_area=183&ref_ area=218&node=bbn4864 (accessed 21 January 2016).

ECB HFCS (2013) 'Household finance and consumption survey', Statistics Paper Series No. 2 (April) The eurosystem household finance and consumption survey. Results from the first wave, https://www.ecb.europa.eu/pub/pdf/ scpsps/ecbsp2.en.pdf (accessed 11 June 2016).

Economist, The (2010) 'Ireland's economy: threadbare', 18 November.

Economist, The (2007) 'The quest for prosperity', 15 March.

Economist, The (2001) 'Charlemagne: David Oddsson, Iceland's eurosceptic leader', 14 April.

EFTA Surveillance Authority (2011) 'Icesave: Iceland to be taken to Court for failing to pay minimum compensation', PR(11)79, 14 December, http:// www.eftasurv.int/press--publications/press-releases/internal-market/ nr/1560 (accessed 7 April 2016).

Eichengreen, B. (2015) 'The Irish crisis and the EU from a distance', paper presented to the IMF conference, 'Ireland shares lessons after its recovery from the sovereign-bank loop', 19 January draft, http://www.imf.org/ external/np/seminars/eng/2014/ireland/pdf/Eichengreen_IrishCrisisEU. pdf (accessed on 22 April 2016).

Eichengreen, B. (2012) 'Throwing out the baby with the bathwater? Implications for the euro crisis for Asian monetary integration', *Journal of Economic Integration*, 27(2): 291–311.

Eichengreen, B. (1997) *European Monetary Unification: Theory, practice and analysis*, Cambridge, Mass: MIT Press.

Eichengreen, B. (1996) *Globalizing Capital: A history of the international monetary system*, Princeton: Princeton University Press.

Elster, J. (1979) *Ulysses and the Sirens: Studies in rationality and irrationality*, Cambridge: Cambridge University Press.

Emanuel, R. (2009) 'Rahm Emanuel: you never want a serious crisis to go to waste', YouTube video uploaded by Jim Swift. 9 February. https://www. youtube.com/watch?v=1yeA_kHHLow (accessed 13 June 2016).

Epstein, Rachel A. (2014) 'When do foreign banks "cut and run"? Evidence from West European bailouts and East European markets', *Review of International Political Economy*, 21(4): 847–877.

EU Directive 94/19/EC of the European Parliament and of the Council of 30 May 1994 on deposit-guarantee schemes, http://eur-lex.europa.eu/ legal-content/EN/ALL/?uri=CELEX:31994L0019 (accessed on 7 April 2016).

Eurobarometer (2012) 'Table of Results', Standard Eurobarometer 77, collected May 2012, European Commission.

Eurobarometer (2007) 'National report. Executive summary', Hungary. Eurobarometer 68, Autumn.

Eurobarometer (diverse years) 'Standard Eurobarometer', http://ec.europa. eu/COMMFrontOffice/PublicOpinion/index.cfm/Survey/ index#p=1&instruments=STANDARD (accessed 20 April 2016).

Eurostat (2016) *Gross Domestic Product for each country* [CPMNACSAB1GQIS; CPMNACSCAB1GQLV; CPMNACSAB1GQIE; CPMNACSCAB1GQHU], retrieved from FRED, Federal Reserve Bank of St. Louis, https://research.stlouisfed.org/fred2/ (accessed 1 June 2016).

Eurostat (2015) 'People at risk of poverty or social exclusion', http://ec.europa. eu/eurostat/statistics-explained/index.php/People_at_risk_of_poverty_ or_social_exclusion#Further_Eurostat_information (accessed 21 May 2016).

Eurostat (n.d.) Undated Eurostat references of individual variables are listed in brackets, eg. [tsdde230]. These can be found on the Eurostat database homepage: http://ec.europa.eu/eurostat/data/database.

Eurostat/AMECO database (n.d.) http://ec.europa.eu/economy_finance/ameco/ user/serie/SelectSerie.cfm

Fairclough, G., and Gulyas, V. (2010) 'Hungary's leader brushes off IMF', *Wall Street Journal* (Eastern edition), A.8, 23 July.

Feher, M. (2014a) 'ECB warns Hungary on central bank policy', *Wall Street Journal*, 7 February.

Feher, M. (2014b) 'European central bank criticizes independence of Hungary's policy makers', *Wall Street Journal* (Eastern edition), 8 February, A.18.

Feher, M. (2014c) 'Hungarian PM vows to continue with economic plan', *Wall Street Journal*, 19 March.

Ferguson, N. (2009) *The Ascent of Money: A financial history of the world*, London: Penguin.

Financial Times (2013) 'Saga ends with Icesave redemption – ruling vindicates Iceland's policy over rest of Europe's', 30 January: 10.

Financial Times (2011) 'Bail-out on ice: Iceland shows that citizens can be put ahead of banks', Leader, 13 April: 8.

Finn, D. (2011) 'Ireland on the turn? Political and economic consequences of the crash', *New Left Review* 67: 5–39.

Fischer, S. (1990) 'Rules versus discretion in monetary policy', in B.M. Friedman and F.H. Hahn (eds.), *Handbook in Monetary Economics*, vol. II, Amsterdam: Elsevier Science Publishers.

Foucault, M. (2004) *The Birth of Biopolitics: Lectures at the College de France*, New York: Picador.

Frankel, J. A. and Rose, A. K. (1998) 'The endogeneity of the optimum currency area criteria', *The Economic Journal* 41: 753–760.

Frankel, J. A. and Rose, A. K. (1997) 'Is EMU more justifiable ex post than ex ante?' *European Economic Review* 41(3–5): 753–760.

FRED [Federal Reserve Economic Data] (2016) 'Long-term government bond yields', https://research.stlouisfed.org/fred2/series/IRLTLT01ISM156N (accessed 21 January 2016).

Friedman, M. (1953) 'The case for flexible exchange rates', *Essays in Positive Economics*, Chicago: University of Chicago Press, pp. 157–203.

Giavazzi, G. and Pagano, M. (1988) 'The advantage of tying one's hands: EMS discipline and central bank credibility', *European Economic Review*, 32: 1055–1082.

Gilmore, E. (2016) *Inside the Room: The untold story of Ireland's crisis government*, Sallins, Co. Kildare: Merrion Press.

Gilmore, E. (2011) 'Frankfurt's way or Labour's way', Google video of Gilmore's 3 February 2011 speech, posted by Michael O'Neill on 25 March 2013, https://plus.google.com/101740968635297455257/posts/j4dBaiKL8w7 (accessed 23 March 2015).

GoH [Government of Hungary] (2008) 'Hungary: letter of intent', in IMF (2008) 'Hungary: request for stand-by arrangement – staff report; staff supplement; and press release on the executive board discussion', IMF Country Report No. 08/361, November, Washington DC: IMF, Attachment 1, pp. 40-46.

GoI [Government of Ireland] (2010) *National Recovery Plan 2011–2014*, http://www.budget.gov.ie/The%20National%20Recovery%20Plan%202011-2014.pdf (accessed 23 April 2016).

González-Páramo, J. M. (2005) 'Inflation differentials in the euro area', Speech at Cámara de Comercio, Industria y Navegación de la Región de Murcia, 23 May, http://www.ecb.europa.eu/press/key/date/2005/html/sp050523.en.html (accessed 11 June 2016).

Gowa, J. S. (1989) 'Rational hegemons, excludable goods, and small groups: an epitaph for hegemonic stability theory?' *World Politics* 41(3): 307–324.

Gowa, J. S. (1983) *Closing the gold window: Domestic politics and the end of Bretton Woods*, Ithaca: Cornell University Press.

Greenhalgh, N. (2010) 'Former govt off the hook on Parex takeover', *Baltic Reports*, 17 August.

Grímsson, Ó. R. (2012) 'Can political science keep up with the twenty-first century?' *European Political Science*, 11: 271–277.

Guðmundsson, M. (2015) 'Iceland's crisis and recovery – facts, comparisons, and the lessons learned', Speech to the Institute of International and European Affairs in Dublin, 27 April.

Gylfason, T., Holmström, B., Korkman, S., Söderström, H.T., and Vihriälä, V. (2010) 'Nordics in global crisis – vulnerability and resilience', The Research Institute of the Finnish Economy (ETLA), Taloustieto, http://www.taloustieto.fi/etlajulk/b242_esipuhe_sisluet_introduction.pdf (accessed 11 June 2016).

Hanley, S. and Dawson, J. (2016) 'East Central Europe: the fading mirage of the "Liberal Consensus"', *Journal of Democracy* 27(1): 20–34.

Hardarson, Ó. T. and Kristinsson, G.H. (2014) 'Iceland', *European Journal of Political Research*, 53: 155–161.

Hardarson, Ó. T. and Kristinsson, G.H. (2013) 'Iceland', *European Journal of Political Research*, 52: 101–104.

Hardarson, Ó. T. and Kristinsson, G.H. (2010) 'Iceland', *European Journal of Political Research*, 49: 1009–1016.

Hardiman, N. and Regan, A. (2013) 'The politics of austerity in Ireland', *Intereconomics*, Leibniz Information Centre for Economics, 1: 9–14.

Hart-Landsberg, M. (2013) 'Lessons from Iceland. Capitalism, crisis, and resistance', *Monthly Review*, 65(05).

Helleiner, E. (1995) 'Explaining the globalization of financial markets: bringing states back in', *Review of International Political Economy*, 2(2): 315–341.

Helliwell, J., Layard, R. and Sachs, J. (eds.) (2016) *World Happiness Report 2016*, Update (Vol. I), New York: Sustainable Development Solutions Network.

Homer (1963) *The Odyssey*, translated by Robert Fitzgerald, Garden City, NY: Doubleday and Co.

Honohan, P. (2012) 'Recapitalisation of failed banks: some lessons from the Irish experience', address to the 44th Annual Money, Macro and Finance Conference, Dublin, 7 September, https://www.centralbank.ie/press-area/speeches/Documents/120907%20Address%20by%20Governor%20Patrick%20Honohan%20at%20the%2044th%20Annual%20Money,%20Macro%20and%20Finance%20Conference,%20Trinity%20College%20Dublin.pdf (accessed 21 April 2016).

Honohan, P. (2010) 'The Irish banking crisis: regulatory and financial stability policy 2003–2008', a Report to the Ministry of Finance by the Governor of the Central Bank (Dublin).

Hudson, M. (2015) 'Stockholm syndrome in the Baltics: Latvia's neoliberal war against labor and industry', in J. Sommers and C. Woolfson (ed.), *The Contradictions of Austerity: The socio-economic costs of the neoliberal Baltic model*, London: Routledge, pp. 44–63.

Hudson, M. and Sommers, J. (2011) 'The spectre haunting Europe: debt defaults, austerity and death of the "social Europe" model', *Global Research*, 18 January.

Hurley, J. (2007) 'Governor's foreword', *2007 Central Bank Annual Report*, Dublin: CBOI, pp. 9–10.

IceNews (2011) 'Nearly 500 questioned by Iceland bank crash investigators', 15 March, http://www.icenews.is/2011/03/15/nearly-500-questioned-by-iceland-bank-crash-investigators/#ixzz45Dy6NapT (accessed 8 April 2016).

Ikstens, J. (2014) 'Latvia', *European Journal of Political Research. Political Data Yearbook*, 53: 198–204.

Ikstens, J. (2012) 'Latvia', *European Journal of Political Research. Political Data Yearbook*, 51: 175–186.

Ikstens, J. (2011) 'Latvia', *European Journal of Political Research*, 50: 1035–1044.

Ikstens, J. (2010) 'Latvia', *European Journal of Political Research*, 49: 1049–1057.

Ikstens, J. (2009) 'Latvia', *European Journal of Political Research*, 48: 1015–1021.

Ikstens, J. (2008) 'Latvia', *European Journal of Political Research*, 47: 1039–1047.

Ilonszki, G. and Kurtán, S. (2009) 'Hungary', *European Journal of Political Research*, 48: 973–979.

Ilonszki, G. and Kurtán, S. (2008) 'Hungary', *European Journal of Political Research*, 47: 998–1004.

IMF [International Monetary Fund] (2015a) 'World economic and financial surveys. World economic outlook database', October 2015 Edition, http://www.imf.org/external/pubs/ft/weo/2015/02/weodata/index.aspx (accessed 11 June 2016).

IMF [International Monetary Fund] (2015b) 'IMF executive board concludes Article IV consultation with Hungary', Press Release No. 15/156, 3 April 2015, http://www.imf.org/external/np/sec/pr/2015/pr15156.htm (accessed 29 February 2016).

IMF [International Monetary Fund] (2012a) *World Economic Outlook April 2012: Growth resuming. Dangers remain*, Washington DC: IMF.

IMF [International Monetary Fund] (2012b) 'IMF statement on Latvia's announcement about early repayment to the IMF', Press Release No.12/476, 10 December, http://www.imf.org/external/np/sec/pr/2012/pr12476.htm (accessed 21 May 2016).

IMF [International Monetary Fund] (2011) 'Hungary: staff report for the 2010 Article IV consultation and proposal for post-program monitoring', February, IMF Country Report No. 11/35.

IMF [International Monetary Fund] (2010a) 'Ireland: 2010 Article IV consultation – staff reports; and public information notice on the executive board discussion', IMF Country Report No 10/209. July.

IMF [International Monetary Fund] (2010b) 'IMF approves €22.5 billion loan for Ireland', *IMF Survey Online*, 16 December, https://www.imf.org/external/pubs/ft/survey/so/2010/CAR121610A.htm (accessed 14 April 2016).

IMF [International Monetary Fund] (2010c) 'IMF approves €22.5 billion loan for Ireland', *IMF Survey Online*, 16 December, https://www.imf.org/external/pubs/ft/survey/so/2010/CAR121610A.htm (accessed 18 April 2016).

IMF [International Monetary Fund] (2009a) 'Republic of Latvia: request for stand-by arrangement – staff report; staff supplement; press release on the executive board discussion; and statement by the executive director for the Republic of Latvia', IMF Country Report No. 09/3, January.

IMF [International Monetary Fund] (2009b) 'Joint IMF, EC press release on the European banking group coordination meeting on Latvia', IMF Press Release No. 09/304, 14 September, https://www.imf.org/external/np/sec/pr/2009/pr09304.htm (accessed 29 April 2016).

IMF [International Monetary Fund] (2009c) 'Concluding statement by participating banks', European Banking Group Coordinating Meeting for Latvia held in Stockholm, Sweden on 11 September 2009, https://www.imf.org/external/np/country/2009/091409.htm (accessed 29 April 2016).

IMF [International Monetary Fund] (2009d) 'Republic of Latvia: first review and financing assurances review under the stand-by arrangement, requests for waivers of nonobservance of performance criteria, and rephasing of purchases under the arrangement', IMF Country Report No 09/297, October.

IMF [International Monetary Fund] (2008a) 'IMF announces staff level agreement with Iceland on $2.1 billion loan', Press Release No. 08/256, 24 October.

IMF [International Monetary Fund] (2008b) 'Iceland: request for stand-by arrangement', IMF Country Report No. 08/362, November.

IMF [International Monetary Fund] (2008c) 'IMF announces staff-level agreement with Latvia on a €1.7 billion stand-by arrangement', Press release 08/332, 19 December 2008.

IMF [International Monetary Fund] (2008d) 'Hungary: request for stand-by arrangement – staff report; staff supplement; and press release on the executive board discussion', November, IMF Country Report No. 08/361.

IMF [International Monetary Fund] (2006) 'Iceland: 2006 Article IV consultation – staff report; staff statement; and public information notice on the executive board discussion', August, IMF Country Report No. 06/296.

IMF [International Monetary Fund] (1998) 'Republic of Latvia: selected issues and statistical appendix', IMF Staff Country Report No. 98/47, May.

Ingebritsen, C. (2000) *The Nordic States and European Unity*, Ithaca: Cornell University Press.

Innes, A. (2015) 'Hungary's illiberal democracy', *Current History*, 114(770): 95–100.

Irish Times (2011) 'Leader', 8 February.

Irish Times (2010) 'Was it for this?' 18 November.

Jabko, N. (2015) 'The elusive economic government and the forgotten fiscal union', in M. Matthijs and M. Blyth (eds.), *The Future of the Euro*, New York: Oxford University Press, pp. 70–89.

Jauer, J., Liebig, T., Martin, J. P. and Puhani, P. (2014) 'Migration as an adjustment mechanism in the crisis? A comparison of Europe and the United States', *OECD Social, Employment and Migration Working Papers*, No. 155.

Johnson, J. (2006) 'Two-track diffusion and central bank embeddedness: the politics of Euro adoption in Hungary and the Czech Republic', *Review of International Political Economy*, 13(3): 361–386.

Jones, E. (2015) 'The forgotten financial union: how you can have a euro crisis without a euro', in M. Matthijs and M. Blyth (eds.), *The Future of the Euro*, New York: Oxford University Press, pp. 44–70.

Jonung, L. and Drea, E. (2009) 'The euro: it can't happen, it's a bad idea, it won't last. US economists on the EMU, 1989–2002', *European Economy*, Economic Papers, 395, December.

Kalačinska, D. (2010) 'Social protest in Latvia 2006–2009: political disenchantment and identity formation', MA thesis, Budapest: Dept. of Political Science, Central European University, www.etd.ceu.hu/2010/kalacinska_diana.pdf (accessed 23 March 2015).

Kalemi-Ozcan, S., Sørensen, B. E., and Yosha, O. (2001) 'Economic integration, industrial specialization and the asymmetry of macroeconomic fluctuations', *Journal of International Economics*, 55(1): 107–137.

Kant, Immanuel (1917 [1795]) *On Perpetual Peace*, Ontario: Broadview Press.

Karolewski, I. P. and Benedikter, R. (2016) 'Poland's conservative turn and the role of the European Union', *EPS*, doi:10.1057/s41304-016-0002-x.

Kelly, M. (2011) 'Ireland's future depends on breaking free from bailout', *Irish Times*, 7 May.

Kelly, M. (2010) 'If you thought the bank bailout was bad, wait until the mortgage default hits home', *Irish Times*, 8 November.

Kelly, M. (2007) 'On the likely extent of falls in Irish house prices', University College Dublin, School of Economics, UCD Working paper WP07/01, February, http://www.ucd.ie/economics/research/papers/2007/WP07.01.pdf (accessed 15 April 2016).

Kelly, M. (2006) 'How the housing corner stones of our economy could go into a rapid freefall', *Irish Times*, 28 December.

Kelpie, C. (2014) '"Ireland stupid to guarantee banks" – Timothy Geithner', *Irish Independent*, 12 November.

Keynes, J.M. (1953 [1936]) *The General Theory of Employment, Interest and Money*, New York: Harcourt Brace Jovanovich Publishers.

Keynes, J. M. (1924) *A Tract on Monetary Reform*, London: Macmillan.

Kindleberger, C.P. (1986) *The World in Depression, 1929–1939*, Berkeley: University of California Press.

Kirby, P. (2012) 'When banks cannibalize the state: responses to Ireland's economic collapse', *Socialist Register*, 48: 249–268.

Kirby, P. (2011) 'Briefing paper on the Irish elections 2011. Facing an angry electorate: Irish politicians desperately seek to convince', February, Friedrich Ebert Stiftung, http://library.fes.de/pdffiles/id/ipa/07867.pdf (accessed 19 April 2016).

Kirchick, J. (2012) 'Wrong way down the Danube', *Foreign Affairs*, 10 July.

Kolyako, N. (2009) 'Godmanis: Latvian government had no choice but to take over Parex Banka', *The Baltic Course*, 4 October.

Kopits, G. (2014) 'Ireland's fiscal framework: options for the future', *The Economic and Social Review*, 45(1): 135–158.

Kopits, G. (2013) 'Constitutional mob rule in Hungary', *The Wall Street Journal*, 27 March.

Kopits, G. and Romhányi, B. (2013) 'Hungary: a short-lived watchdog', in G. Kopits (ed.) *Restoring Public Debt Sustainability: The role of independent fiscal institutions*, Oxford: Oxford University Press, pp. 212–233.

Krugman, P. (1993) 'Lessons of Massachusetts for EMU', In F. Giavazzi and F. Torres (eds.) *The Transition to Economic and Monetary Union in*

Europe, NY: Carnegie-Rochester Conference Series on Public Policy, pp. 241–261.

Krukowska, E. (2009) 'Latvia traders see 53% devaluation, forwards show (Update1)', *Bloomberg*, 4 June.

Kydland, F and Prescott, E. (1977) 'Rules rather than discretion: the inconsistency of optimal plans', *Journal of Political Economy*, 85: 473–492.

Laeven, L. and Valencia, F. (2012) 'Systemic banking crises database: an update', IMF Working Paper WP/12/163, June.

Laeven, L. and Valencia, F. (2011) 'The real effects of financial sector interventions during crises', IMF Working Paper WP/11/45, 1 March.

Laeven, L. and Valencia, F. (2010) 'Resolution of banking crises: the good, the bad, and the ugly', *IMF Working Paper*, WP/10/146.

Lambert, S. (n.d.) 'The Orbán government and public debt', The Orange Files, http://theorangefiles.hu/the-orban-government-and-public-debt/ (accessed 12 February 2016).

Lavery, B. and O'Brien, T.L. (2005) 'For insurance regulators, trails lead to Dublin', *New York Times*, 1 April.

Legrain, P. (2016) 'Ireland's recovery has nothing to do with austerity', *Foreign Policy*, 24 February.

Lenihan, B. (2010) 'Financial statement of the minister for finance Mr. Brian Lenihan TD', 9 December, http://www.budget.gov.ie/Budgets/2010/FinancialStatement.aspx (accessed 11 June 2016).

Lombard, M. (1995) 'A re-examination of the reasons for failure of Keynesian expansionary policies in France, 1981–82', *Cambridge Journal of Economics*, 19: 359–372.

Lucey, A. (2009) 'Europe "amazed" at steps take in budget: Lenihan', *Irish Times*, 27 April.

Lyons, T. and Sheridan, G. (2014) 'Give us €4bn – shower of f**king clowns...', *Independent.ie*. http://www.independent.ie/business/irish/give-us-4bn-shower-of-fking-clowns-29400725.html (accessed 23 March 2015).

Mabbett, D. and Schelkle, W. (2015) 'What difference does euro membership make to stabilization? The political economy of international monetary systems revised', *Review of International Political Economy*, 22(3): 508–534.

MacArthur, J. L. (2011) 'Mortgaging Irish independence. From financial crisis to socialist resistance', *Monthly Review* (March): 40–49.

McGee, H. (2011) 'Gilmore vows to renegotiate "bad deal" on EU-IMF bailout package', *Irish Times*, 4 February.

McHugh, D. (2013) 'Latvia to join eurozone: EU approves 18th euro member', *Huffington Post*, 5 June.

McNamara, K. R. (2015) 'The forgotten problem of embeddedness: history lessons for the euro', in M. Matthijs and M. Blyth (eds.), *The Future of the Euro*, New York: Oxford University Press, pp. 21–43.

Meade, J. E. (1957) 'The balance of payments problems of a free trade area', *Economic Journal*, 67: 379–396.

MFA [Iceland's Ministry of Foreign Affairs] (n.d) 'Icesave: questions and answers', https://www.mfa.is/tasks/icesave/q--a/ (accessed 6 April 2016).

Mill, J. S. (2002 [1891]) *A System of Logic*, Honolulu: University Press of the Pacific.

Moses, J.W. (2011) *Emigration and Political Development*, New York: Cambridge University Press.

MNB [Magyar Nemzeti Bank] (2016a) 'Press release on the loans granted in the second phase of the Funding for Growth Scheme', 6 January, http://www.mnb.hu/letoltes/fgs2-utilization-05-01-2016-final.pdf (accessed 20 February 2016).

MNB [Magyar Nemzeti Bank] (2016b) 'Official Daily Exchange Rates, Euro', http://www.mnb.hu/en/arfolyam-lekerdezes (accessed 30 January 2016).

MNB [Magyar Nemzeti Bank] (n.d.) 'Analysis of the first phase of the Funding for Growth Scheme', http://www.mnb.hu/letoltes/fgs-analysis.pdf (accessed 20 February 2016).

Mundell, R. A. (1961) 'A theory of optimum currency areas', *The American Economic Review* (September): 657–665.

Murphy, A. (2010) 'ECB shift from lender of last resort casts doubt on independence', *The Irish Times*, Business This Week supplement, 26 November: 3.

Myles, R. (2013) 'Iceland triumphs over UK and Netherland in Icesave court battle', *Digital Journal*, 31 January.

NCC [National Competitiveness Council] (2009) *Annual Competitiveness Report 2009. Volume 1: benchmarking Ireland's performance*, Dublin: Forfás and National Competitiveness Council.

Nord LB (2011) 'Ārkārtas Saeimas vēlēšanas', *Latvijas Barometrs* 40, September.

Nyberg, P. (2011) 'Misjudging risks: causes of the systemic banking crisis in Ireland', report of the Commission of Investigation into the Banking Sector in Ireland, Dublin: Government Publications.

O'Brien, D. (2011) 'Banking on Europe: the true story behind Ireland's bailout', *Irish Times*, 23 April.

OECD (2016a) 'Exports of goods and services in Iceland', [ISLEXPORTADSMEI], retrieved from FRED, Federal Reserve Bank of St. Louis, https://research.stlouisfed.org/ (accessed 26 March 2016).

OECD (2016b) 'Imports of goods and services in Iceland', [ISLIMPORTADSMEI], retrieved from FRED, Federal Reserve Bank of St. Louis, https://research.stlouisfed.org (accessed 26 March 2016).

OECD (2016c) 'Data set: average annual wages', OECD.Stat, http://stats.oecd.org/Index.aspx. (accessed 23 April 2016).

OECD (2013) *International Migration Outlook*, Paris: OECD.

OECD (2011a) *OECD Economic Surveys: Iceland*, June, Paris: OECD.

OECD (2011b) *Economic Survey. Ireland*, October, Paris: OECD.

OECD (2003) *OECD Economic Surveys: Iceland*, Paris: OECD.

Ólafsson, S. (2012) 'The Icelandic way out of the crisis. Welfarism, redistribution and austerity', Social Research Centre, December Working paper no.

1:2012.   http://thjodmalastofnun.hi.is/sites/thjodmalastofnun.hi.is/files/
    skrar/the_icelandic_way_out_of_the_crisis.docx (accessed 11 June 2016).
Ólafsson, S. (2011a) 'Icelandic capitalism – from statism to neoliberalism and
    financial collapse', *Comparative Social Research*, 28: 1–52.
Ólafsson, S. (2011b) 'Iceland's financial crisis and level of living consequences',
    Social Research Centre, December Working paper no. 3:2011. http://
    thjodmalastofnun.hi.is/sites/thjodmalastofnun.hi.is/files/skrar/icelands_
    financial_crisis_and_level_of_living.pdf (accessed 11 June 2016).
Oliver, E. (2010) 'Bank bailout cost of €73bn manageable, says ESRI', *Irish
    Independent*, 13 April.
O'Malley, E. (2013) 'Ireland', *European Journal of Political Research Political
    Data Yearbook*, 52: 105–110.
O'Toole, F. (2010a) 'Abysmal deal ransoms us and disgraces Europe', *The Irish
    Times*, 29 November: 11.
O'Toole, F. (2010b) *Ship of Fools: How stupidity and corruption sank the Celtic
    Tiger*, New York: Public Affairs.
Papademos, L. (2007) 'Inflation and competitiveness divergences in the euro
    areas countries: causes, consequences and policy responses', Speech at
    the conference 'The ECB and its Watchers IX', Frankfurt, 7 September,
    http://www.ecb.int/press/key/date/2007/html/sp070907_2.en.html
    (accessed 11 June 2016).
Plato (1987 [*c*. 360 BCE]) *The Republic*, translated by Desmond Lee, 2nd edition,
    Harmondsworth: Penguin.
Polanyi, K. (2001 [1944]) *The Great Transformation*, Boston: Beacon Press.
PM [Iceland's Prime Minister's Office] (2011) 'Statement from the government
    of Iceland on the outcome of the referendum on the Icesave agreements',
    April   10,   https://eng.forsaetisraduneyti.is/news-and-articles/nr/6724
    (accessed 5 April 2016).
PM [Iceland's Prime Minister's Office] (2010) 'The Government of Iceland remains
    fully committed to honour Iceland's obligations', 6 January, https://eng.
    forsaetisraduneyti.is/news-and-articles/nr/4211 (accessed 5 April 2016).
PM [Iceland's Prime Minister's Office] (2009) 'Icesave negotiations concluded
    - outcome presented', 18 October, https://eng.forsaetisraduneyti.is/news-
    and-articles/nr/4008 (accessed 5 April 2016).
PM [Iceland's Prime Minister's Office] (2008) 'Deposit guarantee', 6 October,
    https://eng.forsaetisraduneyti.is/news-andarticles/nr/3033   (accessed   7
    April 2016).
Purfield C. and Rosenberg, C. B. (2010) 'Adjustments under a currency peg:
    Estonia, Latvia and Lithuania during the global financial crisis 2008–09',
    IMF Working Paper WP/10/213.
Raudseps, P. (2008) 'Latvia bank failure dashes hopes', *Bloomberg*, 5 December.
Rawls, J. (1970) *A Theory of Justice*, Cambridge: Harvard University Press.
Regan, A. (2014) 'What explains Ireland's fragile recovery from the crisis? The
    politics of comparative institutional advantage', *CESifo Forum* 2(June):
    26–31.

Regling, K. and Watson, M. (2010) 'A preliminary report on the sources of Ireland's banking crisis', Dublin: Government Publications.

Rey, H. (2013) 'Dilemma not trilemma: The global financial cycle and monetary policy independence', paper presented at the Jackson Hole Symposium, August, http://www.kansascityfed.org/publicat/sympos/2013/2013Rey.pdf (accessed 4 April 2016).

Rimšēvičs, I. (2012) In EC [European Commission], EU balance-of-payments assistance for Latvia: foundations of success, *European Economy*, Occasional papers 120, pp. 16–17.

Rizga, K. (2012) 'The invisible side of Latvia's "success" story: life with "God's mercy and the goodness of others"', *Re:Baltica*, 17 October.

Rokkan, S. (1966) 'Norway: numerical democracy and corporate pluralism', in R. A. Dahl (ed.) *Political Oppositions in Western Democracies*, New Haven: Yale University Press, pp. 70–115.

Rosenberg, C. (2009) 'Why the IMF supports the Latvian currency peg', *RGE Monitor*, 6 January.

RTÉ News (2008) 'ISEQ suffers record one-day fall', 29 September, http://www.rte.ie/news/2008/0929/108565-economy/ (accessed 17 April 2016).

Ruggie, G. (1982) 'International regimes, transactions, and change: embedded liberalism in the postwar economic order', *International Organization*, 36(2): 379–415.

Saeima (2010) 'Committee of the parliament of Latvia: the international loan has been used in accordance with the objective', 26 February 2010, http://www.saeima.lv/en/news/saeima-news/17740-committee-of-the-parliament-of-latvia-the-international-loan-has-been-used-in-accordance-with-the-ob (accessed 23 March 2015).

Salines, M. and Bērziņš, K. (2012) 'Fiscal austerity, structural reforms and reelection: explaining the "possible trinity" in the case of Latvia', in EC [European Commission], EU balance-of-payments assistance for Latvia: foundations of success, *European Economy*, Occasional papers 120, pp. 155–181.

Sassen, S. (1996) *Losing Control? Sovereignty in an age of globalization*, New York: Columbia University Press.

Schelkle, W. (2006) 'The theory and practice of economic governance in EMU revisited: what have we learnt about commitment and credibility?' *Journal of Common Market Studies*, 44(4): 669–685.

Schmidt, V. A. (1996) *From State to Market? The transformation of French business and government*, New York: Cambridge University Press.

Schwartz, H. (2011) 'Iceland's financial iceberg: why leveraging up is a titanic mistake without a reserve currency', *EPS* 10: 292–300.

Scitovsky, T. (1958) *Economic Theory and Western European Integration*, London: George Allen and Unwin.

Seeder, B. (2012) 'Latvian premier seeks euro membership in 2014', *Wall Street Journal*, 20 December.

SIC [Special Investigation Commission] (2010) *Causes and the run up to the collapse of the Icelandic banks in 2008* (Reykjavik) http://www.rna.is/eldri-nefndir/addragandi-ogorsakir-falls-islensku-bankanna-2008/skyrsla-nefndarinnar/english/ (accessed 8 April 2016).

Sigfússon, S. J. (2010) 'Rising from the ruins 1', https://eng.fjarmalaraduneyti.is/minister/former_ministers/steingrimur_j_sigfusson/nr/13555 (accessed 28 March 2016).

Sigurdardóttir, J. (2011) 'The Icesave referendum has been oversimplified', *The Guardian*, 13 April.

Sigurjonsson, F. (2015) 'Monetary reform. A better monetary system for Iceland', a report commissioned by the Prime Minister of Iceland, https://www.forsaetisraduneyti.is/media/Skyrslur/monetary-reform.pdf (accessed 8 April 2016).

Simmons, B. (1994) *Who Adjusts? Domestic sources of foreign economic policy during the interwar years*, Princeton: Princeton University Press.

Simons, H. C. (1936) 'Rules versus authorities in monetary policy', *Journal of Political Economy*, 44: 1–30.

Sinn, H.-W. (2014) *The Euro Trap: On bursting bubbles, budgets and beliefs*, Oxford: Oxford University Press.

Skaar Viken, B. (2011) 'The birth of a system born to collapse: laissez-faire the Icelandic way', *EPS*, 10: 312–323.

Snidal, D. (1985) 'The limits of hegemonic stability theory', *International Organization*, 39(4): 579–614.

Sommers, J. (2015) 'Austerity, internal devaluation and social (in)security in Latvia', in J. Sommers and C. Woolfson (ed.), *The Contradictions of Austerity: The socio-economic costs of the neoliberal Baltic model*, London: Routledge, pp. 17–43.

Sommers, J. (2009) 'The Baltic riots', *CounterPunch*, 19 January, http://www.counterpunch.org/2009/01/19/the-baltic-riots/ (accessed 17 May 2016).

Spain, J. (2008) 'The mega bailout for Irish banks', 10 October, http://www.irishabroad.com/news/irish-voice/spain/Articles/irish-bank-bailout101008.aspx (accessed 16 April 2016).

Statistics Iceland (2010) *Referendum, 6 March 2010*, Statistical Series, Elections, 2010:2.

Steck, G., Grimm, M., Heise, M., Holzhausen, A. and Sauter, N. (2010) *Allianz Global Wealth Report 2010*, Munich: Allianz.

Stiglitz, J. E. (2016) *The Euro: How a common currency threatens the future of Europe*, New York: Norton.

Štokenbergs, A. (2008) 'Cik naudas vajag Latvijai?' DELFI, 10 December.

Stooq (2016) 'Historical data: OMX Iceland All Share Index (^ICEX)', Daily: 31 December 1992 to 23 March 2016, http://stooq.com/q/d/?s=^icex&c=0 (accessed 23 March 2016).

Streeck, W. (2015) 'Why the euro divides Europe', *New Left Review*, 95 (Sept/Oct): 5–26.

Streeck, W. (2014) *Buying Time: The delayed crisis of democratic capitalism*, London: Verso.

Tapinsh, A. (2012) 'Latvia sees good and bad as Russian money haven', *Reuters*, 23 October.

Thorhallsson, B. (2010) 'The corporatist model and its value in understanding small European states in the neoliberal world of the twenty-first century: The case of Iceland', *EPS*, 9: 375–386.

Thorhallsson, B. (2002) 'The skeptical political elite versus the pro-European public: the case of Iceland', *Scandinavian Studies* 74(3): 349–378.

Totaro, P. (2009) 'Iceland may join EU after left-wing victory', *The Age*, 27 April.

US Embassy in Riga (2008) 'Politics and the Parex bailout', Wikileaks cable 08RIGA701, dated 2008-11-17 12:46, https://wikileaks.org/cable/2008/11/08RIGA701.html (accessed 23 March 2015).

Várnagy, R. (2013) 'Hungary', *European Journal of Political Research*, 52: 96–100.

Várnagy, R. (2012) 'Hungary', *European Journal of Political Research*, 51(1): 129–135.

Várnagy, R. (2011) 'Hungary', *European Journal of Political Research*, 50(7-8): 991–998.

Viksnins, G. J. (2008) 'The Georgetown University syndrome and Latvian economic reforms', in D. Auers (ed.), *Latvia and the USA: From captive nation to strategic partner*, Riga: University of Latvia Press, pp. 109–118.

Wade, R. H. and Sigurgeirsdottir, S. (2012) 'Iceland's rise, fall, stabilization and beyond', *Cambridge Journal of Economics*, 36: 127–144.

Wade, R. H. and Sigurgeirsdottir, S. (2010) 'Lessons from Iceland', *New Left Review*, 65: 5–29.

Wagner, H. (2014) 'Can we expect convergence through monetary integration? (New) OCA theory versus empirical evidence from European integration', *Comparative Economic Studies*, 56(2): 176–199.

Warren, E. (2016) 'Senator Elizabeth Warren questions Leonard Chanin at banking hearing on consumer finance regulations', video from a 5 April 2016 Senate Banking Committee hearing titled, 'Assessing the effects of consumer finance regulations', https://www.youtube.com/watch?v=squ2SAhziPo (accessed 11 April 2016).

Webb, M. C. and Krasner, S. D. (1989) 'Hegemonic stability theory: an empirical assessment', *Review of International Studies*, 15(2): 183–198.

Webb, N. (2011) 'The rich just got richer – top 300 now have €57bn', *Sunday Independent*, 13 March.

Weisbrot, M. and Ray, R. (2011) 'Latvia's internal devaluation: a success story?' Center for Economic and Policy Research, December, http://i.fidhouse.com/fidelitynews/wpcontent/uploads/2013/07/latvia-2011-12.pdf (accessed 16 May 2016).

Willis, A. (2009) 'Almunia keeps up pressure on Latvia', *EU Observer*, 14 October.

World Bank (2012) *Golden Growth: Restoring the lustre of the European economic model*, Washington, DC: World Bank.

Wright, R. (2010) 'Strengthening the capacity of the department of finance', report of the Independent Review Panel, Department of Finance, Dublin: Government Publications.

WSJ (2008) 'Excerpts: Iceland's Oddsson', *Wall Street Journal*, 17 October.

Index

www.ingramcontent.com/pod-product-compliance
Lightning Source LLC
Chambersburg PA
CBHW021900020426
42334CB00013B/417